Praise for

The Fuzzy
and the Techie

"A bouncy read by the venture capitalist that suggests sociology and philosophy graduates might be the real winners of the robot revolution. As tech start-ups and websites can be built by putting 'chunks' of other peoples' work and automated processes together, [Hartley] argues, 'techies' could be put out of business. Those 'fuzzies' who studied the liberal arts—with their creative skills and broad understanding of communication techniques and ideas—may well populate Silicon Valley C-suites in far greater numbers in the future. According to Hartley, change is already under way, with many successful start-ups in the tech industry now being established by fuzzies."

—*Financial Times*, "Business Books of the Month"

"For generations, leadership has been viewed as an art form, refined and perfected by a healthy dose of "fuzzy" liberal arts education. But in the tech-heavy world of the twenty-first century, traditional leadership preparation needs to be leavened by STEM. As Scott Hartley brilliantly illustrates, a "fuzzy-tech" partnership is a prerequisite—not just as a guide for governments and businesses in meeting existential challenges, but also as a foundation for emerging leaders; they, not machines, will be the keys to solving the greatest problems of the new century."

—Daniel W. Christman, lieutenant general (retired),
55th superintendent, U.S. Military Academy, West Point

"You can't build a wall to keep the robots out. That doesn't mean we're doomed. Scott Hartley does a masterful job going beyond the headlines to explain why the future needs engineers as much as it does philosophers, and why the two need each other."

—Ian Bremmer, president of Eurasia Group and author of *Superpower*

"This terrific book clearly articulates the importance of the liberal arts in our technocentric world, a view I have long supported. In the end, technology is about making the lives of humans better, and, as the author argues, it is the humanities and social sciences that teach us about the human condition and how it might be improved. A delightful read!"

—John Hennessy, president emeritus, Stanford University, professor of computer science and electrical engineering

"Scott Hartley artfully explains why it is time for us to get over the false division between the human and the technical. If received and acted upon with the seriousness it deserves, we can anticipate real benefits for business and society."

—Tim Brown, CEO of IDEO and author of *Change by Design*

"For fuzzy creatives everywhere, this book is both a tonic and a manifesto. As we enter the age of artificial intelligence, we will need more and more of the human kind, nurtured not by the sciences but the humanities. A compelling and convincing read!"

—Anne-Marie Slaughter, president and CEO of New America

"Scott Hartley's timely and thought-provoking book is a refreshing and important voice in the era of major technological transformation and advances in our world, led by big data, AI, the cloud, genomics, etc. As nature has evolved our brain to be capable of logical reasoning as well as emotional feelings, artistic expressions, and remarkable intuitions, human civilization has always evolved and benefited from the coevolution of arts, literature, engineering, and sciences. Humanity has begun the era of intelligent machines and genomic wonder tools. It has become more urgent and imperative that humanistic thinking and values can help guide the way technologies are designed, experimented, deployed, and communicated. From digital humanities to humanistic technologies, human wisdom should be all in when it comes to designing and defining our collective future. Students, parents, educators, policy makers, CEOs, and entrepreneurs should all read this book."

—Professor Fei-Fei Li,
director of the Stanford Artificial Intelligence Lab

"Great book for all. Blows up the false dichotomy in education between tech and liberal arts. This book shows that not only can both coexist; it is dangerous if they don't both exist side by side in an integrated manner. They make each other more effective. Scott has done an excellent job of making his argument with facts, illustrative case studies, and well-reasoned solutions. An important and enjoyable read."

—Bill Aulet, author of *Disciplined Entrepreneurship* and managing director of the Martin Trust Center for MIT Entrepreneurship

"Silicon Valley is founded on strong engineering cultures, but the biggest challenges of the coming decades will lead Silicon Valley to partner with those who best understand our humanity. Many of the greatest companies are built by fuzzies and techies working together—Scott makes a compelling case that important data and information are increasingly generated by machines, but the wisdom of humans is required to build this data into the knowledge that runs our civilization."

—Joe Lonsdale, cofounder of Palantir

"In this book Scott Hartley succeeds better than anyone I know in articulating the indispensable role a liberal arts education plays . . . One of the impacts of technology has been to democratize freedom, scholarship, and passion. Hartley lays out in plain language that a liberal arts education trumps early specialization in STEM subjects."

—Temba Maqubela, headmaster, Groton School

"I am a 'fuzzy' venture capitalist who owes a successful life in Silicon Valley to the 'techies.' Scott Hartley has brilliantly described the magic that is created when these two tribes work together. His insightful book shines a bright light on this rarely analyzed but highly productive relationship."

—Bill Draper, cochair of the Draper Richards Kaplan Foundation and author of *The Startup Game: Inside the Partnership Between Venture Capitalists and Entrepreneurs*

The Fuzzy
and the Techie

WHY THE LIBERAL ARTS WILL
RULE THE DIGITAL WORLD

Scott Hartley

Mariner Books
Houghton Mifflin Harcourt
Boston • New York

First Mariner Books edition 2018

hmhco.com

Library of Congress Cataloging-in-Publication Data
Names: Hartley, Scott (Business consultant)
Title: The fuzzy and the techie : why the liberal arts will
rule the digital world / Scott Hartley.
Description: Boston : Houghton Mifflin Harcourt, 2017.
Identifiers: LCCN 2017000818 (print) | LCCN 2017001597 (ebook) |
ISBN 9780544944770 (hardback) | ISBN 9781328915405 (paperback) |
ISBN 9780544944374 (ebook)
Subjects: LCSH: Creative ability in business. | Education, Humanistic—
Social aspects. | Telecommunication—Social aspects. | BISAC: BUSINESS &
ECONOMICS / General. | BUSINESS & ECONOMICS / Careers / General.
Classification: LCC HD53 .H3765 2017 (print) | LCC HD53 (ebook) |
DDC 384.301/12—dc23
LC record available at https://lccn.loc.gov/2017000818

Book design by David Futato

Printed in the United States of America
DOC 10 9 8 7 6 5 4 3 2 1

Graphs on page 207 are reproduced with permission from David J. Deming,
originally published in the website summary of his 2016 paper,
"The Growing Importance of Social Skills in the Labor Market."

For my parents

Contents

Author's Note

The terms "fuzzy" and "techie" are used to respectively describe students of the humanities and social sciences (i.e., the fuzzies) and students of the engineering or hard sciences (the techies) at Stanford University. Beneath these lighthearted appellations rest some charged opinions on the relative value of each type of degree, on the importance of the direct vocational application of a college degree, and on the appropriate role of education. Not surprisingly, these are opinions that have bubbled well beyond the vast acreage of Stanford's palm-fringed quads and golden hillsides, into Silicon Valley, and into its metaphorical extension as the economic engine of today's economy.

The divide between fuzzies and techies is a modern incarnation of the chasm physicist and novelist Charles Percy Snow lamented had formed between those in the humanities and the sciences in his famous essay "The Two Cultures." As Snow emphasized, those trained in the liberal arts and those trained in technology and the sciences have much value to share with one another and he advocated building bridges between them. Today, the assertion is widely made that those versed in the classical liberal arts are not well prepared for success in tomorrow's technology-led economy because they do not have the requisite vocational skills in the science, technology, engineering, and math (STEM) disciplines. I will argue that, on the contrary, they have knowledge and skills that are vital to success in this fast-evolving economy.

This book seeks to reframe the debate about the value of a liberal arts versus a STEM education. While taking into account the very real need for more so-called STEM majors, this book seeks to highlight that the debate has turned on a faux opposition between STEM education and the liberal arts. Indeed, as we evolve our technology to make it ever more accessible and democratic, and as it becomes ever more ubiquitous, the timeless questions of the liberal arts, and their insights into human needs and desires, have become essential requirements in the development of our technological instruments.

As a fuzzy, I have grown up in a techie world. I have witnessed the need for collaboration between fuzzies and techies as a child in Palo Alto, as an undergraduate at Stanford, then as an employee of Google and Facebook, and thereafter as a venture capitalist on Sand Hill Road. If we peer behind the veil of our greatest technology, we will see that it is distinguished by its humanity. I have met with the founders of thousands of companies, and the truth is that no matter what you've studied, no matter what your background is, there is a very real and a very relevant role for you to play in tomorrow's tech economy. As "software eats the world," technology requires input and expertise from every corner of society. We need more techies in traditionally fuzzy institutions such as our government, and we need more fuzzies building tech companies. Our technology ought to augment rather than replace, and ought to provide us with great hope rather than great fear.

Finding solutions to our greatest problems requires an understanding of human context as well as of code; it requires both ethics and data, both deep thinking people and Deep Learning AI, both human and machine; it requires us to question implicit biases in our algorithms and inquire deeply into not just how we build, but why we build and what we seek to improve. Fuzzies and techies must come together and the true value of the liberal arts must be embraced as we continue to pioneer our new technological tools.

Scott Hartley

Fall 2016

The Role of the Fuzzy
in a Techie World

One time she was Kate in *The Taming of the Shrew*. Another time she was Adelaide in *Guys and Dolls*. But on her own stage, Katelyn Gleason is the founder and CEO of Eligible, an innovative health-care technology company. A theater arts major at Long Island's Stony Brook University, she never anticipated that she would become an entrepreneur, let alone a tech entrepreneur. But after founding her own company when she was twenty-six years old, and raising $25 million in venture capital from some of the most successful entrepreneurs in American business, she credits her acting experience with contributing significantly to her social skills, confidence, and talent for sales, which were all instrumental in launching Eligible.

Katelyn became a health-tech entrepreneur by chance. She could have been a poster child for the argument against a liberal arts education made so often in recent years: that it doesn't prepare students for the jobs the economy needs filled. Indeed, once she determined that acting might not work out and that she should search for other work, she had no clear idea what kind of job to look for. She did know that she was very good at sales. During college she had supported herself by working as a sales director for a company that published a business directory.

Katelyn says that her acting experience helped with that work by teaching her how to be persuasive in her sales pitches, and also how to deal with the emotional impact of people telling her no again and again. Acting taught her how to quiet her self-doubt and forge ahead despite rejections. She proved so talented at selling that by the time she was twenty, she was managing a sales force of forty. As she looked for job openings in a wide-ranging job search, she was drawn to an advertisement on Craigslist for a job in sales for a web-based startup providing services for health care practices, called DrChrono. The company provided scheduling, billing, and order management for clinical tests and prescriptions. Despite knowing nothing about the health care industry, she knew sales, and she felt confident she could learn what she needed to know to get the job done.

DrChrono hired her as a contract salesperson, and Katelyn began learning about health care and about building a business. She discovered that she was fascinated by the process of innovating a business and loved being part of a small entrepreneurial team. The founders also loved having her. Her sales ability was so impressive that the founders asked her to join them in pitching the company at the highly competitive contest for startups held annually by Y Combinator (YC), a Silicon Valley startup incubator. Winning startups are admitted to a rigorous three-month program, during which time YC founder Paul Graham and a team of successful entrepreneurs and investors offer guidance about how to develop their businesses. DrChrono won a coveted spot, and Katelyn impressed Paul Graham so much that when she decided to leave DrChrono, he advised her that she should found her own health-tech startup, even though she didn't have fancy degrees from an Ivy League school or stellar connections like some of her peers.

Katelyn still knew relatively little about technology, but she did have a clear idea for a business. She had been stunned by the inefficiencies in the way doctors' offices verified patient insurance coverage. It was done mostly by phone and involved time-consuming paperwork, which often led to long delays and to mistakes. Quite often, doctors ended up swallowing the costs of procedures because patients didn't actually have the coverage the doctor thought they did. Other times, patients ended up with crushing unexpected bills. She recalled, "I'd dealt with the front office, and the billing systems. There was one company everyone used called Emdeon." But the technology the Emdeon system was built with was old, and for doctor's offices, connecting their own data systems to the Emdeon system was expensive and time-consuming work. Katelyn had heard about another YC-backed startup called Stripe that offered an easy way for one hundred thousand merchants, from Best Buy to Saks Fifth Avenue to Adidas, to handle all the complexities of accepting payments on the Internet. She boldly decided that she would create a similar system for health care providers, a system faster and easier than Emdeon. Though she had no idea what programming would be involved, she believed she could learn what she needed to know in order to hire software engineers to do that work.

Hunkering down in her apartment in Mountain View, California, in the heart of Silicon Valley, Katelyn threw herself into reading about the technology the system would require. She audited free online programming classes offered by various universities, and spent her days in the public library devouring books. She forced herself to read Apple's software developer kit from start to finish, and asked questions she had on the developer collaboration website Stack Overflow. With that basic knowledge under her belt, she hired two freelance software engineers, and as they built a prototype, she began seeking angel investment. "As a woman with no technical background," she recalled, "I met lots of skepticism, but again, my acting experience developed my resilience to keep forging ahead in the face of so many turndowns." Her acting work also helped her understand how to craft a compelling story about the company, which is essential to convincing investors to provide support. "In theater, the playwright gives you the play, but you have to tell the story," she explained to me in 2016. "I knew I just had to figure out how to tell the right story. When you start rehearsal, you're completely lost. You don't know the characters at all. When you start to build a product, when you start to build a company and you don't even know what your product is going to be, it's exactly the same feeling. You're completely lost. I learned in the rehearsal process that if I worked hard enough, I could gain that internal clarity where I would start to take off like a rocket ship."

In the summer of 2012, Katelyn found herself back at Y Combinator, pitching Paul Graham and team, but this time as a startup founder. She won their backing, and on the heels of their support, she was able to quickly raise $1.6 million to continue building Eligible's product. After launch, the company took off, with a growth rate of 60 percent week over week. In 2013, Katelyn was selected by *Fast Company* magazine as one of its top one hundred most creative people, and in 2015, she was named one of *Forbes*'s 30 Under 30 innovators in health care.

Being CEO of a company is just the latest way Katelyn is under the spotlight, on center stage. She is a fuzzy who joined with techies to solve a problem long overdue for fixing, and she relishes knowing that her company helps process over ten million health insurance eligibility claims per month, bringing efficiency and savings to an industry ripe for improvement.

Katelyn could never have anticipated how her undergraduate experience would prove so valuable in teaching her to dig in and learn what she needed to know about the technology to build her company, or how transferable the skills she had learned about being a confident, highly persuasive communicator would be to entrepreneurship. Rather than be a poster child for the impracticality of getting a liberal arts degree, she became a representative of how applicable the fuzzy skills developed by the liberal arts are, as well as how important they are as complements to technological expertise. Many other successful founders of innovative technology-driven businesses also credit their liberal arts education with preparing them for pioneering new ways of harnessing the power of technology. Founder of corporate communications platform Slack, Stewart Butterfield credits his ability to develop a successful product to following lines of inquiry to their logical conclusion. It's fitting that Butterfield studied philosophy at both the University of Victoria and the University of Cambridge, but his story is not unique. LinkedIn founder Reid Hoffman earned his master's degree in philosophy at Oxford University. Billionaire venture capitalist and cofounder of PayPal Peter Thiel studied philosophy and law, and his cofounder of Palantir, CEO Alex Karp, earned a law degree and then a PhD in neoclassical social theory.

Ben Silbermann, the billionaire founder of Pinterest, studied political science at Yale, while Airbnb founders Joe Gebbia and Brian Chesky earned bachelor of fine arts degrees at the Rhode Island School of Design. Steve Loughlin, founder of RelateIQ, which

Salesforce bought for $390 million three years after he founded
the company, was a public policy major. The cofounder of Salesforce, Parker Harris, studied English literature at Middlebury College. Former Hewlett-Packard CEO Carly Fiorina was a medieval
history and philosophy major, and YouTube CEO Susan Wojcicki
studied history and literature at Harvard. Take a look around Silicon Valley, and many of these exemplars of "tech" are grounded
in educations that taught methods of interrogation and rigorous
thought, with many technology companies formed on the philos-
ophies learned through liberal arts educations. The United States
has no exclusive on this; across the Pacific, the richest man in Asia
is Jack Ma, the founder of the e-commerce giant Alibaba. He was
an English major. While a bounty of opportunity undoubtedly exists for techies as well, and they are in high demand, what's little
understood about today's tech-driven economy is that as technology offers an ever more accessible toolbox, our differentiation—
our very competitive advantage—becomes the very thing liberal
arts programs teach.

The Origin of the Terms

I first heard the terms "fuzzy" and "techie" as an undergraduate at
Stanford University. If you majored in the humanities or social
sciences, you were a fuzzy, and if you majored in engineering or
computer science, you were a techie. This lighthearted moniker—
calling liberal arts specialists fuzzies in contrast to Stanford's heritage as a leading center of technological innovation—has never
deterred students from filling their schedules with liberal arts
classes, primarily because the university promotes a well-rounded
education, and professors firmly believe that success comes from
exposure to a broad range of disciplines.

I chose to be a fuzzy, majoring in political science. I took some fascinating classes that introduced me to recent developments in technology, such as Technology in National Security, and the Entrepreneurial Thought Leadership seminar, for which top technology founders and investors come to lecture. But I nurtured my intellectual curiosity, studying ancient history, political theory, and Russian literature rather than seeking vocational preparation. During college, for two years I worked at the Center for Biomedical Ethics on cutting-edge applied philosophy. From there, I went to work in the domain of technology at Google, Facebook, and Harvard's Berkman Center for Internet and Society. Ultimately I became a venture capitalist, where my job has been to meet with and evaluate tech startups, working with them to help them launch and grow successfully. My education at Stanford taught me that I wouldn't be graduating with a second-class set of skills to those learned by the techies across campus, but rather a complementary set of skills, equally necessary in today's technology-driven economy. My graduation speaker was Steve Jobs, who famously told us in his speech to "Stay hungry. Stay foolish." Jobs also once said how important the humanities and social sciences are to creating great products, and that "technology alone is not enough—it's technology married with liberal arts, married with the humanities, that yields us the result that make our heart sing."

A great deal of media coverage and a number of recent books warn about the threat to jobs from a surging wave of technological innovation that is leading to such breakthroughs in automation as self-driving cars and robot home assistants. We are in the early days of what Massachusetts Institute of Technology (MIT) economists Erik Brynjolfsson and Andrew McAfee dubbed the "Second Machine Age" in their influential 2014 book of the same title. This line of argument suggests that the skills that will secure people gainful employment in this emerging era are those learned by an education in the STEM fields—science, technology, engineering, and math. Earning a liberal arts degree is characterized as an impractical extravagance the workers of the future simply can't afford.

Reading novels and poems, revisiting the debates of ancient philosophy, or studying the history of the French Revolution or the culture of a remote island community isn't likely to get you a decent job in today's more tech-driven economy, and certainly not in the future, or so the argument goes. Microsoft founder Bill Gates caused a stir in a speech to the National Governors Association that state funding in support of liberal arts education should be cut and more money dedicated to higher education in the STEM fields because those are the skills that will get people well-paying jobs. Billionaire cofounder of Sun Microsystems Vinod Khosla, now a leading venture capitalist investing in technology startups, has gone so far as to say that "little of the material taught in liberal arts programs today is relevant to the future." Silicon Valley venture capitalist and software pioneer who created the search engine Netscape Marc Andreessen quipped that those who learn the "soft skills" of the liberal arts in college, rather than the "hard skills" of science and tech, "likely will end up working in shoe stores."

Be Concerned, Not Fearful

The alarm about the future of work, and about the prospects of liberal arts graduates, is clearly founded in genuine concern, but it is also sorely misguided for a number of reasons. First of all, as we'll explore more fully in Chapter 8, though increasingly "smart" and nimble machines will likely be taking the place of some workers, the extent of likely job displacement has been greatly exaggerated. The threat to some jobs is not only clear; it is already present. Robots will assume more and more tasks that can be fully automated, as they've already done with jobs on the assembly lines of so many manufacturers. But the proportion of jobs that can be fully automated is more limited than suggested by forecasts. In many jobs, a number of tasks that can be automated, because they are routine or can be better performed by crunching vast amounts of data, will be taken over by machines. But in many cases, the result will not be to displace human workers; rather it will be liberate people to spend more time on the aspects of their work that require uniquely human skills—nonroutine tasks and complex problem solving that machines can't perform and may never be able to do.

Look no further than the legal profession to see change in the making. In 2015, MIT labor economist Frank Levy coauthored a paper with Dana Remus of the University of North Carolina School of Law called "Can Robots Be Lawyers? Computers, Lawyers, and the Practice of Law." The paper examined the notion that the legal profession is susceptible to automation, and that lawyers will soon be replaced by computers. Their argument was inspired by the advent of software designed to read and analyze legal documents during the discovery process.

After an extensive analysis of the time spent on individual tasks performed by attorneys, Levy and Remus found that they spend the majority of their time analyzing documents, counseling clients, and appearing in court, and many of the skills that make a legal professional especially effective, such as being able to think on their feet and interacting with clients, are, and will remain, uniquely human. They estimate that around 13 percent of legal work could one day be automated—a measurable amount, but relatively modest, especially since the change will happen over the course of many years. Instead of replacing lawyers, automation software will make lawyers more efficient. Machines will handle routine tasks; lawyers will do the rest.

A great irony of the discussion of job displacement is that among the jobs vulnerable to dislocation and automation are many in computer programming—currently hailed as both higher paying and in the highest demand. How might this happen? First, many of these jobs will be transferred overseas to developing economies invested in training masses of highly qualified programmers—places like India, China, and Nigeria. These programmers are no longer simply an inexpensive workforce hired just to do the relatively simple work of building websites; they are being trained to great proficiency. Andela, a startup that aims to train one hundred thousand African programmers over the next decade, has so many applicants that its acceptance rate is under 1 percent. Andela invests as much as $10,000 to train each fellow in the latest software development, fellows such as Olajumoke Oladimeji, a young woman who already had a degree in computer science and electrical engineering from Lagos State University. The fellows are then matched with global companies. Due to the high pay programmers can demand, sending a good deal of programming work overseas is as unavoidable as was sending manufacturing to the developing world. In 1970 one in four Americans worked in manufacturing, whereas today it's fewer than one in ten. The flight of routine computing work will likely follow a similar pattern. Technical skill is important, but a technical education on its own will not automatically ensure employment in the Second Machine Age.

That said, the value of getting a high-quality STEM education, not one limited to learning computer programming languages, but a rigorous grounding in one of the hard sciences or fields of engineering, should not be contested. Work in pure scientific research, as well as in R&D in industry and at the high end of technological innovation, will likely always be secure. Regarding computer programming jobs, there is a current shortfall of candidates to fill them in the U.S. labor force, and the pace of change is rapid. In addition, analysis of the future needs of the job market has indicated that this shortfall will worsen significantly in the coming years. The Bureau of Labor Statistics approximates that there will be one million more computer science job openings by 2020 than domestic candidates qualified to fill them. This is a driving force behind the calls for more STEM majors, and we can't deny that there is a very real need for more techies.

Certainly, more proficiency in the skills needed should be developed, and we might look to countries like Estonia that mandate all first graders learn to code. But the emphasis should *not* be on teaching these skills exclusively, and not only on this nearer-term skills gap. Those being taught the STEM skills should also be afforded the opportunity to develop the proficiencies fostered by the liberal arts, which will make them more agile and employable workers in tomorrow's economy. For example, Ireland's president Michael Higgins said in November 2016 that "the teaching of philosophy is one of the most powerful tools we have at our disposal to empower children." Rather than training legions of people to perform narrowly prescribed vocational tech tasks, we should be balancing this with a liberal arts education that develops more rounded skills and wider perspectives, instilling strengths in both the technical and the fuzzy abilities. The debate over STEM versus liberal arts has obscured the fact that the so-called pure sciences, such as biology, chemistry, physics, and mathematics, are a core component of the liberal arts canon, and that computer science has in many cases also been added to the canon. A false dichotomy has been established between liberal arts and STEM education; students can very well get both at once.

Barriers to Entry Are Falling

But what exactly is the value of a liberal arts education, especially if someone wants to meaningfully participate in pushing the boundaries of the frontiers of technological innovation? Are liberal arts majors truly shut out from the exciting possibilities of the future? A number of misconceptions are involved in that argument. The first part of the discussion includes an overlooked yet rapidly progressing development in technology where well-educated people who are not schooled in the STEM fields can now nonetheless play important roles, and even take the leading role, in applying new technologies to innovating products and services, like Katelyn Gleason achieved so successfully. As her story shows, though gaining literacy in the tech tools is important, a technical degree is not required anymore in order to thrive in many areas of today's tech-driven economy. The barriers to entry for harnessing the power of various technological tools have also been brought so low that those with no technical expertise are now able to gain that literacy much more easily and to collaborate more creatively and efficiently with technology experts while actually driving the innovation of new products and services.

One of the predominant trends in technology over recent decades has been the "democratization" of the tools used for creating technologically based products and services. Tech experts have provided increasingly intuitive interfaces that have rendered using computers so easy that three-year-olds can make their way around an iPad with ease. The emerging voice interfaces, such as Apple's Siri and Amazon's Echo, will continue to improve and will enable nonprogrammers to train and instruct computers to perform many tasks that once required programming. Even now, websites can be built without any programming knowledge whatsoever. Anyone can become a web designer by simply selecting a template and then tailoring it as they like by dragging predesigned elements into it. These sites can also be easily connected to payment services, inventory control systems, and customer relationship management systems. While 3-D printing sounded like a futuristic fantasy just a decade ago, powerful printers are now available to the public at low cost and effortlessly programmed to create any manner of objects, such as custom-designed furniture and clothing. Even just a few years ago, building and maintaining the capacity to store the large volumes of data required for many types of tech-based businesses was prohibitively technical and expensive for all but the savviest of people who came up with an idea for such a business. Now, one need not understand the technical details about how servers work to purchase cloud-based data storage on Amazon Web Services. This isn't to say that all of today's technology tools are effortlessly available; many still require a high level of expertise to make use of them. But in those cases, resources abound for gaining that expertise more readily, and the trend of democratization will continue.

A few years ago, my seventy-year-old father crashed his Litespeed bicycle at over twenty miles per hour and landed on his head, ending up in the intensive care unit with a subdural hematoma. His neurologist recommended as part of his recovery that he undertake a regimen of brain training using Lumosity. This web-based company provides engaging, gamelike exercises for building skills in language, computation, memory, and logic. My father accessed the exercises through Lumosity's mobile phone app, and he enjoyed the experience so much that he was inspired to create an app of his own. He is an industrial psychologist who earned a master's degree from Virginia Commonwealth University, who was not a trained programmer, but he taught himself how to use a programming language called LiveCode, and quickly began creating a working prototype for the product he wanted to build. Using a freelancer website called UpWork, he hired an iOS developer in India to help him. My father released a player-ranking iPhone application just in time for the 2014 FIFA World Cup. He is a shining example of how anyone who is motivated to participate in innovation in this emerging era can do so without any formal technical training. Though my father opted to learn LiveCode, an evolution of a very early Apple Mac program called HyperCard that he'd experimented with decades ago, it certainly wasn't required, and throughout this book, we'll hear the stories of many other nontech-schooled liberal arts graduates spearheading exciting innovations that have the potential to significantly enhance our lives by collaborating with techies to harness the power of sophisticated new capabilities.

The Liberal Arts Skills

While majoring in computer science isn't a requirement to participate in the Second Machine Age, what skills do liberal arts graduates specifically possess to contribute to this brave new world? Another major oversight in the debate has been the failure to appreciate that a good liberal arts education teaches many skills that are not only valuable to the general world of business, but are in fact vital to innovating the next wave of breakthrough tech-driven products and services. Many defenses of the value of a liberal arts education have been launched, of course, with the emphasis being on the acquisition of fundamental thinking and communication skills, such as critical thinking, logical argumentation, and complex problem solving. Fareed Zakaria, in his 2015 book *In Defense of a Liberal Education*, highlights "creativity, problem solving, decision making, persuasive arguing, and management" as the skills taught in the liberal arts. He makes a strong case. But the argument about the general thinking skills that are developed has bypassed attention to what may be the most important factor in why liberal arts majors are particularly well equipped to take leading roles in current and future innovation.

One aspect of liberal arts education that has been strangely neglected in the discussion is the fact that the humanities and social sciences are devoted to the study of human nature and the nature of our communities and larger societies. Students who pursue degrees in the liberal arts disciplines tend to be particularly motivated to investigate what makes us human: how we behave and why we behave as we do. They're driven to explore how our families and our public institutions—such as our schools and legal systems—operate, and could operate better, and how governments and economies work or, as is so often the case, are plagued by dysfunction. These students learn a great deal from their particular courses of study and apply that knowledge to today's issues, the leading problems to be tackled, and various approaches for analyzing and addressing those problems.

The greatest opportunities for innovation in the emerging era are in applying evolving technological capabilities to finding better ways to solve human problems like social dysfunction and political corruption; finding ways to better educate children; helping people live healthier and happier lives by altering harmful behaviors; improving our working conditions; discovering better ways to tackle poverty; improving health care and making it more affordable; making our governments more accountable, from the local level up to that of global affairs; and finding optimal ways to incorporate intelligent, nimble machines into our work lives so that we are empowered to do more of the work that we do best, and to let the machines do the rest. Workers with a solid liberal arts education have a strong foundation to build on in pursuing these goals.

One of the most immediate needs in technology innovation is to invest products and services with more human qualities, with more sensitivity to human needs and desires. Steve Jobs brilliantly recognized this, and he created one of the most highly valued companies on the planet by focusing intensively on that mission. Companies and entrepreneurs that want to succeed today and in the future must learn to follow his lead and consider in all aspects of their product and service creation how they can make use of the new technologies to make them more humane. Jobs drew, in particular, on the insights of the humanities discipline of design. The Macintosh was the first computer to offer users a selection of beautiful typography, which Jobs learned an appreciation of by taking a course in calligraphy at Reed College, in Portland, Oregon. In his Stanford commencement address, he described typography as "beautiful, historical, artistically subtle in a way that science can't capture."

Still, many other liberal arts disciplines also have much to provide the world of technological innovation. The study of psychology, for example, can help people build products that are more attuned to our emotions and ways of thinking. Consider the runaway success of Facebook to appreciate how expertise in understanding "the human factor" can make a difference in the creation of new products, programs, and services. Most of us know Mark Zuckerberg as the lightning-fast coder who lacked social skills and had a hard time with interpersonal relationships. What's been overlooked is that he was a liberal arts student at Phillips Exeter Academy, where students learn around "Harkness tables" and teaching happens through the Socratic exploration of ideas rather than through lectures, and then at Harvard University, where he loved learning Latin and Greek. He even aced an art history final by creating a website that displayed two hundred works of art and allowed his fellow students to offer their comments about the works' importance, an early crowd-sourced study platform. Like his older sister Randi, he studied psychology, and in building Facebook, he applied insights about the innate human desire to connect with one another. While Zuckerberg also possessed prodigious coding skills that allowed him to spearhead Facebook's early development, he tapped into human psychology with Facebook.

Experience in anthropology can additionally help companies understand cultural and individual behavioral factors that should be considered in developing products, and in marketing them. In a newspaper interview a few years ago, Florida governor Rick Scott said he was seeking to shift state funding away from support for people obtaining degrees in psychology and anthropology and toward support for education in the STEM disciplines, remarking, "Is it a vital interest of the state to have more anthropologists? I don't think so . . . If I'm going to take money from a citizen to put into education, then I'm going to take that money to create jobs." Prior to giving that speech Scott ought to have made note of a study by the U.S. Department of Labor that estimated strong job growth for anthropologists, over the average rate of growth for most professions, and on par with the current growth rates for computer software engineers.

Anthropologists in Self-Driving Cars

Carmaker Nissan has enlisted Melissa Cefkin, a PhD anthropologist from Rice University, to evaluate its design and lead company research into human-machine interaction at the Nissan Technical Center. Currently, she leads a team investigating the complexities of the ways in which self-driving cars and humans will likely interact and what the implications of those complexities are for how the cars should be designed and controlled. To consider why her input is necessary, let's take a brief look at the prospects, and the potential pitfalls, of self-driving vehicles.

The engineering feat of getting this technology deployed has been a stunning accomplishment, but many thorny questions remain to be answered about safety. In 2016, the tragic death of a driver of a Tesla car equipped with autonomous navigation autopilot technology highlighted the current limitations automotive designers face when accounting for all dangers. His death occurred in the least complex driving environment—the open highway— when autopilot failed to detect that a tractor-trailer was switching lanes, moving in front of the Tesla. Analysis later revealed that the truck's white body was eclipsed against a bright spring sky. The driver may have failed to spot the truck because he had put his faith in autopilot, taking his eyes off the road to watch a Harry Potter movie. Experts agree that as of yet, many situations that autonomous vehicles might encounter on roads are beyond their ability to safely navigate, such as flooded roads, large potholes, road debris, and temporary traffic controls, for example, detour signs. Now, Cefkin is studying the challenges of self-driving cars navigating within our even more crowded and inherently unpredictable, nonroutine, and complex urban environments.

Dealing with mixed human-machine environments is one of the most difficult challenges facing autonomous car designers today. Ultimately, these environments may be homogenously machine-operated, but for the foreseeable future, these environments will be pluralistic. Where machines could be programmed to be efficient and rule-abiding, humans are messy rule-breakers who analyze situations on a case-by-case basis using a complex set of interpretations that are hard to teach to a machine. Take a busy intersection with stop signs but no stoplights: cars proceed in a way that is determined less by rules than by subtle choreography on the go—a hand wave here, a rude gesture there, some inching forward by the especially eager motorists. Anthropologist Edward Sapir wrote about the nuanced human communication system of gestures, which is "an elaborate and secret code that is written nowhere, known by none, and understood by all." An autonomous vehicle can't yet perceive and understand gestures. The machine knows only to stop at the sign; it's up to Cefkin to figure out what it should do from there and how to manage the complex dance that is human interaction.

To do that, Cefkin needs to identify patterns in human behavior that can help programmers understand how autonomous cars ought to behave on the road. In searching for those patterns, she's borrowing many tools from the world of anthropology—such as the ethnographic practices of close observation of people out in the field and videography of their behavior. A main goal is to help Nissan design a communication system for autonomous cars in interacting with pedestrians and other drivers. Color-coded lights might signal the car's intent to start or stop or stay in place, while some kind of ocular apparatus could be created to let people know whether or not the car is aware of them. Perhaps a video screen can be placed on the front of the cars so that text could be displayed, communicating the messages hand signals once did. In addition to these communication issues, figuring out how autonomous vehicles can be safely introduced to our roads will require accounting for the psychology of drivers, such as some people's irritation when a car is driving slower than the speed of traffic in the "fast lane," not to mention road rage. According to Hans-Werner Kaas, a senior partner at McKinsey & Company, "There is an increasing awareness across all automakers that they have to deal with the psychological issues of these vehicles. They're beefing up their skillset."

Mapping out the myriad logistical issues that must be tackled is only the beginning of making self-driving cars viable. Many complex ethical issues remain. A June 2016 *Science* article entitled "The Social Dilemma of Autonomous Vehicles" rigorously engaged the modern relevance of a 1967 thought experiment put forth by British philosopher Philippa Foot, known as the "trolley problem." In the problem, a trolley is barreling down the track toward five workers. Another worker looking on could switch the trolley to another track with a lever, but there is one worker on the other track. What should the worker operating the lever do? Self-driving cars present a similar conundrum. Should a car be programmed to privilege the lives of the driver and passengers over the lives of a pedestrian or a bicyclist who might veer into the car's path? If the car could avoid hitting someone by swerving sharply to the right, but would thereby crash into a retaining wall, or to up the ante, into a family of three waiting on a sidewalk for a light to change, what should the car do? Though these vehicles have been dubbed "self-driving," in truth (and as we'll discuss more in the next chapter), they are driving according to what they've been taught to do by programmers, chaperoned by code.

Should a car be "taught" to attempt an evasive maneuver in all such instances, but to calculate the risks to its passengers and swerve only as much as will also keep them from harm? Should it be programmed to respond the way the majority of humans do in such circumstances? Is there even a predominant way humans react in such circumstances, and if so, should that behavior be mimicked or optimized? Will programmatic judgment calls coded into software be "recalled" the way failing airbags might today? If the car is capable of a faster response and of calculating all options faster than a human and always selecting the one with the best odds of saving the most lives, then shouldn't laws mandate that the car be programmed to do so, and that in all such circumstances, the car be in charge? Should the option for the human driver to take over the wheel be automatically disabled? Also, if self-driving cars are proven safer and more fuel-efficient, then should car companies be required to increase the pace of developing them? After all, we've required companies to accelerate the development of improving fuel efficiency and decreasing their carbon emissions. These questions only begin to scratch the surface of the issues that must be addressed in introducing these vehicles into our lives.

What if passengers are asked to tap "OK" to accept liability the same way that they might accept terms and conditions when downloading the latest ad-blocker software? Is this sufficient? Harvard psychologist Joshua Greene describes the root of the complexities in his article "Our Driverless Dilemma" in *Science*. Machine decision-making is "more philosophical than technical. Before we can put our values into machines, we have to figure out how to make our values clear and consistent," he writes. For the young ethicists and litigators out there, welcome to a burgeoning field of inquiry. The global law firm DLA Piper has already launched its "Connected and Self-Driving Car Practice," and thirty-three-year-old Elliot Katz, an American studies major from Vanderbilt University and lawyer trained at Cornell, is the global co-chair of the practice, already considering many of these questions.

Tapping Into Liberal Arts Grads

As technology allows for more machine intelligence and our lives become increasingly populated by the Internet of Things, and as the gathering of data about our lives and analysis of it allows for more discoveries about our behavior, consideration of how new products and services can be crafted for the optimal enhancement of our lives, and of the nature of our communities, workplaces, and governments, will be of vital importance. Those products and services developed with the keenest sense of how they can serve our human needs and complement our human talents will have a distinct competitive advantage.

This is why Tinder, the fast-growing dating service, employs sociologist Jessica Carbino, a PhD from UCLA, to help the company understand patterns in matching. Some might see Tinder as a vapid hookup app where users swipe left or right based on their attraction to another user. But to the inquiring social scientist, it's also a vast data trove about human attraction, sociology, and psychology. For example, Carbino has billions of data points from which she can learn about "thin slicing," the term for nonverbal cues people employ in quick decision-making. Data shows, for example, that women find men with softer jawlines kinder, whereas men find women who wear makeup to be more attractive. With 15 percent of American adults on dating apps, many more discoveries about our ways of evaluating a person's appeal and about the intricacies of dating are sure to be made. Tinder is hardly the only company tapping the talents of liberal arts graduates to make products more appealing and effective.

For example, Nathan Jurgenson was a PhD sociology student at the University of Maryland, writing his thesis on "surveillance on social media" from Brooklyn, when he caught Snap founder Evan Spiegel's attention all the way in Los Angeles. Nathan had written on "digital dualism," pointing out the fallacy that the world is "real" while the digital world is "virtual." He put his finger on the sociological reality that to the extent that the real world was stage-dressed for Instagram, it was perhaps more virtual than an authentic digital alternative. The alternative that was ephemeral, transient, and, therefore, more authentic was Snapchat. Younger generations were tired of the artifice behind the art of sharing.

Snapchat was straight talk, and in the age of endless storage and digital abundance, it created scarcity. Spiegel adopted this notion of deconstructing digital dualism and hired Jurgenson. Today Jurgenson is an in-house social media critic, and the editor of the Snap-funded online magazine called *Real Life*, which publishes essays about living with technology.

The wildly successful corporate communications startup Slack, which offers software that allows employees on a team to communicate more efficiently than with email, employs theater majors to help make the messages Slack sends to users more engaging. Just as Siri offers humorous or sassy responses when you pressure her for particular answers, such as "Perhaps you're right," said in a droll tone, Slack's chat bots seek "to provide users with extra bits of surprise and delight" by providing unconventional responses. Editorial director Anna Pickard, a theater major from Manchester Metropolitan University in England, cooks up these kernels of whimsy. When you join Slack as a new user, rather than input your data into fields, you simply "chat" with a friendly bot that asks you for your relevant details. Similarly, Wade and Wendy is a company creating a chat bot powered by artificial intelligence that aims to streamline hiring conversations between candidates and recruiters. Its programmers attempt to codify fluid conversations into static code based on the research and analysis provided by Tommy Dyer, an in-house organizational psychologist who got a very classical liberal arts education based on reading original texts at St. John's College in Annapolis, Maryland.

Much of the criticism of the liberal arts is based on the false assumption that liberal arts students lack rigor in comparison to those participating in the STEM disciplines and that they are "soft" and unscientific, whereas those who study STEM fields learn the scientific method. In fact, the liberal arts teach many methods of rigorous inquiry and analysis, such as close observation and interviewing in ways that hard science adherents don't always appreciate. Many fields have long incorporated the scientific method and other types of data-driven scientific inquiry and problem solving. In development economics, for example, students are taught about conducting randomized control trials that test policy interventions with much the same rigor as clinical medical trials, with groups like the Poverty Action Lab at MIT and the Innovations for Poverty Action at Yale leading the way.

Sociologists have developed sophisticated mathematical models of societal networks. Historians gather voluminous data on centuries-old household expenses, marriage and divorce rates, and world trade, and use data to conduct statistical analyses identifying trends and contributing factors to the phenomena they are studying. Linguists have developed high-tech models of the evolution of language, and they've made crucial contributions to the development of one of the technologies behind the rapid advance of automation—natural language processing, whereby computers are able to communicate with the accuracy and personality of Siri and Alexa. When venture capitalist Vinod Khosla asserted, as he did in a widely circulated 2016 *Medium* post titled "Is Majoring in Liberal Arts a Mistake for Students?," that a liberal arts education limits "the dimensionality of your thinking since you have less familiarity with mathematical models . . . and worse statistical understanding," he neglected to account for how widely these methods of inquiry are being taught to liberal arts majors.

It's also important to debunk the fallacy that liberal arts students who don't study these quantitative analytical methods have no "hard" or relevant skills. This gets us back to the arguments about the fundamental ways of thinking, inquiring, problem solving, and communicating that a liberal arts education teaches, made by Fareed Zakaria among many others. Part of the problem with the misunderstanding about how rigorous the development of these skills can be derives from mischaracterizations of how rarefied, or esoteric, the liberal arts subjects are. Critics love to trot out what *New York Times* writer Charles McGrath called "apocryphal stories" of students "who are expert in the erotic subtext of pre-World War I Croatian folk dance." My father used to warn my sister and me about majoring in "basket weaving." Fortunately, we chose comparative literature and political science instead. In truth, one of the hallmarks of liberal arts education is that students are encouraged, if not required, to study a broad range of subjects, either through a core curriculum that all students must take, or more commonly through taking a number of electives that complement their work in their major.

Specialization is a feature of graduate education in the liberal arts disciplines, not of undergraduate studies. An irony about this criticism is that it is actually in the STEM fields that specialization is more of a problem, with the course loads for many degrees leaving little room for wider-ranging pursuit of intellectual passions or simple curiosities. What's more, computer science programs often churn out graduates who are not versed in the coding languages that will make them effective programmers today. The languages one needs to know to do product development rapidly change. Many such students require additional online training. In fact, Zach Sims, a political science major at Columbia University, co-founded Codecademy, which offers online programming classes, specifically because of this failure of traditional programs. "We found that you can be a good Computer Science major, but not a good programmer. So early on we interviewed people for Harvard and MIT and realized that they might not be the best hands-on programmer," he explained in 2013. Former president of the College of Wooster in Ohio and a senior fellow at the Council of Independent Colleges, Georgia Nugent noted in an article for *Fast Company*, "Why Top Tech CEOs Want Employees with Liberal Arts Degrees," that with technology evolving so fast and the needs of businesses shifting in unpredictable ways, "it's a horrible irony that at the very moment the world has become more complex, we're encouraging our young people to be highly specialized in one task. We are doing a disservice to our young people by telling them that life is a straight path. The liberal arts are still relevant because they prepare students to be flexible and adaptable to changing circumstances." In our ever-faster-changing world, the demand for intellectual agility, creativity, and the curiosity to explore new terrain is higher than ever.

A core aim of liberal arts education is to allow students to pursue their passions, and also to enable them to discover passions. Exposing students to new areas of scholarship and to other cultures, belief systems, methods of investigation and argumentation is at the heart of this mission. The ideal is that a broad liberal arts exposure tugs on the mind, forcing a student to consider positions and opinions that make him or her question perspectives and biases, often fueling late-night debates with classmates. Students are encouraged to select a major based on their intellectual interests as much as, if not more than, on a clear idea of the field of work they will ultimately pursue. A student may enter college expecting to major in economics or English literature, but take a class in urban sociology as an elective and discover an intense interest in urban planning, perhaps deciding to go into urban studies and a career in city planning or government. Perhaps that student will one day bring that knowledge to collaborate with technology experts in order to innovate an efficient urban transportation system that incorporates driverless vehicles, or will consider how demographic analytics could better price real estate.

Central to the philosophy of a liberal arts education is that we may not discover our strongest interests, and the work we would like to devote ourselves to, without exposure to a broad range of knowledge and ways of thinking, and to investigation of the nature of our world and of problem solving. A liberal education is not so much about learning to do a job as it is about learning to learn, and to love learning. It is both about intellectual adventure and about building the fundamental intellectual skills that equip students to continue to pursue new interests for the rest of their lives, whether or not they have a formal education in those pursuits. These fundamental skills—critical thinking, reading comprehension, logical analysis, argumentation, clear and persuasive communication— also prepare students very well for work life.

Georgia Nugent reported in an August 2015 essay for the Council of Independent Colleges that "time and again, graduates in all walks of life (from corporate leadership to crime prevention, from diplomacy to dentistry, from medicine to media) speak passionately of the value of having been introduced to art, anthropology, philosophy, history, world religions, literature, languages—no matter what their college major or their career path. In fact, they often attribute the success they have attained to this undergraduate exposure to many different modes of thought." The innovation of technology-driven products and services also belongs on that list. In a July 2015 *Forbes* article by George Anders, Slack's Butterfield admitted that philosophy taught him well. "I learned how to write really clearly. I learned how to follow an argument all the way down, which is invaluable in running meetings. And when I studied the history of science, I learned about the ways that everyone believes something is true—like the old notion of some kind of ether in the air propagating gravitational forces—until they realized that it wasn't true," he recalled.

The development of these foundational skills is the reason that so many employers are intent on hiring liberal arts graduates, despite the dire warnings of certain tech titans. In a survey published in *Liberal Education* in 2013, 74 percent of employers polled responded that a liberal arts education "is the best way to prepare for success in today's global economy." Employers in the technology sector are very much included. LinkedIn, which owns a treasure trove of data about what kind of people are being hired for which jobs, conducted a study in 2015 revealing that "liberal arts grads are joining the tech workforce more rapidly than technical grads. Between 2010 and 2013, the growth of liberal arts majors entering the technology industry from undergrad outpaced that of computer science and engineering majors by 10 percent."

Companies need intellectual dexterity as much as they need technical expertise. Staying competitive with the pace of innovation today demands it. We'll see again and again in this book how people who earned "fuzzy" liberal arts degrees made bold leaps into totally unknown terrain, connecting the dots between fields, perceiving problems overlooked by experts, and feeling confident in their ability to get up to speed with whatever knowledge they need in order to push forward with an innovative idea. This is not to say that only a liberal arts education fosters this dexterity; many of those who train in technical fields are immensely creative. The point is that a liberal arts education actively encourages such abilities and is of equal importance.

For years, many leading firms in Silicon Valley have been hiring large numbers of staff with little or no technological knowledge, and often no prior experience working at a tech-based company, to bring their expertise in design, sales, brand building, and customer relations management to product development and marketing. What's new today is how fuzzies are playing central roles in coming up with many of the most creative and successful new business ideas and driving core product development. Some of them are applying the specific methods of investigation and analysis they learned in their major field of study, whether economics, sociology, linguistics, or psychology, and some of them are doing work they had no special training for, like Katelyn Gleason. Fuzzies are helping to bridge divides between specialties, making unexpected connections between problems and the technological means of addressing them, and building the cross-functional teams required to pursue the most promising areas of innovation. They are sharing vital insights about how the human factor can and should be accounted for, and how the new technologies can be best used to improve our lives.

The most exciting and influential innovations today—those referred to as "zero to one" innovations by influential startup investor Peter Thiel in his 2014 book with Blake Masters called *Zero to One*—are arising from the merging of fuzzy and techie expertise, producing more powerful ways to solve the most important problems across a wide range of domains like education, health care, retail, manufacturing, policing, and international security. As Mark Zuckerberg argued in an August 2016 interview with Y Combinator president Sam Altman, "I always think that you should start with the problem that you're trying to solve in the world and not start with deciding that you want to build a company . . . The best companies that get built are things that are trying to drive some kind of social change." These innovators are improving the ways in which we foster our children's engagement in learning. They are harnessing knowledge of human psychology and the powers of persuasion to make headway in preventive medicine. They are helping to make government more transparent and democratic, and facilitating higher-quality and more efficient interpersonal communication. Innovators are tapping the potential of the deluge of "big data" and ingeniously making use of the power of such cutting-edge technologies as natural language processing and machine learning. And this era of transformative innovation has only just begun.

Opportunities abound, but so do threats. Any business that is not purposefully spearheading better collaboration between its fuzzy and techie staffs—bringing in people with the right set of skills in understanding the human factor and the possibilities of the new tech tools—risks rapid obsolescence. As leading business strategy specialist Michael Porter wrote with James Heppelmann in the *Harvard Business Review* in 2015, "The evolution of products into intelligent, connected devices . . . is radically reshaping companies and competition," requiring the evolution of new business models and collaboration across the tech and nontech functions.

Every able-bodied working person wants to stay relevant as this wave of innovation builds; college students considering their careers; parents who want to steer their children to success; and entrepreneurs and corporate managers, no matter what sector, must understand the extraordinary potential of merging the fuzzy with the techie. While the rise of robots has been persuasively heralded, the Second Machine Age is less about machines taking over human roles than it is about humans making machines better serve us.

Adding the Human Factor to Big Data

On May 2, 2014, the USS *Blue Ridge*, the command ship of the U.S. Navy's Seventh Fleet, was on patrol in the treacherous waters of the South China Sea. Intelligence detected what looked to be a large hive of vessels in the area known as the Vietnamese exclusive economic zone (EEZ). The data from an intricate web of surveillance devices deployed in the region was displayed on the Global Command and Control System–Maritime (GCCS-M), or "Geeks."

Andreas Xenachis was on duty that day, leading six analysts on a "watch floor," the term for the rotating groups that monitor and analyze the flood of data coming in from the larger fleet C4I— which stands for command, control, communication, computers, and intelligence—operation. His team was responsible for keeping apprised of all data on Geeks, which meant a complex dance of receiving, retrieving, and displaying data about ship movements, satellite data, radar signatures, and newswires. They were also responsible for providing the fleet commander a first-line situational awareness of what the data was indicating and the possible danger to any of the eighty ships, hundreds of aircraft, and tens of thousands of people under his command.

No one on the team that day had ever seen a formation of blips on the screen quite like what Geeks was showing. The blips seemed to be arrayed in a formation somewhat like a layered protection posture, something typically used by a military fleet. It's a formation where a military or "gray hull" vessel might be ringed by smaller ships, providing multiple layers of defense. China and Vietnam have been engaged in a heated dispute for years over Chinese incursions into the Vietnamese EEZ. Might this be a Chinese military operation? Could it be a precursor to an attack? Or was it just a maritime exercise of some sort?

The data could not tell the team on the watch floor precisely how to evaluate the pattern it was showing, or what to advise the commander. Xenachis's team, just like those coordinating the watch floor when his team went to bed, manning the late-night shift, would have to pool its experience in naval operations, background knowledge of the complex situation in the South China Sea, and the specific location of the formation, and communicate moment to moment with the larger C4I team through its dozens of chat rooms and a flurry of phone calls. Exquisitely well-reasoned judgment about the level of potential threat was required; the South China Sea is a tinderbox where one wrong move could easily escalate into a major conflict.

A little history. China, Taiwan, Vietnam, Malaysia, Brunei, and the Philippines have all made territorial claims in the South China Sea, and each country disputes the others' claim. It's no wonder there's interest; there are 11 billion barrels of oil and 190 trillion cubic feet of natural gas in the Sea, and there's a strong interest in energy resources in the region. By 2035, 90 percent of fossil fuel exports from the Middle East are projected to go to Asia. China, flexing its economic might, has aggressively built a series of military installations encircling much of the Sea, and laced the Sea with artificial islands equipped to harbor a growing fleet of naval destroyers lined with airstrips designed for fighter jets. Despite loud protests from neighboring countries, China continues to proceed ambitiously with oil drilling in the disputed terrain, which, based on esoteric legalese, can be claimed by many. In the face of this aggression, the U.S. Navy has stepped up patrols in the Sea, seeking to ensure the freedom of navigation guaranteed under international law. China deems this a violation of its sovereignty, because it claims that its installations technically qualify as islands, therefore giving them exclusive rights to the Sea.

Several provocations have been directed at U.S. ships by Chinese naval vessels. In 2009, Chinese fishing vessels, known to carry out demands of the state, attempted to cut underwater cables attached to a U.S. sonar array. Later that year, a Chinese submarine collided with a U.S. submersible that was conducting underwater surveillance near the Philippines. U.S. defense secretary Ashton Carter has called Chinese actions "out of step" with international norms, and global security experts have questioned whether the world is on the precipice of another Cold War, with a new status quo as one of sustained aggression, one in which miscalculation by China or the United States in response to a perceived threat could spark a major international crisis.

Exercising great caution, Xenachis's watch floor and the C4I team discussed the spectrum of scenarios and explanations for the dense formation of ships they saw. They considered all of the signals intelligence, as well as scholarship, and after analysis of the full circumstances at play in the Sea, they conjointly concluded that the large object around which the smaller vessels were arrayed was a Chinese oil rig, surrounded by scores of fishing boats,

Chinese Coast Guard vessels, and military escort ships. It was later confirmed that the state-owned China National Offshore Oil Corporation was transporting its massive Haiyang Shiyou 981 (HYSY 981) deep-sea drilling rig to a spot just offshore the Paracel Islands—islands all claimed by Vietnam, China, and Taiwan—and that the rig had immediately begun drilling, which led to a months-long confrontation between the Vietnamese and Chinese. The Vietnamese claimed the rig was on their continental shelf, in violation of the UN Convention on the Law of the Sea. In response, China sent as many as eighty ships, including seven military vessels and aircraft, to guarantee the security of the rig.

Zack Cooper is an Asia security expert working with the Maritime Transparency Initiative at the Center for Strategic and International Studies (CSIS) in Washington, DC. "Although there have been a number of operations in disputed waters in the South China Sea, China's placement of HYSY 981 in waters claimed by Vietnam (and Taiwan) led to one of the most sustained confrontations that has occurred in the South China Sea in the last decade," he explains. "This action was destabilizing and risked escalation, but the fact that no major conflict occurred serves as evidence that these types of coercive incidents can be managed . . . Vietnam accepted real risk, which likely surprised Chinese leaders and convinced them to alter their calculations about Vietnam's willingness and capability to challenge Chinese coercion."

The HYSY 981 standoff, as the incident has become known, is representative of the limits of what the vast quantities of data collected today can provide in terms of valuable insight. The Geeks system is indeed a robust tool, providing invaluable real-time information about vessel movements across the entire maritime world. But that data must be interpreted with the wisdom of human experience and creative problem solving. As it turns out, Xenachis's liberal arts education prepared him well for leading his watch floor in that process. Far from technology studies, he majored in political science as an undergraduate at Yale University and international affairs at Tufts University's Fletcher School of Law and Diplomacy. After graduation, he took a position at the Brookings Institution in Washington, DC, where he worked as a special assistant to the president, honing his analytical skills. While he might have been the perfect guy for the job, "if anyone was dropped into such a scenario and faced such an analytic challenge, they would be well served by considering more than just big data," he says.

As an immigrant from Romania, he'd always felt compelled to serve the country that had given him so much opportunity, and so at the age of thirty-one he joined the U.S. Navy as a reserve officer. His hope was to play a direct role in negotiating the complex geopolitical tensions roiling the global community. Xenachis worked initially on the joint staff as an analyst, and was soon promoted to fleet intelligence watch officer aboard the USS *Blue Ridge*, where he received an email inviting him to participate as a geopolitical forecaster of events and become part of one of the most exciting efforts underway to maximize the power of combining human intelligence and on-the-ground expertise with the massive volume and richness of "big data" being collected today—an effort called the Good Judgment Project.

Adding Human Insights to the Power of Technology

One of the most important roles for us humans going forward is to help make the new technologies better at what they do. This isn't to say STEM is less important, but as our technologies become more accessible than ever before, our ability to apply those technologies meaningfully becomes more important. The opportunity to bolster technology's power and apply it more fruitfully is wide-open terrain, and also fertile terrain for those trained in investigating, in problem solving, and in the consideration of the human factors.

A leader in this endeavor is psychologist Philip Tetlock, a professor of management, psychology, and political science at the University of Pennsylvania. In 2011, Tetlock launched the Good Judgment Project (GJP) with his wife, decision scientist Barbara Mellers, and economist Don Moore. For two decades Tetlock has explored the characteristics and pitfalls of how experts make decisions. He's combined the qualitative insights of psychology and political science with the quantitative methods of analysis to evaluate expert opinion, in particular, when expert opinion is reliable and when it's prone to break down.

Tetlock spearheaded the GJP with the aim of solving a problem put forth in a competition sponsored by the U.S. Office of the Director of National Intelligence, which specifically directs the Intelligence Advanced Research Projects Activity (IARPA). IARPA is the intelligence equivalent of the group known as the Advanced Research Projects Agency (ARPA), which was behind the early electronic communications network that became the Internet. In 2010, IARPA created the Aggregative Contingent Estimation (ACE) program, the objective of which was "to dramatically enhance the accuracy, precision, and timeliness of intelligence forecasts on a broad range of event types," meaning international security events like those Xenachis was evaluating in the South China Sea. Tetlock invited Xenachis to join the team he was forming to tackle IARPA's challenge because he had demonstrated an expertise in turning dots on a radar screen into understanding. Anxious to put his abilities to the test, Xenachis immediately signed on to the exciting project, and soon was ranked among the top 2 percent of forecasters.

Each year IARPA publicly poses 100 to 150 questions on foreign policy topics to elicit crowd-sourced forecasting on, for example, the likelihood of chemical weapons inspections in Syria, or whether a woman will be appointed the next secretary-general of the United Nations. The consensus at IARPA was that the answer to ACE would be a "big data" solution, meaning that the solution would be found by the application of sophisticated mathematical analysis to the vast quantities of data IARPA had made available to the contestants. Xenachis recounted that "what ended up happening was very different."

To solve the problem, contributors were given access to IARPA's Integrated Conflict Early Warning System (ICEWS), a large database consisting of historical data about conflict. Teams were given the purview to use any methodology they deemed fit. A number of teams included data analytics experts from top academic institutions in the United States, and they sought purely technological solutions, incorporating a range of analytical techniques, including machine learning. In essence, machine learning is the training of machines to perform tasks autonomously by making enormous quantities of data available to them and then programming them with a set of rules for analyzing it all on their own. Self-driving cars are currently grabbing the most attention, but machines are also being trained to perform many other impressive feats. For example, as we will explore further in Chapter 8, machine learning has enabled Google's DeepMind program, called AlphaGo, to defeat the world champion of the astonishingly complex ancient Chinese board game Go. Until that match, playing Go was deemed well beyond the capability of even the brainiest artificial intelligence machines.

The Wharton team took a different approach from all the other groups. Tetlock built on the latest developments in data science, but he went further. He sought the input of thousands of human contributors with a wide range of backgrounds, including Xenachis's experience with ship movements. He used high-level analytics to perform an initial investigation of the data, but he also factored in human expertise. The results of the competition were astounding. The Good Judgment Project was the only team that showed a significant improvement in forecasting events over that of a control group that used the preexisting method. "The other teams weren't performing any better than the baseline. Despite having fancy tech algorithms, they were missing something. What I think was missing was a human element," Xenachis explained over coffee.

The GJP result is an inspiring testament that in an era of increasingly intelligent technology, the fuzzy still counts, or, in the sage words that form one of the mantras of the U.S. Special Operations Forces, "Humans are more important than hardware." A psychologist with keen insight into the fuzzy strengths and weaknesses of human judgment devised a means of combining the best of what man and machine had to offer. The results were so strong, in fact, that IARPA clawed back the money it had given to other teams and gave it all to the Wharton group to expand their program. The chair of the National Intelligence Council and others such as Harvard law professor and former White House advisor Cass Sunstein have publicly praised the program. Sunstein went so far as to say it was the most important scientific study he's ever read on prediction. *New York Times* columnist David Brooks said if he were president, he'd want predictions such as those provided by GJP on his desk. Tetlock took a skeptic's view, interrogated assumptions, and built an approach that combined human smarts and machine-empowered data science.

Today the Good Judgment Project is empowering a number of public and private sector decision-makers to train their own forecasting experts, who can eventually help them predict developments for which they will need to be prepared. Andreas Xenachis now runs the government team. "What was interesting," he reflected about the IARPA competition, "was that there was an initial assumption that asked, 'How can we automate this? How can we take the human out of the loop?' There was this thinking that they could make the human superfluous. I believe in innovation, but I also believe we shouldn't defer to technological solutions to the point that it takes the human out of the equation—when we still very clearly have a significant value add." As the GJP now expands its reach into the private sector, its new forecasting inquiries include disruptions in vehicle innovations. In partnership with the Program on Vehicle and Mobility Innovation at Wharton, it's polling forecasters about Tesla's autopilot system software updates and electric vehicle adoption in China. Again, it is pairing the fuzzy and techie, building atop very real progress in big data, supplementing it with the social sciences.

Chris Anderson, entrepreneur, author of *The Long Tail*, and former editor in chief of *Wired* magazine, argued in 2008 that the vast quantities of data now being collected would make the scientific method obsolete, as "the scientific method is built around testable hypotheses. These systems, for the most part, are visualized in the minds of scientists. The models are then tested, and experiments confirm or falsify theoretical models of how the world works . . . Data without a model is just noise. But faced with massive data, this approach to science—hypothesize, model, test—is becoming obsolete." In his *Wired* article entitled "The End of Theory: The Data Deluge Makes the Scientific Method Obsolete," Anderson argued that an end of theory was inevitable because with so much data available, analysis will allow for discoveries without the need for humans first postulating what the data might reveal. With enough data, with enough information, we'll simply have knowledge.

But Luciano Floridi, a professor of the philosophy and ethics of information at Oxford University's Internet Institute, refutes Anderson's "end of theory" assertion in his book *The Fourth Revolution: How the Infosphere Is Reshaping Human Reality.* Floridi points out that Anderson's notion is rather unoriginal, and harkens back to an argument made four hundred years ago by the English philosopher Sir Francis Bacon, who contended that if one accumulated enough facts, they could speak for themselves without hypotheses. The same argument was made even earlier by the ancient Greek philosopher Plato, who emphasized that knowledge is more than just information or data; that it comes from knowing "how to ask and answer questions." Floridi concluded that this is an old argument and that "data do not speak for themselves, we need smart questioners." Floridi's assertion is similar to a statement often attributed to Voltaire: we must begin to judge a person on the basis of their questions, not their answers.

A number of breakthroughs in the development of "smart" technologies in recent years have led to arguments that many human capabilities either have already been surpassed by those of machines or will soon be eclipsed. Instrumental to these developments has been the advent of so-called big data, meaning the accumulation of larger collections of data than was technologically feasible until the creation of vast "server farms" or "data centers," which store this data in what is now ironically called "the cloud." At the same time, the migration of business and leisure activity to the web has generated a tsunami of new data to store and to analyze. In addition, increasingly small and powerful sensors are embedded in products of all kinds, from smartphones to cars and household appliances, and are generating data at exponential rates. Our phones and these surrounding sensors can read and write a vast range of data, from visual information to information about the movement of other objects in the sensor's vicinity, as well as environmental conditions and sounds. Some sensors perform what's known as "reality capture," where the atoms of the physical world around us are turned into digital bits.

Another major development contributing to the flood of new data involves the innovation of ever-smaller computer chips and wireless web connectivity. Combined, they are enabling the implantation of objects of all kinds with computing ability as well as the connection of devices to the web. This is leading to the rapid evolution of the Internet of Things, whereby objects all around us will be able to communicate continuously not only with their manufacturers, but also with one another in machine-to-machine interactions. Already, John Deere is making tractors equipped with guidance systems that steer themselves and with sensors that gather information on soil conditions that is transmitted to the company, where it is analyzed to advise farmers about how to improve crop yields.

Some chroniclers of these developments—like Chris Anderson—have argued that the new power of machine learning will fully supplant the human role in analyzing data. I believe the more likely scenario is that humans will find better and more efficient ways to harness the power of big data and machine learning to assist them in tackling a host of outstanding problems that are crying out for better analytics but require both machines and people.

The debate about whether machines will supplant humans stretches back to the middle of last century. MIT professor and pioneer of computing Marvin Minsky argued that artificial intelligence should be the goal and could match human ability, while J.C.R. Licklider, also a professor at MIT, argued that machines would supplement the skills of humans rather than displacing us. It was a debate over artificial intelligence (AI) and intelligence augmentation (IA). Licklider is considered by many to be the Johnny Appleseed of computing for having planted the foundational seeds for seminal developments in computing, including the concepts of personal computers, the importance of human-computer interaction, and even the Internet. He impacted nearly every aspect of today's technology. In his influential 1960 essay "Man-Computer Symbiosis," Licklider argued that there would be no robot apocalypse, but rather that "the resulting partnership will think as no human brain has ever thought and process data in a way not approached by the information-handling machines we know today."

Ever more powerful augmentation is precisely what we are seeing evolve today. The most fruitful work being done with the new technologies combines fuzzy human skills with automated machine ones. And though machine learning might seem to be the ultimate inaccessible techie fortress, far too arcane for anyone but a specialist to make use of the technology, let alone to contribute to improving it, in fact the power of big data and machine learning is being rapidly "democratized." Due to the creation of web-based platforms that allow people to pose problems to be solved, even people with no data analysis experience can assist in asking questions of the data and gain access to a trove of experts in data science to provide answers. Kaggle, a company founded by an Australian economist, is one of these platforms.

The founder of Kaggle, Anthony Goldbloom, grew up in Australia and attended the University of Melbourne, where he graduated with a degree in economics in 2006. He had not anticipated becoming an entrepreneur, but it turned out that his economics training opened the door that led to his idea for Kaggle. After university, he moved to the national capital, Canberra, and went to work as an economist at the Australian Treasury. "I used to work on things like GDP, inflation, and unemployment," he recalled. "None of it was horribly interesting. The Treasury then gave me three months leave to intern for the *Economist* in London, England, and I wrote an article there on predictive analytics. There were all sorts of interesting data locked up inside companies, and I wanted to play with it. There was a lot of data out there, and . . . these companies likely needed help making sense of it." So did all sorts of other organizations, he realized. Goldbloom decided that he wanted to dedicate himself to giving people access to the best tools for solving real-world problems of all kinds. Soon, he was spending his nights and weekends creating the technology that would become the Kaggle platform, and after six months of sleepless nights he quit his job to launch the company.

In short, Kaggle allows companies and researchers to post data to the site, and data scientists from all over the world can compete to perform analysis on it and provide insights, with the winning solutions earning substantial cash rewards for their efforts. Goldbloom has made data science into a highly competitive and highly paid sport. While companies with sensitive data can pay to host closed competitions for experts behind nondisclosure agreement (NDA) walls, much of the analysis done through the platform is open and available to everyone. Kaggle has hosted hundreds of competitions, and its data scientists have made important headway in solving an array of diverse problems.

General Electric, for example, has posted $600,000 worth of prizes on Kaggle, looking for solutions to a number of business challenges. One of those was to help predict runway use and gate arrival patterns for U.S. commercial airline flights. GE provided Kaggle participants with voluminous flight and weather data, and in a four-month competition, the company received over three thousand entries, with the winning team improving industry standard accuracy by 40 percent. That amounts to a savings of five minutes per flight per gate, approximated as an annual savings of $6.2 million for a midsize airline.

In another example, Kaggle helped improve the way doctors treat patients suffering from debilitating eye damage caused by diabetes. For individuals who have diabetes, one of the long-term complications is something called diabetic retinopathy, or harm to the tiny blood vessels in the eye that supply oxygen to the retina. When these blood vessels break, they impact the retina, and in many cases the rupture results in blindness. This is one of the leading causes of blindness in developed countries, and 80 percent of diabetics have some form of retinal affliction. The California Health Care Foundation (CHCF) recognized that if caught early, diabetic retinopathy could be treated with lasers, drugs, and surgery. The CHCF decided to post a challenge, with a $100,000 prize, to find an early detection method. Thousands of images of retinas, healthy and diseased, were posted to the Kaggle platform, and after five months of work, a statistician named Benjamin Graham at the University of Warwick, in England, designed an algorithm that predicted retinal damage 85 percent of the time.

Kaggle, which in 2017 was acquired by Google, is helping solve challenges across every domain. Another powerful result was the creation of a method for the computerized evaluation of essay exams. In education, standardized tests typically feature multiple-choice questions not because these are the best way to test for complex thinking, communication, and collaboration, but because they're the cheapest to grade. Standardized tests are not considered the best way to assess students' knowledge. Essay exams provide a more holistic evaluation of student achievement and are more reflective of skills required in the market.

The Hewlett Foundation wanted to discover whether a means could be found for automating the grading of essays without sacrificing quality. If so, technology could improve standardized testing for cognitive skills by making grading fluid formats like essays more affordable. The foundation sponsored the Automated Student Assessment Prize (ASAP), challenging entrants to use data science to build models that could reproduce scores given by human graders across a data set of twenty-seven thousand handscored long-form student essays written on a wide range of topics. Over three months, they received one thousand eight hundred entries, with the top teams outperforming even commercial vendors. ASAP codirector Tom Vander Ark concluded that "computers can be implemented to validate—not to replace—the work of teachers, lowering costs for school districts and offering better tests that can be graded faster and less expensively."

Where's the "Terrorist Find" Button?

Though many technology innovators see a total removal of the human element from the equation of data analysis as a natural end, others, such as Shyam Sankar, director of Palantir Technologies, are keenly aware of the competitive advantage of enlisting human input. Palantir is a $20 billion company that designs analytics platforms to empower the world's security, law enforcement, and policymaking domain experts, allowing them to fight crime and global terrorism more efficiently by leveraging data science. The company is contracted by some of the most secretive three-letter agencies. Palantir's "forward deployed engineers," as their salespeople are known, can easily find themselves setting up analytics dashboards behind enemy lines, working directly with special operations commanders. In fact, in 2016 Palantir won a $222 million contract to work with the U.S. Special Operations Command.

Sankar received his undergraduate degree in electrical and computer engineering from Cornell University and a master's degree in management science and engineering from Stanford. He's a techie's techie. But he believes in J.C.R. Licklider's vision of complementing human intelligence, intuition, and pattern recognition with powerful machine analytics.

Palantir's technology helps organizations stitch together structured and unstructured data, giving experts in intelligence gathering the ability to search across and ask questions of data from multiple sources, all at the same time. This allows people who are deeply versed in using intelligence to find missing children, fraud, or terrorists, but who often have no expertise in data science, to see patterns that would otherwise be hidden across disparate systems. Sankar's philosophy is that human intelligence augmentation is the only way to stay ahead of such adaptive adversaries as terrorist groups. "Terrorists are always adapting, in minor and major ways, to new circumstances," Sankar noted onstage at TED Global in Glasgow, Scotland, in 2012. "Despite what you see on TV, these adaptations and the detections of them are fundamentally human. Computers don't detect novel patterns and new behaviors, humans do: Humans, using technology, testing hypotheses, and searching for insight by asking machines to do things for them. Osama bin Laden was not caught by artificial intelligence. He was caught by dedicated, resourceful, brilliant people in partnership with various technologies."

In another case, in October 2007, U.S. and coalition forces raided an al-Qaeda safe house in Sinjar, on the Syrian border of Iraq. They found seven hundred biographical sketches of foreign fighters, literally human resource forms about where the fighters were from, who had recruited them, what job they sought, and why they had joined. The only problem was that these forms were crumpled pieces of paper, written by hand in Arabic. Sifting through the forms and interpreting them required human expertise, but the power of machine analysis was also used once the data had been extracted and coded.

The analysts learned that 20 percent of the foreign fighters were from Libya, and 50 percent of them were from just one town. They saw a surge in participation after a speech by a senior cleric in the Libyan Islamic Fighting Group, which immediately alerted them to his rising stature within al-Qaeda. The detection of such a pattern would not have been possible without machines sorting through the volumes of data, but the data would not have been available, or of high quality, without the hands-on process of raiding a safe house, recovering physical assets, and translating and tagging the human resource forms for machine processing. It took both the context and the framing of the problem to put machines to work, and critical thinkers to interpret results.

The many firms, such as Palantir, that are involved in providing data analytics services are generally portrayed as the leading spears of the highest of high-tech approach to deriving valuable insights from "big data." Indeed, the press releases these companies put out tend to portray them as purely tech-driven. That's because the prevailing narrative coming out of Silicon Valley is that technical capabilities are far superior to human ones. But the reality is that every tech company—Google, Facebook, Slack, Palantir, and others—relies heavily on both technical and human inputs.

The emphasis of most techies is on how to gather, store, search, and process big data, which Sankar points out are "necessary but insufficient" to getting the most value from the data. "The imperative is not to figure out *how* to compute," he says, "but *what* to compute. How do you impose human intuition on data at this scale? We start by designing the human into the process." This is why changing the narrative around fuzzies and techies matters; they are in equal parts vital to the development and the deployment of our best technologies.

Bias Behind the Data

The truth is, data is not objective, and the biases within data sets must be accounted for in the analysis of them. "The algorithmic systems that turn data into information are not infallible—they rely on the imperfect inputs, logic, probability, and people who design them," the White House warned in 2016. For example, crime data is not reflective of all crime committed; it is only reflective of reported crime, and the reporting of crime is distorted by many factors. One community may favor calling the police and reporting crime while another may not. Will heavily immigrant communities that are home to people living in the country illegally call the police into their neighborhoods to address minor types of crime at the same rates as communities that have no fear of their members being deported? Will someone with a dozen unpaid parking tickets call to report a petty theft from his car? Reported crime data is, therefore, reflective of a number of nuances around trust and community details that, on the surface, could easily be overlooked.

For example, the Bureau of Justice Statistics has found that certain crimes like hate crimes and sexual assault are chronically under-reported, meaning they're likely to be left out of hotspot maps of reported crime data.

The Human Rights Data Analysis Group (HRDAG), a nonprofit based in the Mission District of San Francisco, which is dedicated to applying rigorous data analysis in order to address human rights violations all around the world, conducted a study of bias in crime data, and how algorithms can amplify bias in the response of police departments. One study, published in *Significance,* the Royal Statistical Society's magazine, investigated the efficacy of a predictive policing algorithm published by PredPol, a company focused on predicting and preventing crime through data science. The algorithm is intended to inform police departments regarding the optimal locations for deploying officers with the aim of preventing probable crimes.

Authors Kristian Lum and William Isaac decided to apply the algorithm, which is one of the few to have been publicly released in a peer-reviewed journal, to data that they pulled from the publicly available records on drug crimes in Oakland, California. Lum and Isaac supplemented that data set by gathering data on the distribution of drug crime in Oakland from a number of other sources, such as the National Survey on Drug Use and Health. Their data showed that drug use is roughly even across all ethnic groups, while the corresponding drug arrests are not. According to a 2013 report from the American Civil Liberties Union (ACLU), African Americans are 3.73 times more likely to be arrested for marijuana possession than whites, even though the groups use marijuana at roughly the same rate. The ACLU blames racial profiling, stop-and-frisk procedures, and arrest quotas for the discrepancy. HRDAG also found that while drug *crime* was fairly evenly distributed across the city, drug *arrests* were concentrated in only a few locations, primarily West Oakland and Fruitville, two predominately nonwhite, low-income communities.

Therefore, information about where crime was occurring was likely statistically biased, and if police officers were dispatched in higher numbers to those neighborhoods with the higher reported crime rates, as the algorithm suggests, then the bias would be exacerbated, because with more police in those neighborhoods, more arrests would likely be made. The higher arrest data would then be fed into the algorithm, creating a distorted feedback loop because the algorithm would process that information as confirmation that its prediction of higher crime in those neighborhoods was correct, further reinforcing the initial bias. In the first-ever report on big data and civil rights, the White House highlighted the powerful new opportunities, but also warned that "without deliberate care, these innovations can easily hardwire discrimination, reinforce bias, and mask opportunity." With algorithms being piloted to provide recommendations to judges in San Francisco courts, these considerations go well beyond traditional law enforcement. Technology writer Om Malik calls it "data Darwinism," where your digital reputation might become your gateway to access.

Cathy O'Neil, former director of Data Practices at Columbia University's Graduate School of Journalism, and author of the best-selling book *Weapons of Math Destruction: How Big Data Increases Inequality and Threatens Democracy*, takes caution a step further. As she states, "Big Data has plenty of evangelists, but I'm not one of them." She argues that algorithms can be, as she says, "used as weapons" to perpetuate discrimination. They can use math to camouflage bias. O'Neil highlights five characteristics these harmful algorithms possess: they target certain groups of people; they're opaque so that the people who are targeted by them don't understand how they work; they affect a large number of people, or have "scale"; their creators define their success in a way that isn't shared by the people targeted by them (a common definition of success: to save an organization money); and they create pernicious feedback loops.

Claudia Perlich, a data scientist and an adjunct professor of business intelligence and data mining at New York University's Stern School of Business, offers another eye-opening example that illustrates O'Neil's point. In a talk entitled "All the Data and Still Not Enough," she discussed a data-mining competition she has won on multiple occasions, one known as the Knowledge Discovery and Data Mining Cup. In 2008, Siemens Medical challenged competing research teams to rank order candidate regions extracted from fMRI breast images by the likelihood that they contained breast cancer. Teams were provided a data set of 100,000 such candidate regions, drawn from 1,712 patients. One hundred and eighteen of the patients included at least one malignant candidate region. Siemens also told them to look at 117 features in each image, some of which might have predictive ability to show if the patient had cancer. Teams were asked to build a predictive model that looked at these 117 features and see how well the model could diagnose the candidate regions and ultimately the patient.

Perlich's team was from IBM's Watson Research. As they explored the data set, they noticed that there seemed to be a very high incident rate for patients with low patient ID numbers, far exceeding the expected approximately 10 percent. When adding the patient ID to their predictive model (something no data scientist worth her salt would normally consider), they observed a notable increase in predictive performance. The patient ID was in theory a randomly generated ten-digit number that merely identified the patient, and it should have had absolutely nothing to do with the incidence of breast cancer in fMRI data. But what they found indicated otherwise. The patient IDs were clustered into bins. In one bin, 36 percent of the patients had malignant regions, while in two other bins, only 1 percent had cancer. Of all of the features in the data that should show correlation with breast cancer, the patient ID was the last one, and so Perlich's team was perplexed. Upon further examination, the best hypothesis explaining this effect was that the data must have been pulled from four sources. Gathering data from a diversity of sources is generally a good practice in data analytics. But in this case, those who put the data set together did not explicitly record the fact that some patients were from breast cancer *screening* facilities, and others were from cancer *treatment* facilities. As a result, the patient IDs having different numeric regions became very predictive because the incidence of cancer would be much higher in the treatment facilities. Though Perlich's team had built a highly predictive model that looked at thousands of features in fMRI imagery, on further inspection they realized that the only thing the model could reliably predict was whether patients were being treated for cancer or in the process of being diagnosed. On first blush the model had seemed highly effective, but it was almost too good to be true, and experience told them to interrogate it further. Leakage in the data had clouded the model's predictive ability.

"How do we start to regulate the mathematical models that run more and more of our lives?" Cathy O'Neil asks. "Data is not going away. Nor are computers—much less mathematics. Predictive models are, increasingly, the tools we will be relying on to run our institutions, deploy our resources, and manage our lives . . . These models are constructed not just from data but from the choices we make about which data to pay attention to—and which to leave out. Those choices are not just about logistics, profit, and efficiency. They are fundamentally moral."

Such human errors in the collection and interpretation of data must be corrected by human analysis, and this is work for which those trained in the humanities and social sciences are well equipped. They bring valuable perspective about the social contexts in which data is collected, as well as the needed skills for interpreting and communicating the revelations found in data. We can't eliminate bias from society, but we can pair fuzzies and techies to train our algorithms to better sift for, and mitigate, our shared human foibles.

Data Literacy Must Complement Data Science

Leslie Bradshaw, who studied gender, economics, anthropology, and Latin at the University of Chicago, was named by *Fast Company* as one of the one hundred most creative people in business and the woman "making data science cool." Bradshaw cofounded the interactive design firm JESS3 and is today at the forefront of digital product creation. Since 2012, she's also been an advocate of what she calls "data literacy."

"To deepen the benefits of Big Data, we must put the social sciences and the humanities on equal footing with math and computer science," she wrote as part of the American Dreamers project, an experiment in publishing put together by creative agency Wieden + Kennedy, the same agency that came up with Nike's famous slogan, "Just Do It." Bradshaw defines data literacy as "an understanding of the fundamental problems that can crop up along the way [in data gathering and analysis], from strategy to data collection to filtration to analysis to presentation."

Those schooled in the humanities and social sciences can play an important role in advancing data literacy, Bradshaw argues, both among those practicing data science and among the public to whom findings are being presented. This is because they are especially attuned to the types of social issues and psychological biases that must be factored into the assessment of how data sets have been created, and also because they are particularly well trained in the methods necessary for clearly presenting the findings of data. Bradshaw emphasizes that data literacy requires three essential "treatments" of data sets and the analyses run on them: the putting of the data into the larger social context from which it has been collected; the clear presentation of the data through effective visualizations; and the storytelling about the findings that makes those findings both clear and compelling. Explaining her mission to improve data science, she writes, "My dream . . . is a future of More Meaningful Data. And for that, we need: the data gathered and parsed; the data analyzed, interpreted, and contextualized; and the data visualized, narrated, and made accessible. Currently, however, the cult of the mathematically-inclined, computer-science-educated 'data scientist' is not allowing for the full potential of Big Data to be put to use."

People who have studied the social sciences have been taught not only to look for sources of bias and opinion that may be shaping the analysis of data, but also to think of the questions that must be investigated if we are to improve the application of data analysis to solving myriad social problems. How might data be gathered and analyzed in order to illuminate ways in which preschool education could better prepare children for learning? What insights might be discovered about how blighted inner-city economies can best be put on the track to job creation? What can the newly voluminous data we can gather reveal about factors contributing to depression or the incidence of diabetes? These are just a few of the areas in which social science has provided methods and perspectives that can be applied both to gathering more robust and relatively unbiased data and to analyzing it more effectively.

As for the humanities, those schooled in design can bring artistry to the visualization of data findings that makes what would otherwise be formidable spreadsheets of unintelligible figures immediately comprehensible. Those trained in writing with clarity and narrative flair can tell stories about data findings that make them both comprehensible and memorable, assuring they have greater impact. "Embrace the English majors, philosophers, and journalists of the world as equals," Bradshaw advises data scientists, for "you will create more accessibility and therefore more engagement with your data."

Tackling Long-Standing Mysteries

In 2015, employers surveyed by the National Association of Colleges and Employers listed "ability to work in a team" as the most desirable attribute of new college graduates, even ahead of problem solving, analytical, and quantitative skills. Yet "teamwork" remains an ambiguous and poorly understood term. Google launched a study it called Project Aristotle to determine why some work teams perform better than others. Google is a notoriously data-driven company; it even measured the productivity increase when a manager greets his or her new hire on the first day of work. (The answer? A striking 15 percent.)

Laszlo Bock, the author of the 2015 book *Work Rules!* and a senior advisor at Google, where for a decade he ran People Operations (known as human resources at most companies), says, "We try to bring as much analytics and data and science to what we do on the people side as our engineers do on the product side." In that spirit, a research team of psychologists, sociologists, and statisticians was formed within the People Operations group to find an answer to one of the most vexing mysteries in business: What makes some teams more effective than others?

The group spent several years analyzing a wealth of data about the characteristics of over two hundred teams at the company. They questioned fifty years of academic research, looking at what motivated teams, if they had shared values, and how much they socialized outside the office. They analyzed teams composed of friends, and others made up of total strangers. They looked at teams with identical makeups, with varying performance.

Ultimately, the research group found that *who* was on a team mattered far less than *how* they interacted. They found that how teams managed debate, disagreement, and consensus mattered. Groups had unwritten rules of culture. Some were aggressive, where people interrupted one another frequently, while others were conversational. Some teams featured experts who let it be known that they knew what they were talking about, while others held open discussions. What they ultimately found was that one of the biggest drivers of team performance at Google was what's known as psychological safety, or the ability to take risks and to be wrong.

Google's research confirmed the conclusions of a 2008 study by psychologists at Carnegie Mellon, MIT, and Union College, who found that high-performing teams had high collective intelligence, and the driver of collective intelligence was contribution. The best teams had fluid leaders who took advantage of everyone's relative strengths and fostered norms of openness, or "equality in distribution of conversational turn-taking," as reported in Charles Duhigg's *New York Times* article "What Google Learned from Its Quest to Build the Perfect Team." In teams where one person dominated, performance often broke down. Google also confirmed that, as in the 2008 study, high "average social sensitivity" was extremely important. Teams that were made up of members who spoke equally and were sensitive to the moods, personal stories, and emotions of their teammates performed better. Google took a rigorous, data-driven look at its own performance, and found that having high "average social sensitivity" mattered most.

There could perhaps be no more compelling testament to the power of combining fuzzy and techie forces than the fact that one of the world's leading companies in both gathering and analyzing data, with the professed corporate mission to "organize the world's information and make it universally accessible," found that even with the most brilliantly trained analytical minds and the most powerful technology tools, both of which Google employees have in spades, the greatest success comes from attending to human factors like leadership and softer skills.

As Project Aristotle uncovered, noncognitive "social skills" are of exceptional value to companies. The 1998 Occupational Information Network (O*NET), a survey administered by the U.S. Department of Labor, defines social skills as "1) Coordination; 2) Negotiation; 3) Persuasion; 4) Social Perceptiveness." David Deming, a professor of economics at Harvard's Graduate School of Education, has evaluated the benefits of social skills by looking at team production, where workers with comparative advantages in performing certain cognitive tasks better than their peers "trade tasks." Traditionally, trading tasks is seen to have coordination costs, but Deming argues that "social skills act as a kind of social antigravity, reducing the cost of task trade and allowing workers to specialize and coproduce more efficiently." In essence, social skills grease the wheels of teamwork, bringing down the costs of collaboration.

As our technology does more routine work, we're left with

nonroutine, complex work for which we each harbor different passions and abilities. Teamwork, trading tasks, and consequently social skills are increasingly important in this world. As the liberal arts teach us about ourselves and what it means to be human, they teach us empathy, which is at the root of social skills; it is such social skills that facilitate task trading, collaboration, and therefore greater productivity.

In considering how we account for gaps and biases in our data, in how we should administer new tools, and in how we build our teams, we must appreciate the crucial role of the fuzzy as a complement to the techie.

THREE

The Democratization of Technology Tools

I first met Peter Platzer, the founder of Spire, a startup pioneer in sending small and relatively inexpensive satellites into space, sitting in a San Francisco café appropriately called the Sextant, named after the device once used by sailors to navigate by the stars. Spire is deploying small satellites that can help fill in disconcerting gaps in the tracking of ships at sea that have continued to persist despite the advent of Global Positioning System (GPS) technology. Improved maritime domain awareness can mitigate piracy, illegal fishing, and human trafficking. And vessel tracking is just one of Spire's prospective uses. Onboard sensors—which measure the bending of radio waves bounced through the atmosphere—are also helping improve the accuracy of weather forecasts. These "soundings," or collections of raw atmospheric pressure and temperature data, can feed into weather prediction models, not only helping people plan for beach holidays and ski trips, but also helping inform industries such as agriculture and insurance.

Peter and his founding team at Spire are a testament to how accessible so many technology tools have become, allowing people from all walks of life to spearhead the development of many exciting innovations today—innovations that tackle problems, well beyond the traditional scope and expectations of Silicon Valley, that are crying out for solutions.

Satellites have been among the most sophisticated, and inaccessible, of all technology tools. They're not only incredibly expensive to build, but they must be launched by rockets, and the cost of launch alone can range from about $55 million to $260 million, depending on the size and weight of a satellite. The result has been that even as powerful as the ability we now have to monitor conditions and events on the planet's surface from space is, there remain many limitations due to the cost constraints of sending up more satellites. Access to satellite time is also prohibitively expensive for many companies and organizations that could benefit from their capabilities due to the comparatively short supply for the demand. Spire has been able to build much smaller satellites that are still powerful tools because many of the highest-tech components required have been made so affordable and so comparatively easy to package into products.

To consider how these small satellites can be used to help solve a host of thus far intractable problems by collecting and democratizing new types of data, let's take a close look at the issue of ships that go missing.

Since the beginning of navigation, the sea has been a siren, beckoning humanity to sail across and over the horizon. But the globe's vast expanses of open water are as treacherous as they are bewitching, and tracking ships as they traverse the roiling, storm-tossed waters has always been a vexing problem. From as early as 31 BC, when Roman general Agrippa's naval attack on the forces of Antony and Cleopatra at Actium, in modern-day Greece, put Augustus Caesar on the throne as the first emperor of the Roman

Empire, the secrecy with which oceangoing vessels can maneuver has been one of the most challenging security issues, both for naval commanders and for commercial shippers. These days, satellites continuously scan the seas, but there are many holes in their coverage, and ships frequently go missing, sometimes to gain a commercial advantage and other times due to foul intent.

The Democratic People's Republic of Korea, or North Korea as it's more commonly known, has caused international scandals by hacking into Hollywood studio email accounts and testing ballistic missiles without warning. The country is also complicit in clandestine activities on the high seas, specializing in smuggling arms and trafficking narcotics.

International security experts were alarmed when a North Korean ship called the *Mu Du Bong* disappeared off the electronic commercial shipping grid for nine days in July 2014. Under international maritime law, ships are required to be equipped with transponders that send regular, programmed signals using what is known as the Automatic Identification System (AIS), a global communications network that helps provide safety and tracking on the open ocean. Transponders don't usually turn themselves off, so foul play was expected regarding the *Mu Du Bong*. This wasn't the first such occurrence; North Korean naval commanders have a history of such misbehavior.

Perhaps the most infamous incident involves the *Chong Chon Gang*, a 509-foot ship capable of carrying over nine thousand tons of cargo. The massive vessel disembarked from its slip in the North Korean port city of Nampo to enter service in 1977, launching into a storied career of arms trading, safety infractions, and other such violations. The ship was registered to Pyongyang-based company Chongchongang Shipping, which is widely understood to be a front organization run by the storied Central Committee Bureau 39 of the ruling Korean Workers' Party, often referred to by the Orwellian moniker "Office 39."

Office 39 routinely engages in illegal activities to generate hard currency for the government—basically, it's a highly organized crime syndicate set up and run by the North Korean regime that, until his death in 2011, reported directly to Kim Jong-il. Its moneymaking schemes have been creative and highly adaptable from year to year; Sheena Chestnut Greitens, a researcher at the Brookings Institution and the University of Missouri, has linked its operations to everything from making methamphetamine and the best counterfeit U.S. dollars in the world—so good the U.S. Secret Service calls them "supernotes"—to trafficking in endangered species, engaging in insurance fraud, and manufacturing knockoff cigarettes and consumer goods. It's even sold counterfeit Viagra (and the *Washington Post* says it works). Andrea Berger, a North Korean expert at the UK's Royal United Services Institute, a think tank, says, "Office 39 is extremely important. It's generally regarded as the regime slush fund." According to an official European Union Commission Implementing Regulation against North Korea, Office 39 has representation in places as far-flung as Rome, Bangkok, and Dubai, and its subsidiaries are "involved in facilitating North Korea's proliferation financing projects," circumventing UN sanctions, laundering illicit money through offshore banks in Macao, and using that money to fund the state's nuclear weapons ambitions.

In March 2009, Somali pirates chased the lumbering and aging *Chong Chon Gang* through the Arabian Sea, firing guns and rocket-propelled grenades from surrounding speedboats. Unlike the case of the 2009 hijacking of the *Maersk Alabama*, made famous by the movie *Captain Phillips*, the *Chong Chon Gang* repelled the pirates. But due to reported damage from the attack, the vessel made an unannounced stop in Tartus, Syria. North of Lebanon, on the Mediterranean coast, Tartus was a troubling port of call for the wounded ship because it's also the site of a large Russian naval base; in fact it's the largest outpost of Russian power in the region and its only military installation outside of the former Soviet Union. Maintaining the base is arguably one reason that Russian president Vladimir Putin has helped prop up the draconian regime of Syrian president Bashar al-Assad even as civil war has ravaged the country and hundreds of thousands of people have died. The vessel's stop seemed suspicious, and some maritime analysts doubted that it was made due to the need for repairs. A year later, in February 2010, Ukrainian authorities detained the *Chong Chon Gang* as it passed through the Black Sea for reasons that were again unclear.

By July 2013, the *Chong Chon Gang* made its way to Cuba, into waters ninety miles off the American coast. For ten days after leaving Cuba, the ship went missing from the AIS system, having turned off its AIS transponder. Then, as the ship was attempting to leave the Gulf of Mexico to begin its eight-thousand-mile journey back to North Korea, it was spotted near the Panama Canal by Panamanian authorities. After an intense five-day standoff, Panamanian officials boarded and combed the ship. At first, it appeared to be carrying only two hundred thousand sacks of brown sugar in its massive hold. But aware of the ship's reputation, the searchers dug further, and hidden amidst the sugar, they found two Soviet-era antiaircraft missile batteries, nine disassembled air defense missiles, two MiG-21 fighter jets, and fifteen engines. While the North Korean government claimed that Cuba was simply sending the old parts to North Korea for repair, many experts asserted that Cuba had clearly violated UN sanctions banning the sale of weapons to North Korea.

Because of this history, when only a year later the *Mu Du Bong* went off-grid, the working assumption was that it could have been up to similar misdeeds. The ship was heading north from Cuba, toward the United States, when its signal went dark and the captain "lost his bearings," or so he claimed. The transponder turned on again only after the ship accidentally ran aground on a reef off the coast of Mexico. Its hull was empty, so it's impossible to know what kind of cargo it had been carrying. But the fact that a major foreign ship that could have easily been loaded with weaponry could secretly approach U.S. shores illustrates the security imperative of improved maritime tracking. Supplemented by GPS and imagery data, Spire's relatively inexpensive satellites offer an additional ability to provide that service, plugging the gaps between land-based surveillance systems and space-based signals intelligence.

Because of the curvature of the earth, land-based AIS systems can typically only see ships within fifty miles of shore, which doesn't come close to covering the two hundred miles of the exclusive economic zones that give countries special rights over the use of the waters along their coasts. What's more, the satellites responsible for tracking ships beyond that fifty-mile range take readings far less frequently than desired. This isn't by choice; the scanning frequency is limited by the number of satellites in operation, so constrained by the great expense of both building and launching them.

In fact, ships not only can but also do regularly disappear off the tracking grid, and it's nearly impossible to determine where they travel. If a ship is moving at a manageable speed of thirty knots, then from the time of the last AIS reading, that ship can travel anywhere within a roughly 200-mile radius. That might not sound like much, but because a ship is free to move in any direction, that radius of 200 miles equates to a search area of 125,000 square miles. This not only makes locating North Korean ships like the *Chong Chon Gang* and *Mu Du Bong* that turn their transponders off highly improbable, but also hampers search and rescue missions for ships in trouble. The small satellites (often called nano-satellites) that Spire and other firms are building will eventually make the costs of expanding coverage and taking readings much more affordable. Because the ocean scanning frequency is a function of how many satellites are in orbit, as the costs of deploying nano-satellites fall, it becomes both less cost prohibitive for firms like Spire to deploy many satellites and less expensive for companies and governments to purchase access to this enhanced signals intelligence. Other sensors already aboard Spire satellites make many additional kinds of readings possible, such as providing better data about emerging weather patterns and more rigorous scrutiny of illegal fishing, and can offer access to these various data streams on a subscription basis, just like Amazon Web Services might offer cloud computing. In a country like Indonesia, which has seventeen thousand islands, subscription data streams from space are perhaps one of the only scalable ways to manage illegal fishing within its waters.

Spire is a company that represents how the increased accessibility of technological tools is opening the field of innovation up to anyone who, with a good education and a good idea, can apply the tech to a problem that needs solving. Platzer didn't study at a classic liberal arts institution, but he did study a pure science—physics —one of the core scientific disciplines of a liberal arts education. The debate over the importance of more STEM graduates has tended *not* to acknowledge that the pure sciences—physics, mathematics, biology, geology, and many others—are in fact part of the liberal arts canon. A false dichotomy has been promulgated. There is an essential difference, however, in the liberal arts approach to STEM education, which is that students are not advised to think in strictly vocational terms about their studies, but rather are encouraged to take courses in the humanities and social sciences as well—and required to do so at many liberal arts schools—helping them to appreciate the value of these other fields of endeavor. More fundamentally, they are encouraged to follow their passions in deciding how to apply their learning.

Platzer is a physicist who chose to apply his scientific training to a passion for space, and some of those around Platzer and the Spire leadership are clearly hard-core techies, those that studied and deeply understand the nuances of electrical engineering, for example. But just as many provide the context as to how Spire's new data will be applied. These individuals, such as Theresa Condor, who today runs corporate development, have studied subjects like international trade and development. They might understand a subject such as illegal fishing or human trafficking, and they provide the impetus to orient the company's data around solving a dire challenge. They help ensconce the product in parts of the economy that are ripe for change, such as better understanding real-time flows of trade and how weather patterns affect markets.

What's important to note is that the evolution of technology and the rapidly declining cost of increasingly powerful sensory devices have made possible the progress of the budding commercial space industry, and opened it to individuals not traditionally versed in rocket science or space technology. It has become possible to create smaller satellites using off-the-shelf components, which are much less expensive to launch, and these satellites collect data that can be applied to all sorts of ideas and markets.

For example, Condor's background in international trade, having studied it at Columbia's School of International and Public Affairs and the London School of Economics, and her work running Citibank's Latin America trade syndications desk undoubtedly helped the team at Spire understand the value of real-time satellite data on shipping locations. While a vital and hardworking team of techies assembled the pieces, it was Condor's experience negotiating shipping contracts while living in Bangladesh with the U.S. Agency for International Development (USAID) that gave meaning to the scope of what the satellites could do. There is enormous value in gathering richer data sets provided by more satellite coverage, but understanding the applications requires a consideration for global conditions and events. And many of these experts are fuzzies, like Theresa. By Stanford's standards, Platzer would be called a techie. But he is also a science major who has taken a liberal arts approach to developing both scientific and soft skills, and he did not pursue a vocational route in his education. Today he is a leading innovator in one of the highest of high-tech fields, but his brilliance has been in surrounding himself with fuzzies as well as techies to apply space data in rich new ways.

Companies like Spire are possible because comparatively tiny and cheap off-the-shelf versions of satellite components have become available to the general consumer—they don't have to be specially developed, and these components give the smaller satellites powerful capabilities at greatly reduced cost. While earlier satellites were generally the size of small cars, costing millions of dollars, Spire's are the size of wine bottles and cost only hundreds of dollars to build. As Platzer told *SpaceNews* in 2015, "It's the iPhone-ization of space. We can change what our satellite does, remotely on Earth, by changing the software." The rapid development of commercial space flight, such as the rocket-launching

service offered by Elon Musk's company SpaceX, also made sending the satellites into orbit economically feasible. Nano-satellites
are so small that they can piggyback onto larger payloads, ride
sharing into space at comparatively low cost. With roughly twenty
nano-satellites deployed in 2016, Spire is growing quickly and planning to ultimately deploy a network of over one hundred satellites.

Indeed, entrepreneurship is always a risky endeavor, but with
the new tech tools that are so accessible to anyone with a passion
for an idea, the possibilities for joining the vanguard of innovators
are truly unbounded. Let's take a look at some of the incredible
tools now available and how they can be assembled in novel ways
to create breakthrough innovations, with no deep training in technology required.

Assembling the Technological Building Blocks

Next time you're late meeting someone and are opening the Uber
app to call a car to your doorstep, consider the assembly of building blocks that have made Uber's service possible. The company
needs access to an extraordinary amount of data regarding car locations, traffic conditions, and routes to destinations, but it didn't
need to build its own storage capacity to hold all that data. Until
it became economical to build its own data centers, it could use
Amazon Web Services, one of the leading cloud computing options, to take care of that at a cost one hundred times lower than
in the year 2000. While the app uses text messaging to communicate with riders and drivers, Uber didn't have to develop its own
texting system; it uses technology provided by Twilio, another of
the booming breed of web service providers, which enjoyed a successful IPO in June of 2016. Nor did Uber have to try to create its
own mapping technology; it uses Google Maps. For emailing rid-

ers' receipts, it uses an email provider called SendGrid, an online payment company. Braintree manages all of Uber's transactions.

These building blocks are only a few among the others that are now available to everyone for creating innovative products and services. Look under the hood of nearly any startup today and you'll see an assembly of a dozen or so underlying technological building blocks that the company has not had to develop itself but has only had to combine in a smart and innovative way. "Full stack developers" have given way to "full stack integrators." Just as great chess players say that they see the board not as composed of a set of individual pieces but as made up of what they call chunks of pieces that work in conjunction with one another to create strategic formations, entrepreneurs can now compose their companies from groupings of available services. "Chunking," a term that originally comes from cognitive psychology, refers to how information is processed by the brain, greatly reducing complexity in how we remember dates, telephone numbers, or sequences to play chess. The advent of technology services and prefabricated components is similarly greatly reducing the complexity of innovation.

In 2012, I wrote an article in *Forbes* arguing that Silicon Valley no longer has a lock on the most exciting technological innovation, that "innovation is a demographic, not a geographic, phenomenon . . . Silicon Valley remains a bastion, and a gravitational force. But the walled gardens are withering, and the access class is becoming an asset class." Whereas the technology sector was once accessible only to the comparative few, and it was primarily the techies who drove technological innovation, today truly anyone —including anyone with a background in liberal arts—can participate in our digital world, and combine these tools in new ways to pioneer genuine innovation. In fact, many of the tools are free and are easily accessed through the web. Moreover, as innovation in the underlying technology infrastructure continues, which will make even more powerful tools even more accessible, there is ample opportunity for fuzzies to apply the tools to a broad range of problems they perceive.

We've already learned about how Kaggle and the Good Judgment Project are making the highest-quality data analytics accessible. They are only two such services. Forrester Research issued a report in 2015, *The Forrester Wave: Big Data Predictive Analytics Solutions*, that identified thirteen other big data analytic solutions services providers, including IBM, Dell, Microsoft, and Oracle. And data analytics are only one of many technologies being made more available. Much of the democratization has been spearheaded by techies and has developed as a natural consequence of simplified architecture and interfaces, but some leading innovations driving technology's accessibility have actually been pioneered by fuzzies.

Services for Hire, from Prototyping to Customer Management

The most basic requirement for launching any technology product or service today—and really a product of any kind—is creating a website. Just a few years ago, doing so required either learning HTML or hiring a web developer, generally for a fairly hefty fee. Today, a bonanza of free and affordable off-the-shelf tools allow a total novice to create a beautifully designed site. All one needs to do is simply select a template and then do some customization of it by clicking on and dragging into it predesigned elements, such as rotating carousels of photographs or a shopping cart feature. Services also facilitate buying a domain name and the ongoing management of the site, from providing hosting and e-commerce services to streamlining integrations with data analytics of customer traffic services. If a higher level of customization is desired, these platforms allow for programming, and additionally, some even offer expert programmers for hire, though freelance web developers are also widely available.

For the design and the creation of products, designers and engineers with expertise in all types of design—mechanical engineers, industrial designers, graphic artists, and interaction designers, among others—can now be hired through a number of platforms, such as Behance, Dribbble, and Framer. All of them showcase designers' work and facilitate lining them up for projects. Behance cofounder Scott Belsky, who sold the company to Adobe in 2012 for a figure reported to be over $150 million, was an expert in neither design nor in the technology to create the Behance platform. He had cultivated a strong interest in design, however, from a number of elective classes he took as an undergraduate at Cornell University in a major it offers called design and environmental analysis, and he had studied the science of creativity under Professor Teresa Amabile while getting his MBA at Harvard Business School.

In 2006, Belsky partnered with Spanish designer Matias Corea, who earned his bachelor of fine arts from Barcelona, Spain's Escola Massana, and together they focused on a perceived irony about the professional needs of designers. As Belsky recounts, he realized that "many companies, books, and conferences existed for creativity; it was all about inspiration and ideas. The funny thing is that the last thing Creatives need are 'more creativity and ideas.'" Instead, he understood that they needed a clear way to promote their work better, and to get appropriate credit and better remuneration for it. "Organizing portfolios by who did what helps people showcase work and helps others discover it much easier," he explained. "Transparency is an essential step toward meritocracy . . . If I know who did something amazing, then I can hire them to do something amazing for me; and by the way, if I know how great they are, I'm going to pay them more." That perspective was vital to attracting top-quality talent to the platform and in propelling Behance to becoming host to more than eight million public design projects.

Framer is an early-stage startup, based out of Amsterdam, that is spearheading another approach, emphasizing the need to bring fuzzy designers and techie web developers together in a community of collaboration. Building on top of another widely used Dutch design startup called Sketch, based out of The Hague, Framer allows users to visualize design and code at the same time. Using what it calls Auto-Code, Framer allows manipulations to the image on the right side of the screen to live-update to the underlying code that describes the image on the left. In other words, you can create designs in Sketch, export them to Framer, and automatically get the corresponding code. If you manipulate the code, you see changes in your image; if you manipulate the image, you see how it updates your code. There's a whole world of rapid prototyping tools, like Zeplin out of Istanbul, Turkey, that auto-generate code based on visual images. These tools make parts of front-end web or app development as easy as copy and paste.

The creation of product prototypes has also become easier and less costly. One of the earliest barriers to becoming an entrepreneur is the fact that one might have to pursue it on the side, while holding down another job until you can prove a concept or generate traction. Today, tools abound to develop physical product prototypes and web product prototypes with less time and money, making getting off the ground that much easier. Consider again my seventy-year-old father, who built an iPhone application by first drawing on a napkin what he wanted to build. He then transferred those drawings to a comprehensive screen-by-screen explanation of his app using Apple's presentation software Keynote. He then figured out the basic commands the app needed to be able to handle, and began reading on the web what he needed to learn. He taught himself some aspects of code, but when he ran into challenges, he was able to hire a programmer in India to help him. Because he had so specifically designed and wireframed his app, they were able to build it cheaply and quickly. Once he'd identified in detail the problem he was solving and how a user would navigate, he was able to guide the programmer through the logic and the designer through the necessary storytelling. The highest-order challenge was having the idea.

For those who want to create physical product prototypes, the rapidly evolving technology of 3-D printing allows an entrepreneur to digitally send product designs to the printing machine and to create a prototype in a range of materials that can be fed into the machine, whether plastic, metal, or even ceramics. The inputting of the design is done with computer-aided design software, which is fairly easy to master, though this work can also be readily contracted for.

Shapeways, which originated in the Netherlands, is a company that has built a marketplace of designers for hire and provides a 3-D printing "factory of the future" for product creators. In this factory, industrial-size machines take the physical material that is fed into it and then squeeze it out of a fine nozzle in extremely thin layers, following the pattern that will create the object desired, layer upon layer. Objects of all kinds are now being 3-D printed, from furniture to musical instruments, to specialty household fixtures, to drone accessories and prefabricated materials for buildings. Such 3-D printers turn designs in digital bits into atoms, and the industry is growing at a blistering rate. McKinsey Global Institute forecasts that the 3-D printing industry could grow in economic impact to as much as $550 billion by 2025. Much the same way, companies like Lexington, Kentucky–based MakeTime make available Computer Numerical Control (CNC) machines that can produce parts and prototypes on demand, using the spare capacity of qualified machine shops across the United States. Having studied psychology at DePaul University and architecture at the Savannah College of Art and Design and the Southern California Institute of Architecture, MakeTime founder Drura Parrish understood both digital fabrication and the appeal of the sharing economy to leverage underutilized assets. Whether created by techies or fuzzies, these companies are broadening all of our access to create.

Off-the-shelf electronic components also permit innovators to create prototypes for all sorts of electronic products at reasonable prices. One of these providers, Arduino, is an open-source platform offering hardware components, such as circuit boards, and a software library with code for controlling the hardware. Arduino components can be very easily assembled and programmed by people with no training in electrical engineering. For example, Chad Herbert decided to use Arduino to create a low-cost and easily portable device that could monitor his son's sleep. His son has a form of epilepsy and he would sometimes have seizures while he was sleeping. The existing monitors were expensive, costing roughly $400 to $500, whereas Herbert's device cost a tenth as much. The monitors were also bulky, making them difficult to transport. Herbert simply built a device by tailoring a design and some code that were already available in the Arduino library. And Hebert isn't a techie; he's a soccer coach, concerned father, and editor in Baton Rouge, Louisiana, after having studied journalism at Southeastern Louisiana University. He's emblematic of the accessibility of even hardware creation.

Anyone curious and driven enough to learn how to use these tools can find workspaces where equipment, instruction, and guidance are readily available. These "hack spaces" have popped up in droves in cities worldwide. One example, TechShop, with locations in seven states, offers a membership and provides access to millions of dollars' worth of equipment for product fabrication, including metalworking tools, laser-cutting devices, an electronics lab, 3-D printing, and classes. For $150 per month, these platforms can draw out the creative "maker" in any of us. But of course anyone can access all the tools they need from the cloud, by sending design files to MakeTime. "We just want to be the largest U.S. machine shop that anybody has access to," says Parrish, referring to his digital marketplace for distributed manufacturing.

Another tool helpful for hacking together prototypes is basic videography. Innovators can create a video that shows how the product *will* work before any of the heavy lifting is done. Dropbox founder Drew Houston made such a video to share his vision with potential users and investors before he had done much of the sophisticated coding needed to actually bring Dropbox to life. The video highlighted the basic functionality of the file-sharing service, and it generated hundreds of thousands of visitors to his site and expanded the number of people interested in his prereleased product from five thousand to seventy-five thousand overnight. Similarly, Spire, which was then called Nanosatisfi, raised initial development capital by posting a video to the crowd-funding site Kickstarter. There, 676 different individuals contributed $106,330, which helped the startup get off the ground, literally, pulling together the components to build and launch its first satellite. While nobody's trying to be the next Martin Scorsese, freelance videographers are widely available, and coupled with crowd-funding platforms, this simple storytelling can help anyone raise money to launch an idea.

Once a prototype exists, services are available for testing consumer reactions, such as TestFlight, which is owned by Apple and allows the makers of mobile apps for Apple's iOS system to get feedback from beta testers. The Google Play native app beta tester is another such program. These and other services facilitate the adoption of the "lean startup" approach to product development, made famous in 2011 by serial entrepreneur Eric Ries in his best-selling book *The Lean Startup*. Feedback on a minimum viable product (MVP), tested by early-adopter customers, can help iteratively perfect a product, allowing a creator to build, then measure, then learn. A number of other services make surveying users and testing consumer responses to early product versions a breeze. Consider Optimizely, which allows innovators to perform what's known as A/B testing, comparing customer responses to two versions of a design, such as a website's shopping cart, or multivariate testing, which allows for testing of many versions at once. Optimizely allows anyone to visually edit their web, iOS, or Android interfaces without writing a line of code, changing variables on the fly, and to then conduct A/B or multivariate testing of the changes. Eighty percent of apps are deleted after their first use, so Optimizely facilitates rapid testing and analysis so that anyone can develop an effective product.

To build the infrastructure to support a company's operations, a plethora of additional technology services are available. Cloud computing companies, like Amazon Web Services, facilitate the storage, management, and retrieval of vast quantities of data at greatly reduced costs from just several years ago. According to Kleiner Perkins, one of Amazon's and Google's earliest investors and one of Silicon Valley's most successful venture capital firms, the cost of storing each gigabyte of data has decreased by a factor of four since 2010, from roughly twenty cents to about a nickel today. To put that in perspective, as of July 2015, YouTube reported that users were uploading 400 hours of video every minute, or roughly 210 million hours of video each year. At the conservative estimate that each minute of video is about 40 megabytes in file size, that's 500 million gigabytes of data that YouTube receives each year. In other words, cutting the cost of storing that data by a factor of four could save Google as much as $75 million per year. And that's not even accounting for storage redundancy, where the same information is kept multiple times over, meaning the cost savings are even more pronounced. Services for receiving payment, controlling inventory and shipping logistics, running a sales operation, and conducting ongoing customer relationship management are competing furiously to support startups.

Powerful marketing and advertising tools, most notably Google's AdWords program and Facebook advertising, are helping innovators target potential customers with much greater precision than ever before, while other new social media tools, such as Pinterest and Instagram, provide entrepreneurs with valuable insight into consumer trends. These services enhance marketing capabilities, but even more profound than these tools that have long been designed for fuzzies and business managers is the fact that even coding is becoming more accessible.

Learning to Code Democratized

For those who would like to learn to create web-based products and services from the ground up—that is, by mastering the coding required—a new breed of educational platforms allows novices to get up to speed on any of the coding languages quickly. This is possible because the languages have become much easier to learn in recent years. Whereas once being a programmer meant writing binary code made up of ones and zeros to control electronic currents and voltage to manipulate physical components, higher-order coding languages like Basic, C, and then C++ transformed coding into a process of using language, and increasingly accessible languages have been created, such as JavaScript, Ruby, and Python. Much like Russian and English have different symbols, or syntax, but share underlying meaning, and Google Translate and other online tools can help one translate text from one syntax to the other, computer programming is moving toward greater universality. What matters more than whether you can speak Russian or English is the content and the meaning behind your words. Similarly, what matters more than if you can code in Java or Ruby is logic, what questions you're asking and trying to address. Whereas programmers once had to write code from scratch, today GitHub, an open-source community of developers and collection of accessible repositories, offers a treasure trove of tried and tested libraries and blocks of code to "fork," meaning to copy and build upon. And whereas a great deal of time was once spent checking for errors, modern editing programs, such as Sublime Text, offer color-coded feedback and editorial guidance that is the equivalent of spell-check for coding.

Similarly, frameworks such as Ruby on Rails offer even greater abstraction by employing what's known as "convention over configuration" philosophy. These frameworks standardize "conventions" for performing common tasks, such as integrating with a database. Whereas Ruby might require twenty lines of code if a developer were to configure it originally, Ruby on Rails brings it down to two lines of code by allowing the developer to use the convention, making standard tasks extremely easy to perform, highly reliable, and more secure than in the past. And these frameworks aren't confined just to Ruby. Rather, there are frameworks for nearly all languages. Django is a framework for Python, while Express is popular for JavaScript.

YouTube is justifiably famous for cat videos, but it also offers a treasure trove of tutorials in almost all programming languages, available for the price of watching only three seconds of advertising (the platform even offers viewers the option to skip over the ads). If you want more curated pedagogy, there's the well-known Khan Academy, with short and remarkably effective lessons for free. For the development of iPhone apps, Apple offers what it calls "playgrounds," where anyone can learn to code. They provide a library of "snippets," which are blocks of code for specific types of tasks, and a QuickType keyboard that makes coding more intuitive. Apple's playgrounds offer a fast track to building complicated applications for anyone willing to read the basic how-to instructions, also on the Apple website. Massive open online courses (MOOCs) offer instruction in most computing languages as well as every other aspect of technological innovation, all for free, and many of these courses are straight out of Ivy League lecture halls. In fact, Richard Levin, the CEO of Coursera, one of the most successful MOOC companies, served as the president of Yale for twenty years.

Other private educational companies, such as the previously mentioned Codecademy, cofounded by Columbia University political science major Zach Sims, are "teaching the world how to code" by breaking down coding into bite-size lessons for easy online consumption. Codecademy allows people to learn interactively through the company's website, named by *Time* as one of the world's fifty best. Over twenty-five million learners around the world have used Codecademy. Treehouse, based in Portland,

Oregon, offers thousands of hours of in-depth videos on how to code for twenty-five dollars per month. Over 180,000 students in 190 countries have learned technical skills in thirty minutes per day. Many businesses rely on these services to up-skill and cross-train their workforces in the use of the ever-changing tech tools. Companies like Twitter, Airbnb, and AOL use Treehouse. General Assembly (GA), cofounded by Yale sociology graduate Matthew Brimer, also offers both online and hands-on instruction. One of its most popular workshops, called Dash, is free and offers hours of tutorials in HTML, CSS, and basic JavaScript. More than a quarter million people, myself included, have taken the class, which was created by Nathan Bashaw. One might assume he's a techie, but in fact he studied political theory, constitutional democracy, and philosophy at Michigan State University, and he attributes his success in developing the class to his liberal arts background, explaining, "My broad liberal education prepares me to think critically and creatively, to make connections that others don't see, and to articulate arguments effectively." GA also offers face-to-face teaching, drawing on such fuzzy insights into the most effective methods for teaching techie skills, primarily by getting students involved immediately in creating programs and building products.

When I sat down with Brimer at GA's New York office in 2016, he said that the philosophy behind founding GA was that with such rapid evolution of technology today, "your education should always be in beta," the engineering term for "a work in progress" product. Indeed, many of the students who attend the company's classes are programmers who are adding new languages to their repertoire. "The coding languages of tomorrow don't even exist yet. Education shouldn't be something you receive, or a box you check. It should be something that grows along with you, throughout your life," Brimer sagely commented. With fifteen GA campuses in cities around the world, $100 million in venture capital funding, and seven hundred employees as of 2016, General Assembly is a new urban community college, open to anyone who wants to learn or improve their technology skills. In other ways, it's an intellectual gymnasium, a place where you can, in essence, hit the weights and stay in top-performance shape. Moreover, through GA's Opportunity Fund, lower-income students can attend its three-month immersive courses for free. Students like Jerome Hardaway, a Tennessee-based air force veteran who served in Iraq and Afghanistan, took advantage of the Opportunity Fund, placing first in his web development class. A criminal justice and political science graduate from Florida State University, today he runs an organization he founded called Vets Who Code, helping others like him consider technology.

Another nontechie entrepreneur who availed himself of GA's offerings in order to learn how to execute his vision is former emergency medical technician (EMT) and volunteer firefighter in Allegheny County, Pennsylvania, and police officer in Los Angeles County Rahul Sidhu. His company, SPIDR Tech, is a leader in the field of data-driven policing, which has the potential to make important headway in addressing some of the biases in police work, such as the disproportionate arrests of minorities discussed earlier. Our always-on cell phones have been empowering citizen journalists to expose abuses and have sparked awareness of prejudice on both sides of policing, but subsequent advances in improving policing have lagged. Sidhu is seeking to change that by building a new CRM, or community relationship management, tool.

Sidhu was struck by the gap between the collection of vast amounts of data in policing and the effective use of it. "When you pull over a vehicle as a cop, you get on the radio, and you read the plates," he explained, "you relay your location, and the dispatcher on the phone goes into the dispatch software and creates an event. They specify the officer's name, where the traffic stop is happening, and the software creates a time stamp. Then the officer asks to run the check on the driver. This pings the DMV database, and that's where we get the name, address, ethnicity." In this way, policing has learned to make highly effective use of data, but there is a great deal of progress to be made in gleaning insights from analyzing the storehouses of information about the locations, dates, times, and many other aspects of crimes. Sidhu realized that collecting police data into a larger pool and conducting in-depth analysis of it could help optimize resources as well as expose biases. For example, the data might show that a particular officer pulls over more drivers of a particular type, or at a particular time or place. This might prompt inquiries into how to be more consistent or how such biases could be mitigated.

Sidhu began thinking about how he could stitch together the various kinds of data that police forces collect, such as that from GPS devices in patrol cars, dispatch data, and the DMV record, to facilitate better analysis of it. "I loved law enforcement and being a cop," he said, "but so many things I saw on a daily basis were so far behind other industries. Data was behind."

Sidhu had marshaled technical resources to build a product before. At the University of Pittsburgh, he'd cultivated a passion for emergency medicine. He worked as an EMT, and he had a patient die just ten minutes after he dropped her off at the hospital. That inspired him to develop a tool that enabled paramedics to perform EKGs in the field and send the results to hospitals before arrival, allowing paramedics to streamline delivery of critical patients. He worked with medical professionals and engineers to build the device, and he developed the confidence to steward tech resources even though he himself wasn't a techie. In fact, when he started, he knew nothing about coding, and he decided to learn.

He took a 720-hour intensive course at GA in all aspects of web and mobile development. He then took a 160-hour immersive course in sales and business development that taught him how to pitch the product and manage sales and customer relationships, and a twelve-week intensive course in user experience design, which explored the design process and product management skills for creating prototypes, then testing them, and moving forward to build a final product. When his CTO, a full-time Google employee, wasn't willing to leave his job to start a company, Sidhu's web development instructor, Kenaniah Cerny, asked him out to lunch and offered to step in. Sidhu also asked Glendale police officer Elon Kaiserman to take charge of business development, thinking back to a moment they'd shared, facedown in a sandpit at the Los Angeles County Police Academy, when they'd committed to work together in the future.

SPIDR Tech now offers a wide range of services to police forces, using data to identify sites where traffic accidents are most likely to occur and to better monitor and allocate officers' patrolling time, and also to communicate more effectively with the communities they police by sending out automatically generated public reports about arrests and crime levels. The establishment of better relationships with communities is at the core of Sidhu's vision, and admittedly something that's vitally needed across America today. "This isn't just a tool," he said, "it's something that can overhaul culture. If you have an agency using data to see where officers are struggling, where they're doing well, the parts of town that require a little more patrol than others, or if you're using data to issue reports to any citizens who call for police service, then you're enabling the force to impact the community. You don't just end up changing the culture of the police department; you end up changing the culture of the entire community."

Mike Schirling spent twenty-five years in the Burlington, Vermont, police department, over seven of those years as chief of police. He was witness to three computer system overhauls during his tenure. Early on, he recalls, "we had typewriters and carbon paper to do affidavits." With one hundred officers, the Burlington police force is the largest in the state, but even so, it receives many more service calls a year—over forty thousand—than it can handle. Schirling became excited about SPIDR Tech, which helps automate follow-up communication regarding calls from the public and in dealing with arrests, as well as helping police share information with the community about exactly how the department is responding, thus building trust. He became an advisor to the company following his retirement from the police force.

What's most interesting about SPIDR's services is that they've been developed atop a number of existing resources, requiring no new investment by police forces in terms of additional tech hardware. The founders worked with existing vehicle and police hardware, and employed software tools to use it in new ways. "Most police departments have GPS units in the cars, but use them for real-time tracking of their assets," Rahul explained. "We've built algorithms to look at this same GPS data over time, not to say where they are, but to start predicting where they might have to go next. The same GPS data, looking historically, can be repurposed to understand patrol presence and correlations with crime rates." As big data can only go so far, SPIDR's community relationship management platform uses technology to extend, as much as possible, human engagement into a citizen's pocket via their smartphone.

Liberal arts graduates can tap into all of these remarkable resources to apply their insights into human needs and desires to create breakthrough solutions. And those, like Rahul, experienced in the very real-world spectrum of human problems to be tackled can lead the charge in finding new ways to apply these tools to improve our lives. As we saw with the limitations of big data, all of the marvelous new technologies require human input, and insight into human desires and foibles, for their potential to be realized. In the following chapters, we'll meet a host of innovators who are grounded in the liberal arts, and who are figuring out how to make our machines more humane, if not necessarily more human. They're devising ways to improve our health and happiness, our educational systems, and our economy, and to increase the transparency and efficiency of our governments. All this demonstrates that with ever more powerful tools, we still require the timeless qualities that make us human.

FOUR

Algorithms That Serve — Rather Than Rule — Us

One innovative fuzzy who is making groundbreaking use of the new generation of technology is Katrina Lake. She has collaborated with Eric Colson, one of the most talented programmers of what's known as "recommendation algorithms"—the data-mining mathematics that serve up suggested items to shoppers on Amazon and the songs you might like to hear on music service Pandora. Katrina's company, Stitch Fix, was described by *Forbes* as being in the game of "fashionista Moneyball."

Like many of her fellow economics undergraduates at Stanford, Katrina found her way into a job in business consulting after graduation, specializing in strategy for retail companies at the Parthenon Group, working with companies like Kohl's and eBay. She also realized that some retailers, such as Macy's, hadn't much changed the way they were doing business in decades. An ironic result of her immersion into the retail sector was that she didn't have much time to shop for herself. In fact, she was so time-crunched that she ended up outsourcing all of her wardrobe shopping to her trustworthy, stylish sister.

When Katrina finally got some free time, she decided to head away for a weekend outdoors on a camping trip in the remote Northern California wilderness. Shopping for a tent online was a daunting experience; she found herself overwhelmed by the number of options. She had no idea what she wanted, and she didn't have time to do research before making her purchase. Buying a tent really shouldn't be this hard, she thought. Suddenly she realized that there was a gap in the retail services industry; there was a need for efficient, specialist assistance in making purchases. Her economics training had taught her that breakthrough innovations generally result from spotting such gaps and then devising a powerful and cost-effective approach to address them. She figured that if she was having so much trouble figuring out what tent to buy, lots of other people must be having the same problem with all sorts of other items.

She was confident she had the kernel of a good idea, but she wanted to get her MBA at Harvard to conduct further research into how she might develop a business model based on the idea. To complement her academic work, she also took a marketing job at fashion retail startup Polyvore, where she learned the skill of leadership from CEO Sukhinder Singh Cassidy, formerly Google's president of Asia Pacific and Latin America Operations. She also learned about the human touches that create superior shopping experiences, even for online retailers.

Companies can create loyal followings even in the face of intense competition from behemoths like Amazon and Walmart when they apply a high-quality aesthetic design sense to selecting appealing and trendy items and to featuring them in the most enticing ways. Polyvore was smart about capitalizing on this opportunity, but the company was also tapping one of the most powerful human-centric innovations that have arisen from the creation of the Internet—*social networking*. Polyvore was one of a new breed of what are called social commerce sites, which provide various ways for shoppers to participate in enhancing the shopping experience of fellow shoppers, from offering advice about items they might like to creating displays of outfits they've put together, much in the way a personal shopper might suggest outfits to clients. Pinterest is the highest-profile example of this kind of social commerce, but a host of other e-commerce sites are tapping this potential as well.

Those two jobs provided Katrina with a solid understanding of traditional retail along with innovative online business models. Learning about how some of the most successful online retailers were using recommendation algorithms, she decided that she was going to create the Netflix of shopping, but with a twist. Her company would be a Netflix that incorporated stylists with the human touch in order to enhance the quality of selections offered to shoppers. Her company would also add the personal communications touch she had seen driving the success of social commerce. In short, she wanted to create a fashion commerce brand that would save shoppers time by taking responsibility for choosing items for them, not displaying an endless panoply of items and leaving it to the shoppers to struggle with choices, as she had when picking a tent. Stich Fix aimed to become an online personal shopper and would cultivate relationships with customers, who would be clients that Stich Fix learned about, getting to know their tastes and styles over time.

The site would not overwhelm visitors with pages of items or provide conflicting customer reviews. It would have no shopping cart and no buy button. Instead, Katrina envisioned Stitch Fix using a powerful recommendation algorithm to weed through the masses of clothing items from a wide range of brands, in a full range of styles, and create an initial selection of items to match a client's personal tastes. Those suggestions would then be sent to a staff of personal stylists to evaluate them and make a final pick of items to be sent to clients.

Clients would receive a box at home containing five items, a fashion "fix," as the company dubbed each delivery. They could try the items on in the comfort of their homes, just like sunglass company Warby Parker had pioneered, at times that were convenient for them, and they would be able to return any items they didn't want to purchase. Stitch Fix would additionally pick up the cost of return postage. For this business model to work the recommendations would have to be outstanding; without strong sales, the costs of inventory management, hiring the staff of personal stylists, and shipping would quickly sink the startup.

Katrina's vision was bold—so bold that some twenty venture capital firms turned her down as she sought funding, often based on the fact that she had no technical skills in building the recommendation technology necessary to make the program work. But the vision was also tantalizing, and the potential of the model seemed so strong that, ultimately, she was able to convince three vital players she needed to pursue her idea.

Steve Anderson of Baseline Ventures, who was notably the first investor in Instagram, was equally excited about Stitch Fix. He invested $750,000 in 2011. With the capital she needed to make some key business and technical hires, she then approached Michael Smith, the chief operating officer (COO) of Walmart.com, to build the traditional retail infrastructure for the company. Katrina certainly wasn't thinking small; Smith had overseen all operations in the COO role at Walmart.com over nearly a decade at the company, from supply chain management to customer service.

She could have found few more qualified business logistics professionals to work with her. As it turned out, Smith was interested in joining a startup, and came on board.

Finally, Katrina reached out to the man behind the Netflix recommendation algorithm, the VP of data science and engineering for the company, Eric Colson. Why not? She was building the Netflix of shopping. At Netflix, Colson had built an eighty-person team to create what was widely viewed as the gold standard in recommendation algorithms. At Stitch Fix, he has now built a comparable team, but, in line with her vision of an algorithm-enabled personal shopping service, the data team supports the work of more than two thousand five hundred human stylists. Colson was the perfect partner in blending the fuzzy and techie, as he also appreciated how important human input would be to giving Stitch Fix the competitive edge to make it successful.

Colson was an economics major as an undergraduate, like Katrina, and his studies had exposed him to the fields of information systems and management science, which fascinated him. He went on to get two master's degrees, one in information systems at Golden Gate University in San Francisco, California, and then another in statistical learning at Stanford, which deals with those mathematics that are at the core of recommendation engines. While pursuing his degrees, Colson conducted research on developing ways to blend the distinctive talents of humans with those of the new generation of artificial intelligence machines. Working with Katrina to scale Stitch Fix gave him the opportunity to prove his contention that, as he and his coauthors wrote in one of his research papers, "hybrid machine-human recommendation systems can combine the best of both large-scale machine learning and expert-human judgment."

For a data scientist who loved building recommendation engines, the Stitch Fix model was an enticing challenge. While recommendations are generally expected to account for only a portion of sales at most online retailers who make use of recommendation algorithms—accounting, for example, for about 35 percent of sales at Amazon—100 percent of sales at Stitch Fix would be earned through recommendations. Colson wanted in, and he assumed the role of chief algorithms officer, perhaps the newest addition to the C-suite titles.

In order to optimize recommendations, the Stitch Fix system starts by asking shoppers to sign up as clients and then to answer a series of more than sixty questions about their tastes in clothing and accessories, as well as about their physical attributes, such as height, weight, clothing sizes, and age. Stitch Fix uses application programming interfaces (APIs), in particular an API from Pinterest, to enhance the company's understanding of clients' tastes by allowing them to select Pinterest pages that display types of items and outfits that they like, or that generally reflect their personal aesthetic. This option has proved so popular that 46 percent of Stitch Fix users have availed themselves of it, creating visual pin boards from which Stitch Fix can understand preferences.

All of this data is fed into the computer system. The algorithm then crunches through both the client data and vast amounts of data that the company has input about all of the items in the Stitch Fix inventory, looking for appropriate matches to the client's preferences. Each item in the inventory has been elaborately tagged with between 50 and 150 unique descriptors, from the basic type of material to the color and fit, such as slim leg versus bootleg for blue jeans, and more refined characteristics of style, such as whether it is bohemian or classic. The algorithm then creates a list of items for possible inclusion in the initial set of five to be shipped to the client, ranked by the probability it has calculated that the person will love an item. Colson calls this part of the system the "M algorithm," referring to his machine-learning systems. Then comes the part he calls the "H algorithm," the decision-making by the human stylists.

Each list is sent to a stylist, along with the probabilities the machine has calculated that the client will like the items, with all of the information the shopper provided about her tastes. To make the final selection of the five items, the stylist applies a nuanced understanding of fashion aesthetics and of cultural factors involved in clothing selection, such as types of looks that are trending as newly popular in the shopper's area of the country and which styles are considered "age appropriate" for a shopper. "We make no attempts to get the machines to act like humans. Nor should it be the other way around," Colson said at Data Driven NYC in 2016, a lecture series on data science put on by FirstMark Capital. "We want each to leverage their unique abilities . . . We have these wonderful complementary key resources that we leverage." But Colson hasn't stopped there. He has taken the process of augmenting human abilities a step further.

His team is even using algorithmic learning to help mitigate biases in the judgment of the stylists, which are subconscious but can be detected by sophisticated data analysis. For example, each stylist has their own style preferences and also their own sense of what styles are modern versus traditional, hipster versus fashion-forward. Stylists also inevitably have personal biases about which items would look best on a shopper, which may conflict with the shopper's desires. So Colson has programmed the algorithm to look for such biases in the set of selections sent by each stylist to shoppers over time. He then continuously refines both the routing of shoppers to stylists and the tailoring of the set of items that are sent to the stylists to choose from, in order to make better and better matches. For example, if a stylist sees only the age of the client, they may have a different bias than if they see age and a photo. By seeing both, the stylist might learn that one older client has a younger aesthetic, and perhaps a young client has an older aesthetic. They may act on any number of biases. By viewing the stylist's behavior as a data science "classification problem," Colson's team treats the stylist as unchangeable, rooted in their ways, and instead uses its algorithm to refine the choices given to the stylist to account for and help mitigate their bias. In other words, Stitch Fix never tries to change a stylist; Stitch Fix uses technology to ensure that each stylist delivers the perfect "fix."

By combining and melding human and machine strengths in this way, Stitch Fix has become the primary method by which 39 percent of its clients now shop. The company is growing at a fast yearly clip. That growth has also spurred an infusion of additional venture backing from some of the most respected investors in Silicon Valley, such as Uber board member and Benchmark Capital partner Bill Gurley. Gurley noticed that his assistant was spending her discretionary income on Uber and a then-unknown styling service Gurley came to discover as Stitch Fix. "Katrina Lake is one of the best I've ever worked with," he's admitted. With Gurley in her corner, Katrina has also been able to make executive hires of top experts in the fashion business, such as Julie Bornstein, the former CMO and chief digital officer of Sephora and head of e-commerce for the millennial lifestyle brand Urban Outfitters.

Katrina Lake was not intimidated by the technical challenge of creating her own online company. She realized that the resources of Silicon Valley were open to her, that the tech world is not a walled garden accessible only to tech gurus. She also understood that those who have tech skills are deeply in need of the kinds of talents that fuzzies have to offer, helping not only to bring the human touch to technology, but also to make creative connections, such as how a subscription service model like that of Netflix could be applied to a retail fashion business. Netflix had been around for a decade, but it took someone hungry and foolish enough to try to apply the Netflix core model to fashion. Today, having taken Stitch Fix public in the fall of 2017, Katrina not only runs a four-thousand-person company, but at the age of 34 she's one of America's richest self-made women (after only Taylor Swift).

Humans Are Behind the Curtain of Artificial Intelligence

The ability of algorithms to sort through and respond to the overwhelming amounts of data being gathered about an individual's interests and behaviors opens up a wealth of opportunity to serve human needs and desires better—a potential that businesses, not to mention governmental institutions, have only begun to tap. The vast improvements in the power of algorithms have led some analysts to predict that they will increasingly manage and perhaps later replace human workers, but the standout innovators actually working to craft better and better algorithms tend to see the future differently.

Like Colson, they advocate using algorithms to augment human talents and they caution about the limits of pure math in replicating human skills. Another leader in the application of algorithms to create a breakout service is Paul English, the founder of travel booking website Kayak. He is undeniably techie, having studied computer science as an undergraduate at the University of Massachusetts Boston. He's exactly the kind of guy you'd think would discount the role of humans, yet, like Colson, he thinks humans and machines work best together.

English is a big fan of building artificial intelligence into products with technology like chat bots, but he calls himself an "AI realist." Today English is using new tech tools to reinvent travel booking for a second time, launching a company called Lola. The service uses a chat interface—referred to as a chat bot or messaging app because of some automated response features—to allow people to book trips conversationally from their mobile phones, no pesky searching and filtering required. For example, if you chatted, "I'm looking for a flight from San Francisco to Austin next Friday," the chat bot might respond by asking "Are you traveling alone?" or "Is this a one-way trip or do you need a return flight?" But Lola's chat function can handle only a limited number of the tasks the service must perform, so English also employs a staff of human booking agents. He appreciates that human needs can be quite complicated, and algorithms can quickly become flummoxed by requests. While providing basic information about flights is straightforward, consumer preferences in booking hotels, for example, involve all sorts of psychological factors, such as how trendy a hotel is, or the thread count of the sheets one hotel uses versus another. And the same person might have quite different preferences in some instances than in others. For example, when you're on a business trip, a hotel close to the airport might be preferred, while one in the center of the action of a bustling city might be the choice while on vacation. "It's going to be some time before AI can take the majority of requests," English said. He also highlights that it's going to take an extremely high level of confidence in the quality of service that bots can offer before brands like American Airlines or Hilton Hotels allow their services to be managed by machines. Until then, humans will continue to play a significant role directing artificial intelligence for human benefit. "At Lola, my new company . . . people have pointed out the irony that at Kayak, we maybe put some travel agents out of business, because we made self-service really, really simple . . . Now for Lola, I'm going to spend my next ten years working on how to make travel agents really cool and powerful and trying to revolutionize the offline business." With 46 percent of travel bookings in the United States still happening in person or over the phone, English asks, "What is the role of humans in travel planning? Are there ways in which humans can be better than computers? Can humans be better than AI? And how do humans and AI work together? Should we, as entrepreneurs, . . . be building human-led AI, or should we be building AI backed by humans?" His five-person AI team works intimately with his twenty-person travel agent team. Both sides are vital.

The fact is that the most sophisticated "thinking" machine programs being developed today are being used to complement human intelligence rather than supplant it. Behind the scenes are people scurrying about to keep up appearances, supplementing the machines in case there's a glitch in the system. X.ai, a New York–based startup, created a digital assistant named Amy, who aims to "magically schedule meetings." In theory, the user needs only carbon copy Amy on an email with a scheduling request, and it can calendar a meeting between those parties on the email thread, eliminating much back-and-forth. X.ai promotes Amy as powered by artificial intelligence, but in many cases, the scheduling requests are beyond the comprehension of Amy, and the program gets confused. Currently, the company is attempting to build a fully artificially intelligent digital assistant, but the process to get there is deeply reliant on humans behind the scenes, stitching together gaps in the capabilities of the technology.

One such behind-the-curtain human was Willie Calvin, a twenty-four-year-old public policy major from the University of Chicago whose job it became to keep up the pretense that Amy, the digital assistant, could handle any situation with ease. While Amy has received kudos for coming across as exceptionally human, having what's been described in the press as "eloquent manners," a big part of the reason Amy seems so human is because sometimes it's not Amy at all. Sometimes it's a person, like Calvin. The truth is it's hard to "magically schedule meetings."

At Facebook, a company with nearly limitless resources and engineering talent, the messaging team is developing a digital assistant called "M," which is embedded in Facebook Messenger. The program uses natural language processing to decipher the meaning of user requests and then execute on them. But M does not operate without a human touch. It relies on a band of Facebook employees called "M trainers," many of whom have backgrounds in customer service, who perform the tasks the program can't handle. If the task is booking a car service to take the user to an event, the M program could use the Uber API to take care of that itself. But if the request requires a personal touch, like delivering cupcakes to a birthday party, the AI will hand that task off to an M trainer, who might call an on-demand concierge service like Task-Rabbit or Postmates and hire someone to pick up and deliver those cupcakes.

Devising new applications for combing the talents of humans and algorithms is rich terrain for those with the inclination to investigate human behavior and the problems we need solved, and to devise better solutions for improving our lives. Of course, some of these problems, like delivering cupcakes, probably don't need solving at all. Journalist Nick Bilton, author of the 2013 book *Hatching Twitter,* reported in *Vanity Fair* that "SF tech culture is focused on solving one problem: What is my mother no longer doing for me?" This is what journalist Kara Swisher has called "assisted living for millennials." Those with a liberal arts background in considering the nature of human life and society, the quirks of our psyches, and the norms behind our behaviors, and who have been taught creative thinking and communication skills, are prime candidates to play leading roles in finding meaningful ways to apply the technology. Technology companies have barely scratched the surface of such opportunities to make their products and services more humane and therefore more appealing.

Machines Gone Wild

Pedro Domingos is a professor of computer science at the University of Washington and the author of over two hundred technical papers in data science. In 2014, he won the highest award in data science, the SIGKDD Innovation Award, given for outstanding technical contributions in the field of knowledge discovery in data and data mining. He had invented a new open-source technique for mining data streams. In his 2015 book, *The Master Algorithm: How the Quest for the Ultimate Learning Machine Will Remake Our World,* which heralds the advance of algorithms, he also concedes that "computational complexity is one thing, but human complexity is another . . . Computers are like idiot savants, learning algorithms can sometimes come across like child prodigies prone to temper tantrums."

Tay, the name given to an artificial intelligence–powered "female" chat bot that Microsoft released to the web in March 2016, was one such savant. Tay was a bot powered by machine learning. Tay was trained on social data from Twitter and conversations from messaging apps Kik and GroupMe. Microsoft decided to make Tay a member of Twitter, and suddenly the data with which the bot was learning was live Internet content, directed at her from all sorts of Twitter members. Capable as Tay was, within minutes of the bot going live on Twitter, users began to see through her programmatic responses and sent messages to see what they could get Tay to say. Some users commanded Tay to repeat their own statements, many of which were very offensive, and Tay dutifully obliged. Others, part of the online message board called 4chan, began to coordinate together, escalating an already crass digital prank. When asked about the Holocaust, the bot responded egregiously with a clapping-hands emoji. Microsoft quickly pulled Tay from the site and announced it would make "some adjustments."

Some of the most thoughtful coverage of the Tay debacle was written by tech-savvy fuzzies such as John West, a front-end developer who studied philosophy as an undergraduate at Oberlin College. Prior to writing for the online magazine *Quartz*, West worked as a programmer, and being both a fuzzy and a techie, he offered an especially trenchant analysis of the Tay affair, writing, "The question we always ought to ask ourselves before leaping headlong into the unknown with new technology is: Who benefits?" Another writer, Leigh Alexander, a reporter at the *Guardian* newspaper, offered keen insight about how Microsoft had not considered the social norms at play on Twitter, writing, "Microsoft apparently hasn't learned anything from the countless headlines about how Twitter users like to talk to visible women—everything from gleefully anarchic trolling to threats and abuse—otherwise it would have seen this coming." Fuzzies, grounded in the liberal arts concern for protecting and enhancing the quality of our lives and not only invested in the pure mission of advancing technological capabilities, are needed to bring caution and sensitivity to innovation. It's possible to be experimental and conscientious and to move fast without necessarily breaking things. Without attention to the human factors in the ways that technologies are deployed, we run the risk of many more serious consequences than Tay's bizarre offenses.

The negative consequences so far have been unintentional, and that's one reason that diversity of thought and expertise in contemplating human issues is so important. To keep step with the increasing power of algorithms, companies must make a greater effort to embed thoughtful human analysts into the product development process, just like anthropologist Melissa Cefkin is helping Nissan by designing autonomous vehicles, in order to ensure that machines are well integrated into our lives. The damage that might be done by an algorithm gone wild should not be underestimated. Author Michael Lewis managed to make the esoteric subject of high-frequency stock trading fascinating in his 2014 nonfiction work *Flash Boys,* when he vividly chronicled from the inside how algorithmic programs written to game the market played out and went horribly wrong. The result was the so-called Flash Crash of May 6, 2010, a trillion-dollar stock market dive that happened in just thirty-six minutes. Highly technical traders pushed thousands of very small electronic contracts, or indications of interest in buying or selling a security, into the market, then preemptively cancelled them if there was demand to execute them. These tiny contracts were used to "spoof" the market, influencing the trading of stocks in a given direction so the flash traders could make money by having taken a profitable position in those stocks in advance. Those involved were indicted on charges of fraud and market manipulation, and regulations were changed to outlaw these duplicitous technical tricks hidden within the bowels of machines. But with new regulations come regulatory arbitrage, and a host of new tricks to get around limitations. So while that particular misuse of algorithms has now been accounted for, the potential abuses are unlimited, and the results are often not betrayed by a dramatic revelation like the Flash Crash.

A more admirable use of algorithms in the financial markets has been developed by one of Lewis's protagonists, Brad Katsuyama, who was the whistle-blower on these stock scalpers. He is now using algorithms to create greater equality in the marketplace. In June 2016, the Securities and Exchange Commission (SEC) approved his trading platform, IEX, as an official stock exchange, and an alternative to the New York Stock Exchange (NYSE) and NASDAQ. Indeed, we must channel our tech, as it is also the only tool capable of mitigating its own misuse. Much like credit card companies manage their own fraud, using a host of data-driven and machine-learning techniques to patrol their own environments, perhaps there is a role for the distribution of regulatory authority that asks our greatest techies to partner with fuzzies to help manage the dangers these same tools can provide if not wholly considered.

These days, algorithms govern a great deal about what content is shown to us online, whether it's what we see in our Netflix movie queue, our Facebook News Feed, or our Google searches. Serious questions must be asked about how the selection process is influencing our lives. In 2016, the *Wall Street Journal* used Facebook's Graph API to extract articles from the site that were widely shared by people who self-identified as "very liberal," or "very conservative," and then to construct two representative News Feeds, a "Blue Feed" and a "Red Feed." This exercise revealed how significantly algorithmic selection was skewing the content to which readers were exposed and how algorithms create "echo chambers" that merely reinforce people's views rather than opening their minds to a wider range of perspectives. While it's true that publications like the *New York Times* have long selected their own front-page headlines, thus framing the issues, what's different today is that these functions are hidden behind the veil of technology believed to be "data driven," and therefore objective. In the wake of the Donald Trump presidential election, many pundits pointed to how the polls "got it wrong." The polling data was powerless to predict a groundswell of political frustration in America. Aaron Timms, an Australian lawyer and journalist who is the director of content at Predata, a New York–based predictive analytics startup, instead argued that "humans failed, not Big Data . . . We need both better data and sharper reporting . . . the marriage of techies and fuzzies to which good technology always tends." Data will confirm or deny according to will, lest we interrogate it fully. We must ask questions of those algorithms "objectively" serving us content. After all, what is editorial?

To that end, Facebook does make robust attempts to counter the echo chamber effect, and it will be greatly assisted in that effort, as it has been all along in finding new ways to serve users' needs, by a vast complement of fuzzies that the company has hired to work alongside its techies. Naomi Gleit, who transferred from Harvard to study science, technology, and society at Stanford a year before Mark Zuckerberg moved to California, was so deeply engaged in the mission of understanding how technology affects the nature of our lives that she wrote her senior thesis about Facebook in 2005. She was so determined to become a part of shaping the powerful new social tool that Zuckerberg and his team were building that she dropped by their Palo Alto office continually for months until they finally offered her a job as an assistant. Today, she's a vice president of product, and after "Zuck," as he's known, Naomi is the most tenured employee.

Another early employee who brought human sensitivity to the development of the Facebook platform right from the start was Soleio Cuervo, who majored in music at Duke University in North Carolina and who plays both the violin and the saxophone. Soleio helped design many features, such as the now-ubiquitous "like button," and credits music with enabling him to succeed in the tech world. "Music helped me operate within an existing system and expand on that system," he explained. His ability to seamlessly maneuver from jazz to classical, or from sax to violin, turned out to apply equally well to the improvisational process of building a startup. Despite early braggadocio that everyone at Facebook pushed code, the company has benefited greatly from hiring liberal arts majors like Gleit and Cuervo, equal contributors to the core Facebook product, and instrumental to the tremendous success of the company.

There Is Much Good to Be Done

Of course, cautionary tales should in no way be taken as suggesting that algorithms are inevitably fraught with danger, or that we should not be finding lots of new ways to apply them. Frankly, there is really no turning back, and algorithms do countless hidden and wonderful things. Algorithms are already ubiquitous, and they're enhancing nearly every aspect of our lives, from how we search the web, to how autocorrect alters our text, to how we navigate with GPS and use our phones to take and send pictures. If you apply filters in Instagram, or change the audio settings on your stereo, algorithms are at work everywhere. The point is not that they are dangerous; it's that they must be developed with a sensitivity and depth of understanding about how they can best serve our needs. And that's where fuzzies are playing a major role.

One such liberal arts grad, thirty-two-year-old Shivani Siroya, has applied her academic background in international relations from Wesleyan University and in health economics from Columbia's School of Public Health, as well as her background at the United Nations Population Fund and Citigroup, to help the underprivileged in developing countries gain access to desperately needed financial capital. While she is based in Santa Monica, California, much of her work is in Kenya. Microfinance banks grant loans to poor business owners, usually in developing countries, who don't have a credit history—which means that lenders generally don't have a good way to judge whether or not to lend to a particular entrepreneur. These loans are often quite small.

Traditional lenders usually have to send staff into the field to meet with borrowers in order to evaluate their creditworthiness, an expensive process that means interest rates on microloans can be really high, sometimes exceeding 25 percent. As a result, small and medium business owners, the engine of a developing economy, are often left behind, unable to borrow the necessary capital to grow their businesses.

But Shivani and her company, Tala (formerly known as InVenture), are reimagining this system. Tala harnesses the huge amount of personal data that accumulates on a person's cell phone—text messages, call records, location and travel information, lists of contacts—and uses it all to evaluate the risk of lending to the phone's owner. It's a system that capitalizes on the popularity of smartphones, and their ubiquity even in the world's poorest countries. "We picked the smartphone data because we felt that it was the closest proxy to someone's daily life," she explains. And she should know; she interviewed four thousand five hundred owners of small and micro businesses across India and sub-Saharan Africa before having sufficient clarity around the market.

Shivani partnered with techies to create a platform where a potential borrower downloads the Tala mobile app onto their smartphone and makes a request for a financial loan. Tala then uses an algorithm that has been developed to analyze ten thousand data points on the customer. Tala has found, for instance, that people who make more calls after 10 p.m., when the call rates are lower, tend to be better borrowers. Perhaps this is because they are detail-oriented people who make the effort to methodically understand their options or who read the fine print, or perhaps it's because they're savvy go-getters who find out the best way of doing things by talking to many people around them. Tala has also observed that if the majority of a person's calls are longer than four minutes, they should be considered a less risky borrower because they can build better relationships over the phone. The company evaluates these and a number of other data points, such as bank withdrawals and deposits, social media, and demographics, to make a holistic assessment of the borrower.

Tala began in East Africa, India, and South Africa, and plans to expand to more parts of the world that are normally overlooked by the finance industry. Tala debuted in 2014, and within two years 125,000 previously un-creditworthy Kenyans had borrowed money, an average loan of one hundred dollars each, and their default rate was around 5 percent. More than three-quarters of the borrowers came back to get another loan, apparently satisfied with their first experience.

Tala isn't the only tech company that is trying to disrupt microlending; in fact, it's a hot space contested by many fledgling startups. A company called Branch also uses an app to determine creditworthiness, and doles out loans that average around thirty dollars with interest rates between 6 and 12 percent. Another company, Lenddo, has created an algorithm that assesses credit risk and verifies identity based on nontraditional sources, such as social networking data. Lenddo is live in twenty countries, and financial firms and telecom companies can plug into Lenddo to score, evaluate, and verify applicants in the emerging middle class, people who might not have the traditional qualifications to be approved. These are precisely the kinds of life-enhancing benefits that algorithms can provide, by seeing signals in the data that broaden access to life's bounty. Indeed, algorithms and machine learning can be used to enhance the most human of our skills, such as our creative expression. One example of this is an innovation that is providing powerful input with which to improve our ability to tell stories.

Sophie Lebrecht studied psychology at the University of Glasgow in Scotland and went on to earn her PhD in cognitive neuroscience from Brown University. After, she got together with the head of Carnegie Mellon's psychology department, Michael J. Tarr, to found a company called Neon Labs, which sells an image selection tool that assists companies by choosing images that tell more emotionally resonant stories with online media. Neon applies a machine-learning algorithm to suggest various images that companies can use to elicit emotional engagement. In other words, Neon is trying to use data science to figure out the subconscious appeal of images. This is becoming more and more of a pressing need as companies continue to be inundated by a flood of new imagery, and the time for those creating content to engage viewers diminishes. In fact, our brains make decisions about what content to engage with or avoid in as little as seventeen milliseconds, which is so rapid that we can be said to be not actually conscious of making the choice. Lebrecht's PhD dissertation investigated how the brain's visual system constantly assigns these micro positive or negative reactions to our surroundings, something Lebrecht calls "micro-valence," borrowing the term "valence" from chemistry, where an atom's valence is its positive or negative charge. She turned that work into a patent. Today Neon is built on this research and uses neuroscience to predict consumer preferences by mapping the affective triggers for positive valence, or, in other words, what makes us like stuff.

With people bombarded by more and more images in ads, articles, and videos across multiple devices, capturing their attention in these brief moments is becoming increasingly difficult. Neon helps content creators optimize the images they show. Companies pump video made up of millions of frames or images into the Neon tool, and the program algorithmically analyzes these images with its neuroscience-based machine learning. The program evaluates each image and tags it according to one thousand different variables, such as its coloration and the facial expressions contained in it. The images are then compared with a seed library of images, for which the company has created data about how people emotionally reacted to them. If an image propelled into the tool has similar characteristics to one in the seed library that has performed well in the past, Neon flags it as one that the company might want to use. Neon then ranks all of the images identified for the company, helping the creator pinpoint the image that will most effectively capture the most attention in a micro-moment.

In short, Neon empowers, rather than replaces, human storytellers. Let me put this into perspective. Consider the work of those who have to select highlight footage for television viewers. During the 1996 Olympics in Atlanta, NBC broadcast 171 hours of sports coverage. Twenty years later, for the 2016 Olympics in Rio de Janeiro, NBC broadcast 356 hours of content per day, and an unprecedented 6,755 hours during the course of the thirty-first Olympiad. Similarly, during the 2016 Super Bowl, forty NBC cameras recorded hours of football on 4K cameras at 120 frames per second, while professional photographers on the field shot as many as two thousand images each. Neon's pioneering machine-learning technology makes navigating vast collections of imagery easier, helping leading media, advertising, and research labs identify dramatic highlights and moments that matter. In 2017, to share its technology more broadly, Neon decided to partner with Carnegie Mellon University and open-source its artificial intelligence platform under the name Neon Open.

Sophie Lebrecht, Shivani Siroya, and Katrina Lake have all built on liberal arts degrees and brought together fuzzy-techie teams to realize a vision about how the new power of algorithms could be applied to better serve a human need. The door remains wide open for more people like them to ensure that this extraordinary technology is harnessed to serve us rather than rule us. The greatest threat is not technology; it is our prioritization of technology at the expense of other subjects, the liberal arts, and how we ask the big questions so that our tools are put to good use. We must nourish technology, not through exaltation, but by bringing to its development and application the diversity of thought.

FIVE

Making Our Technology More Ethical

Donald Norman is a longtime advocate of smart design. Currently the director of the Design Lab at University of California, San Diego (UCSD), in his 1988 book *The Psychology of Everyday Things* (later called *The Design of Everyday Things*), he discussed what he termed the "psychopathology of everyday things," capturing the inanity of badly designed products, such as leaky teapots and swinging doors that trap us, and a need for "user-centered design." In his follow-up book in 1992, whimsically titled *Turn Signals Are the Facial Expressions of Automobiles*, the message was actually quite serious: product designers must strive to make products much more responsive to human needs and desires while also taking into consideration how the inventions they're crafting can be thoughtfully integrated into our lives. Norman wrote that innovations, especially those in the technology sector, should enhance the quality of our lives, rather than cause frustration.

"Much of modern technology seems to exist solely for its own sake," he wrote, "oblivious to the needs and concerns of the people around it, people who, after all, are supposed to be the reason for its existence . . . My goal is neither to attack nor to defend, but to understand just how the interaction between human and technology takes place, to discover where and why difficulties appear, and then to try to do something about them. You might say that my goal is to socialize technology, to humanize technology."

In writing about automobile turn signals, Norman highlighted that "machines are social devices" because they interact with people, and as such, they must be designed to be responsive to the ways in which we think and behave. In other words, machines must be crafted with sensitivity to our fuzzy human nature. Just as humans have developed a repertoire of physical hand signals or facial gestures for communicating with one another, automobiles need turn signals as technological semaphores between drivers. Little could Norman have foreseen the arrival of self-driving automobiles, which will require sophisticated means of communicating with humans—communication patterns anthropologist Melissa Cefkin is developing at Nissan.

Donald Norman is widely acknowledged to be one of the fathers of the human-centered design movement, the focus of which is to make technology products more humane. He embodies the superiority of product creation to be achieved by combining the skills of the fuzzy and the techie. Norman received his undergraduate degree in computer engineering and then a PhD in the pioneering fuzzy-techie field of mathematical psychology, in which he studied computer modeling of the workings of the human mind. After almost thirty years conducting highly influential research into human-machine interaction as a professor of psychology at UCSD, Norman went to work for Apple in 1993, helping the company fulfill Steve Jobs's vision of creating "technology married with liberal arts, married with the humanities . . . that make our heart sing." There, Norman created the field of "user experience," and the legion of human-centered design specialists who followed in Norman's footsteps have helped to make significant strides toward Jobs's advised goal, with Apple products leading the way.

At the same time, the wave of technology products designed to primarily assist and delight us has also introduced many unwanted "revenge effects" into our lives—that is, the unintended consequences of using them—such as the addiction to playing video games and the stress of keeping up with the emails, text messages, and social media notifications that overwhelm us. Designers have only scratched the surface of the potential for creating technology products with a deeper sensitivity to human needs, to help assist us, further our goals, and improve our lives.

In this chapter we'll explore how a new generation of innovators is taking the original vision of Donald Norman and Steve Jobs further by applying the skills, insights, and sensitivities cultivated by the liberal arts to technological innovation. Fuzzies lead some of the fastest-growth tech companies today because they're crafting everyday solutions that take advantage of powerful new technology, but do so with deep empathy for and understanding of how their innovations can help solve pressing human problems.

Following the path laid out by Norman and Jobs is University of Victoria philosophy major Stewart Butterfield, founder of the messaging app Slack. Butterfield had long been an entrepreneur, having previously built and sold photo-sharing company Flickr to Yahoo for $25 million in 2005, at the age of thirty-two. After leaving Yahoo in 2008, Butterfield founded a gaming company called Tiny Speck. When the writing was on the wall that Tiny Speck wasn't going to succeed, he thought he might have a product to spin out based on the internal communications tool he had built to help his team avoid email. He turned out to be very right. He founded Slack, and in less than three years, his new business was valued at $4 billion and had garnered over 2.7 million daily users.

Butterfield had empathized with the need to cut down on the number of emails people must keep up with at work—he understood the overwhelming feeling of facing four hundred work emails after a three-day weekend all too well. Slack helps users navigate the digital email jungle. According to the McKinsey Global Institute, interaction workers spend upwards of 28 percent of each workday in email and 19 percent in information gathering. Slack investor and early Facebook executive Chamath Palihapitiya says, "They [Slack] are going to destroy email. They are going to create a network effect across all companies, and what it's going to do for people—which is something which I think is so important —is that they're going to give you back time."

Gentry Underwood once ran the design firm IDEO's Knowledge Sharing domain. He focused on "social software," or large-scale collaboration platforms and tools built with human-centered technology. He studied the fuzzy-techie field of human-computer interaction at Stanford, earning a degree in symbolic systems. But he left the startup world to earn two master's degrees, one in psychology from Santa Clara University and one in anthropology and community development from Vanderbilt University in Nashville, Tennessee. From those studies, he learned the practice of ethnography—how ethnographers go out in the field to observe people in action, from tribes in Borneo to workers in a twenty-first-century office. He applied his ethnographic studies to building a more humane email inbox and founded a company called Orchestra, which offered a mobile product called Mailbox that let users delightfully swipe emails to "snooze" them for later. Before the startup could even release its flagship iPhone app, in 2013 Dropbox bought the one-month-old app for $100 million.

This new fuzzy-techie era of product development has only just begun, and there is tremendous opportunity to apply the perspectives and methods of research of the humanities and social sciences to improving product design. As Donald Norman said, design is more than making things pretty: "Design is a way of thinking, of determining people's true, underlying needs, and then delivering products and services that help them. Design combines an understanding of people, technology, society, and business," and that requires all of us to participate.

Advancing Design Ethics

In order to cultivate in his employees at Apple the human-centered design ethos that he championed, Steve Jobs brought scholars in the humanities to the company to teach courses, creating Apple University, launched in 2008 under the direction of former dean of the Yale School of Management, Joel Podolny. Apple University's goal is to educate employees about a range of product and design skills. The curriculum also includes classes that focus on the importance of beauty, simplicity, and efficiency in product design.

One of the academic all-stars at Apple University was Kim Malone Scott, a Slavic studies major from Princeton who ran Google's multibillion-dollar AdSense business before joining Apple's faculty. Another is Josh Cohen, a polymath who earned his PhD in philosophy at Harvard while studying with the fabled philosopher John Rawls, and who has taught politics, philosophy, and law as a professor at MIT, Stanford, and UC Berkeley. In one of his lectures, he highlighted the design principles that landscape architect Frederick Law Olmsted applied in creating the plan for New York City's Central Park. One of those principles was that in order to foster a better appreciation for the beauty of nature in urban dwellers, every path through Central Park should be curved so that each step would reveal a new vista of gorgeous greenery. Olmsted's goal was to surprise and delight, also one of Apple's objectives when crafting new products. He also wanted to democratize the natural beauty then reserved largely to the elites, who could escape New York City for more pastoral settings. Scrolling through streamlined Apple interfaces on your iPhone, you might experience a joy somewhat akin to that of walking along the curved paths of Central Park on a spring evening.

Curricula in the humanities and social sciences have a great deal to offer technologically oriented product designers in creating products that are not only more appealing, but also more humane. Taking a page from Apple's playbook, Google executives also endeavor to foster a more thoughtful and human-centered approach to the design of the company's products and services. Until 2016, Tristan Harris was Google's "product philosopher." Like Donald Norman, Tristan steeped himself during both his undergraduate and graduate studies in the methods for bringing the fuzzy into technology creation. Tristan is a leading proponent of ethical design, meaning the design of products according to the principle that they must foster the human good. Today he leads a global movement to bring "design ethics" to technology.

That's a mission in perfect alignment with the original goals of liberal arts education. Fostering ethical behavior was at the core of the ancient Greek conception of the liberal arts. People educated in philosophical inquiry, with good communication and critical thinking skills, would be equipped for responsibly participating in civic life. They would be prepared for exercising, and defending, the freedom that the invention of democracy allowed them to conduct their lives according to their own aspirations, but also taught to respect the mandates of the common good. Tristan is working to bring that same ethos to technology innovation, inspired by his own liberal arts education.

Like Gentry Underwood, Tristan studied human-computer interaction at Stanford, a program that combines instruction in computer science with instruction in linguistics, philosophy, and psychology. Its aim is to cultivate a better understanding of how machine "intelligence" might be developed and how it can best complement human thinking and feeling. Tristan also studied under Stanford professor and psychological researcher B. J. Fogg, who founded the university's Persuasive Technology Laboratory (PTL). Fogg pioneered investigation into how technology can be employed to change human behavior by focusing on how people develop habits. PTL has conducted analysis of the psychological appeal and effects of spending time on Facebook, how technology can be designed to help people adopt positive habits, such as physical exercise, and quit bad ones, such as smoking. In 2007, Fogg taught a course on Facebook in which students used techniques of "mass impersonal persuasion" to influence twenty-five million people, and in 2008 he taught a course called Psychology of Facebook. Fogg's persuasive technology researchers in their Peace Innovation Lab are even exploring how "emerging social behaviors and insights are promoting new paths to global peace." Tristan also studied under the tutelage of professor Terry Winograd — the same professor who taught Google founders Larry Page and Sergey Brin.

Much as Page and Brin had been captivated by the largely untapped potential of the web to democratize access to information, Tristan was inspired by the possibilities to enhance the information services provided to online readers. In 2007, like Page and Brin, he quit pursuing work on his degree in order to start a company, which he called Apture. Tristan developed a technology that allowed the readers of web-based text to click on any word and up would pop a small box within the article leading to a host of relevant information collected from all around the web. In short order, the company was enhancing storytelling and helping to provide greater context on the web. After garnering over a billion page views per month across such sites like the *Economist*, Reuters, and the *Financial Times*, Apture was purchased by the folks at Google in 2011 for a reported $18 million. Tristan was twenty-seven at the time. He was then brought into Google as a product manager and he immediately began to focus on bringing ethics to the designs he was working on—respecting human needs and advancing human good for Google's billions of users.

One of Tristan's initiatives at Google was to instill employees with an understanding of the psychology of mindfulness by stressing the importance of focusing on the present and fully experiencing life in the moment instead of being constantly distracted by text messages, emails, and phone calls. He helped organize a meeting between Google's top product designers and Thich Nhat Hanh, a leading practitioner of mindfulness training and Vietnamese Buddhist monk, in a bid to advance the cause of a movement Tristan founded, and runs today, called Time Well Spent. Tristan believes that our beloved technology devices are undermining our ability to spend our time well, diminishing, and therefore disrupting, our ability to exercise our full potential for meaningful interactions, cultivation of relationships, and concentrated creative thought.

Tristan was an avid amateur magician as a child, which gave him an acute understanding of the limits of the human mind in resisting distraction. Magic's sleight of hand is all about diverting the eye. At the Wisdom 2.0 Summit, an annual conference that brings together experts in various fields to discuss how technology can foster human well-being rather than undermine it, he spoke about Time Well Spent, and that he founded it in an attempt to reverse the trend of technology hijacking people's attention. Herbert Simon, a former professor of information science at Carnegie Mellon, famously framed the concept of the "attention economy," by which he meant an economy in which people's attention is the prized commodity highly sought after by companies. He warned that a "wealth of information creates a dearth of something else . . . It consumes the attention of its recipients." The great irony of the information revolution, he pointed out, was that the wealth of information becoming available was creating a poverty of attention. Today, Tristan is raising awareness about the risks of attention-seeking technologies. He's working to encourage the development of products that protect our time and enable greater focus and quality of experience.

At the heart of the problem is the fundamental economic incentive to compete for our attention. The builders of mobile phone apps, along with the creators of new web services and designers of electronic games, earn their money primarily by encouraging people to spend more time engaging with them. "Whether you're building a meditation app, or an informative website, you're all competing for attention, which means that you win by being more clever at getting people to spend time and to come back. There's a whole industry that's helping people to do this, and it becomes a race to the bottom of the brain stem to seduce instincts into getting us to spend time," Tristan said recently. Ethical design questions this "race to the bottom of the brain stem" by identifying the ways our time is hijacked and then encouraging the development of products and services that *respect* our time. Tristan asks, "Is technology amplifying human potential, or amusing ourselves to death?" Are computers still, as Steve Jobs said, "bicycles for our minds"?

When we are tagged in a photo on Facebook we receive an email notification. Companies continually sending us such alerts have convinced us there's a chance we'll miss something—a moment, new Tinder match, Snap, or Twitter mention—so we have to immediately check. We're also subject to the subtle coercion of social obligations companies urge on us, like "Tag this person in a photo" or "Endorse your new LinkedIn connection." We're told that our Facebook message has been "received" and then that it's been "read," putting pressure on the recipient to reply. "Didn't you get my text message? I sent it an hour ago."

These design features tug at our social mores, capture our attention for a moment, and distract us from whatever other, probably more important, endeavors we were pursuing. These are the moments when we have been hijacked by our technology. Linda Stone, a former Apple and Microsoft employee who's now on the Social Computing Advisory Board at the MIT Media Lab, coined the term "continuous partial attention." This mode of "semi-sync" communications is neither real-time nor deferred. It's a process of constant minor interruptions that delude us into thinking that we're highly engaged across a number of shallow conversations, but in fact, we're just continually, partially attuned.

Every time we enter a password to unlock our phone to see an Instagram like or a new WhatsApp message, we get drawn into a distraction. It might not seem like much, but according to Deloitte, the consultancy, the average American checks his or her phone forty-six times per day. With 185 million smartphone users, that's over 8 billion distracted moments every single day. The impact of product decisions, because of widespread adoption, is tremendous.

We often talk about multitasking in the technology age as though we're all able to work on two or even twelve things at the same time. The more the better, we boast. Of course, is any of this valuable? Imagine you sit down to look over a spreadsheet, then pause to check your email. Soon enough, your phone rings, so you pick it up and jot out a quick text to your spouse. What you're really doing is focusing on one task until you're interrupted and pick up another . . . and then another. Experts call this behavior "rapid toggling between tasks."

Gloria Mark is a professor in the Department of Informatics at the University of California, Irvine, who studies the impact all this toggling has on workers' productivity, plus their mental and emotional states. She studies what she calls "interruption science." She has found that our technology is rewiring how we attune ourselves to the world around us. We allow ourselves more interruptions because we start to draw our behaviors, and even new values, from what we have been conditioned to via technology.

In one study, Mark sent researchers into the offices of typical American companies and watched how often workers were interrupted or "self-interrupted" themselves. The answer was every three minutes. Moreover, she noted that it could take a worker twenty-three minutes to regain focus on a task. In contrast to 2004 research that indicated that information workers switched tasks roughly every three minutes, Mark has found that today that number is closer to every forty seconds.

Of course, not all interruptions are bad, and some are even helpful. Mark has found that as long as an interruption is brief and doesn't require a lot of deep thinking, it usually doesn't have a huge impact on your immediate workflow. People who respond to email through self-interruption, rather than a computer-driven desktop notification, for example, are more productive. An interruption related to the task at hand can actually help someone become more productive and focus more on work.

A major cost of all those interruptions, however, is stress. Next time you hear a multitasker's hauteur about performing amazing simultaneous feats, remember that stress is its silent externality. In one experiment, Mark assigned workers a typical office task: simply responding to a batch of emails. One group was left to work uninterrupted, while the other was constantly bombarded with phone calls and instant messages. When all the workers were tested to measure stress, interrupted workers displayed much higher levels of stress, frustration, and a feeling of time pressure than those who worked without distractions. Yet despite the higher stress levels, the interrupted workers completed tasks quicker than the nondistracted group. Mark measured the ability to answer specific questions via email, and as such was also able to measure quality. She found that the distracted workers used fewer words, but the quality of their answers didn't suffer markedly. Mark thinks that once people expect to be interrupted, they actually work faster to compensate for the perceived cost of that interruption. Obviously there is no one perfect way to work, but it's important that researchers like Mark shine a light on how technologies are affecting us, and help inform advocates for design ethics like Tristan Harris.

Shedding light on the mechanisms by which our attention is hijacked, one phenomenon Tristan has also written about is how technology innovators have used the psychology of variable rewards to hook us into returning so compulsively to our email inboxes or to playing a game like Candy Crush Saga. B. F. Skinner, a behavioral psychologist at Harvard, figured out in the 1950s that by varying the ratio of reinforcement, respondents toggled between liking a reward when they had it and craving it when it wasn't there. Because the reward's delivery was randomized, variable ratio scheduled rewards are known to be highly addictive. As respondents never know when they might receive the next reward, they become more fixated on pursuing the reward. This is the principle behind the addictiveness of slot machines. Tristan asks, "What makes more money in the Unites States than movies, baseball, and game parks combined?" The answer is slot machines. Natasha Dow Schüll, an anthropologist and professor of media, culture, and communication at New York University, who wrote the 2012 book *Addiction by Design,* found in her research that slot machines get people "problematically involved" at three to four times the rate of other gambling. These slot machines, known as "one-armed bandits" for taking your money one pull of the side lever at a time, are not unlike today's one-finger bandits, meaning our smartphones. As Tristan argued in an essay for German publication *Der Spiegel,* "Smartphone addiction is part of the design."

"I have a slot machine in my pocket," Tristan explains. In fact, a few billion people around the world do, too. "Every time I check my phone, I'm playing the slot machine to see what I'm going to get. Every time I check my email, I'm playing the slot machine to see what am I going to get. Every time I scroll news feed, I'm playing the slot machine to see what's going to come next." Tristan proposes that in light of such manipulations, perhaps we have a certification for ethical design akin to the LEED, or Leadership in Energy and Environmental Design, label that recognizes best-in-class "green" buildings. He even considers whether there ought to be the equivalent of a Food and Drug Administration (FDA). Should we consider helping people think about their diet of information consumption, creating the equivalent of the food pyramid for our intellectual nutrition? He's not thinking small. "Imagine a digital 'bill of rights,'" he suggests, "outlining design standards that force the products used by billions of people to support . . . them in navigating toward their goals." He inspires the hope that perhaps we're beginning to see the digital-generation's James Madison, John Jay, and Alexander Hamilton, the authors of *The Federalist Papers*, hashing out, as the Federalists did for the basic rights and responsibilities of citizens and our governments, the rights and responsibilities involved in technological design. While some of this thinking is at obvious odds with other Libertarian thinkers in the Valley, that is precisely why this conversation, this debate, ought to be brought into the open.

Such a notion may seem naively utopian, but the fact is that products could easily be developed with an emphasis on helping us use our time well, and they might also be quite lucrative. "What if technology was designed differently . . . conscious of how much time we wanted to spend with it," asks Tristan. "What if you said, 'I want to spend thirty minutes on my email,' and then it [the email system] was on your team, to help you spend time the way you want it to?" Tristan's techie credentials complement his fuzzy perspectives powerfully in advancing his argument. He knows how technology is developed, and he knows how it could be developed differently. "Companies like Apple and Google have a responsibility to reduce these effects by converting intermittent variable rewards into less addictive, more predictable ones with better design," he wrote in a widely circulated piece, "How Technology Hijacks People's Minds," on the blog *Medium* in 2016. "For example, they could empower people to set predictable times during the day or week for when they want to check 'slot machine' apps, and correspondingly adjust when new messages are delivered to align with those times." By asserting the responsibility of product designers to take account of the possible ways in which their products are undermining human well-being, Tristan puts the spotlight on the influence technology designers now wield in people's lives. His voice provides leadership and momentum for the case that designers have ethical obligations to follow.

Protecting Our Freedom to Choose

In addition to protecting our time, advocates of design ethics want to make technology innovators and consumers more cognizant of how technology can constrain our freedom of choice. As we learned with the powerful algorithms of Stitch Fix, sometimes-constrained choice can be immensely helpful for people. On the other hand, it's important that we also remain conscious of how the constraint on our choices may be limiting our ability to take actions we would prefer. One of the creative and forceful voices shining a light on this issue is Joe Edelman, an engineer who built the community algorithms at Couchsurfing, a forerunner to Airbnb. Today Edelman is a technology activist and philosopher at the Center for Livable Media based in Berlin, Germany. His work examines how technology can be better designed to help people make choices they really want to make, rather than those that companies lead consumers to select. In his 2014 paper "Choicemaking and the Interface," he argues for a radically different approach to the design of the menus that have become nearly ubiquitous in technology products. They should be designed, Edelman contends, to allow people to make choices that are *good*, not just *convenient*. As we spend more and more of our lives looking at a screen, menus play an increasingly important role in our lives—indeed, many of our key decisions are made by scanning a list of options. As fallible human engineers and designers create all our products, our menus will never be fully free from individualized perspective. At the very least, Edelman says, menus should be free from bias and manipulation. But he goes one step further: Ideally menus should help the user live better. They should help us make selections that align with our values.

Specifically, Edelman wants interfaces to help users avoid decisions that they later come to regret, especially when they could have identified a better choice if only they had taken the time and effort to think about it. He calls it "Durable I-Wish-I-Had-Known Regret" (DIR) and says that bad screen menus often drive users to make choices that lead to this sense of remorse. "Shitty menus," he writes, "may be missing information about time costs, money costs, whether hoped-for outcomes are likely, whether unexpected outcomes are likely, whether there are less-costly or otherwise better options for similar outcomes, and even whether our hopes themselves are likely to change." In other words, our technology products are missing the equivalent of a surgeon general's warning on a pack of cigarettes, or an FDA-required nutritional label on all food items. You can still light up a smoke, or drink that 410-calorie Starbucks Frappuccino instead of the 80-calorie black coffee, but at least you have full information, with menus that provide you with transparent choices.

To illustrate his point, Edelman turns to a famous scene from a film cherry-picked for tech nerds. In *The Matrix,* the protagonist, Neo, is offered a choice of a red pill or a blue pill. And so he considers only those two options. "Neo does not think or consider that perhaps he wants to go for a run, or that later he wants to have a lobster dinner, but only if he can afford it and his girlfriend can come along," Edelman says. "No, Neo simply chooses from the options given." And so it is with us. When we're given a set of options to choose from, we usually select the item that we prefer from that set of options—but that doesn't necessarily mean that's what we prefer most of all. We simply consider the local maximum, the best relative choice, not the best absolute choice we could make. To combat this, Tristan navigates his apps only by searching for them directly on his phone. This "consciousness filter" ensures intentionality in all that he does. On the back of his laptop, he even has a Post-it that reads, "Do not open without intention."

Since navigating through an interface is really just a series of choices, our engagement with interfaces is inherently limited. We move through the interface by choosing from options that some tech designer decided might be relevant or interesting or important to us—but how are they to know? If beta tests show positive user feedback, and A/B tests demonstrate lift in consumer engagement, does this make it right? There are a host of questions that founders, designers, developers, and investors could, and perhaps should, be asking, not the least of which concern how the design of menus may be manipulating us subconsciously.

Take the case of the typical menu for tipping cabdrivers on the screen of New York City taxis. For rides over fifteen dollars, the Taxi and Limousine Commission (TLC) sets the default tip amounts, displayed as three large buttons on a touch-screen menu, at 20 percent, 25 percent, and 30 percent. Of course, one can enter a custom tip, but most passengers take a look at the greasy smudge marks on the screen and do as little touching as possible, pecking at one of those three buttons, often the middle one, leaving a 25 percent tip. Two scholars, Kareem Haggag of the University of Chicago and Giovanni Paci of Columbia University, analyzed data for thirteen million New York taxi rides, looking at the impact that these tipping "defaults" had on passenger behavior. What they found was that these defaults increased tips by over 10 percent, which, to the average driver earning $6,000 per year in tips, added up to an extra $600 per year just because of the menu. That's great for the drivers, but do taxi riders really want to be tipping so much?

Joe Edelman wants to address the issue of such subtle manipulations, whether they are intended or not. He wants interfaces to be designed to take personal preferences into account. To illustrate his point, he redesigned a hypothetical iPhone lock screen to optimize the morning of a specific user—and not some generic idea of a user that will be used to supplant all the real users who will come in contact with this lock screen. This interface is designed for a unique individual, personalized according to individual preferences. Let's use a hypothetical user named Susan as an example. To use the lock screen to optimize the morning for her, she is asked to describe her ideal morning. If Susan wants to wake up, get some fresh air, do yoga, write in her journal, and then go to work, that's the outcome for which the design will optimize.

On Edelman's version of the lock screen, in the morning there are no time-stamped notifications about Facebook conversations Susan is behind on, emails she needs to read, or entertainment she should to watch, because those things are not part of Susan's ideal morning. Instead, the lock screen simply reminds Susan what time her first work meeting is and lets her know if there are any friends who would like to journal or do yoga with her today. A widget at the bottom of the screen lets Susan choose from a set of adjectives to describe her ideal day—Adventurous? Quiet?—and then shows her only those friends and apps that will help her have that kind of day. Without presuming to know how the user *should* live their life, designers might remain open to giving the user more choice into how they might *like* to live their life.

Donald Norman understood how powerful the effects of even the smallest obtrusive features of the technology we bring into our lives can be on our way of thinking and behaving. He wrote, "Our social judgments, our skills, and even our thoughts are indelibly affected by the nature of the technology that supports us. Worse, the impact is so pervasive, so subtle, that we are often unaware of how much of our beliefs have been affected by the arbitrary nature of technology . . . Technologists tend to create what technology makes possible without full regard for the impact on human society. Moreover, technologists are experts at the mechanics of their technology, but often are ignorant of and sometimes even disinterested in social concerns."

Let me give you an example. Consider the technology that has enabled scrolling on a computer. Scrolling technology first appeared in the design of a computer mouse, allowing a user to move continuously down a page while reading without needing to lift a finger to point at an arrow. It was wonderfully convenient. When Apple designers incorporated the technology in the design of its iPod by creating the scroll wheel, we could suddenly navigate thousands of songs with only the slightest flick of our thumb. This design tweak then inspired the widespread implementation of the scroll feature in websites and apps, facilitating how we compulsively check our emails, Instagram photos, and Facebook News Feed. Here's the end effect: If it weren't so easy to scroll through so many photos and comments, perhaps we wouldn't be doing nearly as much of it. We probably think of ourselves as choosing to do so, but the design of our technology reduces friction in specific and sometimes calculated ways, ways that "nudge" us to act one way or the other.

Of course, the concept of nudging behavior through design interventions is nothing new. In 2008, Cass Sunstein, a law professor at Harvard, and Richard Thaler, a behavioral science and economics professor at the University of Chicago, coauthored the best-selling book entitled *Nudge: Improving Decisions About Health, Wealth, and Happiness,* building on the work of acclaimed economics Nobel laureate and Princeton psychology professor Daniel Kahneman. "Nudges," as Sunstein and Thaler call them, are design tweaks that can steer behavior, exactly the kind of conscious reframing of "choice architecture" for which Tristan Harris and Joe Edelman advocate.

Understanding the myriad ways in which technology is influencing our behavior and raising awareness about those effects has become vital work for fuzzies. In a sign of Google's growing interest in the valuable perspectives that fuzzies have to offer, the company brought in Damon Horowitz, now a philosophy professor at Columbia University, to act as a temporary in-house philosopher from 2010 to 2013, helping the company consider how to cope with issues regarding user privacy.

Horowitz is a bridge builder, working to combine the knowledge and perspectives of technologists with those of people educated in the liberal arts. He began his college career at Columbia University, taking its famous Great Books seminars. While he earned a degree in philosophy, he was frustrated by society's lack of progress on many fronts. Artificial intelligence seemed a panacea and a form of new progress, and so he decided to change course and pursue a technical master's degree at MIT's Media Lab. The bridges built by the liberal arts educational experience can encourage people to travel both ways, after all. His 2011 article in the *Chronicle of Higher Education* titled "From Technologist to Philosopher" discussed the heady thrill—the power—of being a programmer. "Once you've built a few small systems that do clever tasks—like recognizing handwriting, or summarizing a news article—then you think perhaps you could build a system that could do *any* task." As Horowitz recounted, "I had a high-paying technology job, I was doing cutting-edge AI work, and I was living the technotopian good life. But there was a problem . . . All I had really done was to create a bunch of clever toys—toys that were certainly not up to the task of being our intellectual surrogates." That's when he decided to return to his liberal arts roots and pursue a PhD in philosophy; the new perspectives he learned in his graduate studies dramatically changed his approach to developing technology.

"When I started graduate school," he wrote, "I didn't have a clue exactly how the humanities investigated the subjects I was interested in," and "I realized just how limited my technologist view of thought and language was . . . I didn't just get a few handy ideas about how to build better AI systems. My studies opened up a new outlook on the world . . . I became a humanist. And having a more humanistic sensibility has made me a much better technologist." He applied his new understanding to bringing more of the human element into search engine technology, cofounding the "social search engine" company Aardvark, which allowed users to ask questions and connect in real time with other people who had also signed up for Aardvark and specified particular interests or expertise that aligned with the scope of the question. For a question such as "What bars should I visit in Chicago?" Aardvark was easier than Google, because it was immediate, chat-based with another person, and built right into Gmail.

This innovation, and the team that had built it, was so impressive that Google bought the company for $50 million in 2010. Horowitz urges all technologists to go back to school and get a degree in the humanities, because "the technology issues facing us today—issues of identity, communication, privacy, regulation —require a humanistic perspective if we are to deal with them adequately . . . Getting a humanities Ph.D. is the most deterministic path you can find to becoming exceptional in the industry. It is no longer just engineers who dominate our technology leadership, because it is no longer the case that computers are so mysterious that only engineers can understand what they are capable of. There is an industrywide shift toward more 'product thinking' in leadership—leaders who understand the social and cultural contexts in which our technologies are deployed."

Fortunately, he and other technology innovators bringing the key insights of the liberal arts into technology are forging the way toward designing more ethical machines. One of the most exciting areas of progress is in the innovation of "digital therapeutics," meaning programs and devices that assist people in leading healthier and happier lives.

Making a Difference in Preventive Medicine

When Sean Duffy graduated from Columbia University in 2006, he thought the world was binary. He thought he could love and do only one thing, and he had always thought that would be health care. Sean was drawn to health care because he wanted "to give back to the world," as clichéd as that sounds. As an undergraduate, he had participated in Columbia's mandatory "core curriculum," a program requiring rigorous study of literature, contemporary civilization, art, music, and the frontiers of science. There, Sean learned about neuroscience and, fascinated by it, decided to make that his major. Duffy still expected to pursue a medical degree, but after graduating he was drawn by his intellectual curiosity and the heady pulse of Silicon Valley. He decided to hold off on applying to medical school. He heeded the siren call instead and applied to Google, where he got a job in the People Analytics department.

Thus began Duffy's journey of learning how to combine the differing perspectives of fuzzies and techies. His job with the People Analytics team taught him about managing people and organizational psychology. But being at a leading hub of technology innovation, he acquired a deep understanding of how software developers think. He saw the ways in which they approach problems, and he picked up the necessary vocabulary to communicate well with them. He also learned a great deal about technology itself. "I learned what can be done with a tool, even if I didn't know how to build the tool," Duffy recalls.

As he developed a better grasp of technology and how it can be designed to serve human needs, as so many of the products being created at Google were intended to do, he began to consider the possibility that he could combine his newfound appreciation of technology with his lifelong interest in health care. He left Google in 2009 to pursue a joint MD/MBA degree at Harvard. But he wasn't done with his preparation for building health technology yet. After only a year in Cambridge, Massachusetts, he dropped out and took a job at IDEO, the well-known Silicon Valley design firm, as a health design specialist. When he arrived in the Valley this second time, a new company called Fitbit had enraptured many. Attaching a pedometer to a person's wrist to count how many steps they took was lauded as the breakthrough development to shrink the world's overweight and obese populations. Tech journalists prognosticated about the profound impacts the innovation would have on people's health, but Duffy wasn't so sure. He recognized that data alone wouldn't change people's commitments to lead healthier lives, and actually assisting them in truly changing behavior would require a human touch.

Duffy began exploring the possibilities of digital health products with an IDEO colleague, Dennis Boyle. They thought it was important to look beyond wrist accelerometers and explored how they could affect chronic disease. The Diabetes Prevention Program (DPP) Research Group had published an important study on a lifestyle intervention for people who were prediabetic. The study found that type 2 diabetes, which afflicts 8 percent of American adults, was preventable using lifestyle interventions that focused on behavior modification, predominately diet and exercise. Among those who met the goal of losing 7 percent of their body weight, the incidence of diabetes fell by 58 percent. The results were profound. Duffy wondered: What if he could apply his background in neuroscience, his nontechnical experience at Google in managing people and understanding their behavior, his medical studies, and his design thinking from IDEO in a singular way that could target this type 2 diabetes problem? Deep down, he was a fuzzy, and he understood that with the right techies he could tackle this issue. His ability to ask the right questions gave him a comparative advantage over those taking a data-only, technology-only approach.

While still working at IDEO, Duffy began assembling a team of computer engineers in San Francisco, as he read more about the clinical processes for intervention and behavior change. The DPP's clinical trials had relied on human counselors coaching patients and staying in close touch with them. That intervention worked, but the method wasn't scalable. It would be economically impractical to do such intensive counseling for the millions of Americans who are at risk for diabetes. But technology could be developed to scale the therapy, and to do so in a way that preserved the human touch.

In order for the interventions designed to be effective, though, Duffy would have to understand the thoughts and feelings of the patients more fully. In 2011, before his technology team wrote a single line of code, then twenty-seven-year-old Duffy flew to rural Georgia with his cofounder to sit down with patients who had been diagnosed with prediabetic conditions. What he found was scary. "The people we talked to felt abandoned. After finding out they were at high risk of a deadly disease, they were—at best —handed a pamphlet, told to change their lifestyles and to lose weight," Duffy recalls. These patients were on their own, without social support or any ongoing medical guidance. Physicians had passed the buck, and it was up to patients to manage their disease, even though very few knew how, or had the discipline to change. Ironically, across the state, the Atlanta-based Centers for Disease Control and Prevention had issued a call for help, labeling chronic, rather than infectious, disease "the public health challenge of the twenty-first century."

Duffy decided that he had to figure out a way to maintain the same behavioral interventions, levers for motivation, and psychological elements of an in-person program while scaling it up through digitization. He had to put behavioral nudges into a person's pocket and help them conquer the preconditions that put them at risk of type 2 diabetes. He founded Omada Health and began to call the work the company would do "digital therapeutics." In short, he would artfully surround participants with all they needed to make positive lifestyle changes. The solution was one part techie and one part fuzzy, evidence-based science supplemented with a small-group social network, a personal health coach, and digital tracking tools like an Internet-connected bathroom scale that would update personal progress. Duffy decided to change the menu of choices for the millions of at-risk patients and partner with techies to bring scale to a practice that he knew could fundamentally improve human lives.

Duffy proceeded to raise more than $80 million in venture capital to support building the product, and after five years of development, Omada Health is delivering on his vision. Omada's central product takes into account a patient's food intake and exercise habits, social and emotional tendencies, and readiness to change, which is gauged by the patient filling out an online questionnaire. Omada's software program then assesses the patient's location, personality type, life stage, and other factors that help place the patient in a small group of individuals who have been determined to be like-minded and able to support one another. The technology also assigns the group a coach. Together, the group members and coach push one another toward achieving their goals, a central one of which for all of the patients is to lose 7 percent of body weight, the amount that the DPP linked to a 58 percent reduction in risk of type 2 diabetes. Throughout the entire process, the whole group is informed of each member's progress, which creates social peer pressure, but is also a source of empathy and motivation. Omada scientists have found that 80 percent of people who enter the program succeed in losing the prescribed 7 percent of their body weight. "You need all the ingredients to make the recipe," Duffy says. "Our program resembles a symphony."

When Duffy and his team began building Omada, experts in the medical community indicated that if the company published corroborative data about the program's results, traditional medical reimbursement by health care providers for patients might not be far behind. As I made my way into Duffy's San Francisco office in the spring of 2016, he walked toward me with a grin and a stride that told me he had news for me he couldn't wait to share. "The Centers for Medicare and Medicaid just approved reimbursement for digital therapeutics. We are the first-ever broadly digital service to be reimbursed under the Affordable Care Act." Duffy likened this moment to the dawn of anesthesia in the world of surgery. Prior to the advent of anesthetics and strong analgesics, surgeons were constrained by what they could attempt. It wasn't that they were incapable of doing more, but the sets of restrictions around risk and what society was willing to accept were narrower.

With anesthesia, those constraints broadened as drugs were able to push back thresholds of pain and surgical possibility. Similarly, digital therapeutics will push the boundaries, making preventive medicine more effective.

Other innovators are now on the cusp of creating digital therapeutics, and the best of them are also combining the human touch with technological power. Steven Johnson, a contributing editor of *Wired* magazine and the author of a number of books about the likely future of technology and how technology affects our lives, wrote an article entitled "Recognising the True Potential of Technology to Change Behaviour" that argued, "In the same way that the internal combustion engine and the light bulb allow us to overcome our relatively feeble powers of motion and perception, so digital technology can be directed to overcoming our relatively feeble powers of reasoning, self-control, motivation, self-awareness and agency—the factors that make behavior change so difficult."

Digital Therapy for the Masses?

Two other innovators who are proving this case are combining their talents in technology with their knowledge of psychotherapy in order to offer a powerful new, low-cost, and private form of therapy that is helping to move the needle on mental health.

Roni Frank and Oren Frank are on a mission to inspire all those who are suffering from mental pain, so many of whom opt to endure in silence rather than to seek therapy. They founded Talkspace, a technology-based therapy platform that, for a small fixed fee of thirty-two dollars a week, gives patients access to as much time with a licensed therapist as they need, provided through text messaging, recorded audio, and video. The Franks are working to transform the addictive devices in our pockets into lifelines for anyone in need, and less than three years after launching Talkspace, their one thousand certified therapists offer tailored services to over three hundred thousand users.

At the start of her working life, Roni Frank was a software developer. When she and her husband, Oren, went to couples therapy, the experience changed her life. Not only did the therapy help her deal with emotional challenges; she decided she wanted to become a therapist herself. She crossed the fuzzy-techie divide and enrolled in a master's program at the New York Graduate School of Psychoanalysis. Upon her graduation, she decided to combine her newfound psychological expertise with her prior technology expertise to create Talkspace. She had learned that fifty million Americans are diagnosed with mental health–related illnesses each year, and in spite of that massive population of sufferers, only one-third of that group ever pursues treatment.

People are frequently locked out of traditional therapy in part due to prohibitive prices, but also due to the stigma of seeking therapy, which, though it has lessened over recent decades, is still a deterrent in many circles. She knew therapy could be more accessible, more discreet, and made digitally available. Patients could be provided with certified, trustworthy therapists digitally, and in doing so, the costs of treatment could be brought down considerably. Whereas traditional therapy can cost over $150 per hour, Talkspace's counseling costs under $130 a month. Since privacy was another concern discouraging mentally ill people from seeking treatment, Roni Frank hoped that her totally discreet application might encourage more sufferers to come forward and seek help as well.

Roni's husband, Oren, was a technologist working in advertising at the time she developed her idea, and he was enthusiastic about cofounding a startup focused on this problem. Working out of a small loft on New York's Upper West Side, the Franks are try-ing to change the face of therapy by offering a gateway opportu-nity. With the service being so discreet and so low cost, they hope that those who might be particularly reluctant to seek help, such as teenagers who are worried about alarming their parents or war veterans who feel embarrassed by their difficulty in dealing with the trauma they have experienced, will be inspired to get the help they need. One potentially large market to be served is college fraternities such as Alpha Tau Omega (ATO), which is partnering with Talkspace to offer therapy to its ten thousand undergraduate members across 140 chapters. "In a frat setting, it's probably rare for a guy to speak up," says Austin Haines, president of the ATO chapter at the University of Florida. "It's very likely that someone in the fraternity is struggling with their mental health."

Therapists have been as avid about Talkspace as the clients who have joined because the company has built a suite of patient management tools for them to better manage their practice, a por-tal through which they can interact with a new diverse clientele, and a community of practitioners from whom to learn. The key insight that has helped Talkspace succeed hasn't been its tech; it has been the Franks' keen understanding of therapy and the needs of patients and psychologists. Over five hundred thousand peo-ple have tried Talkspace, and a thousand therapists across all fifty states are working on the platform. More important, organizations are beginning to see the value of offering a lightweight form of therapy as a benefit to employees, students, or alumni.

On a crisp fall day in Manhattan, I went to see an innovative marketing installation Talkspace had commissioned, an example of what's called experiential marketing. In Madison Square Park, adjacent to the famous Flatiron Building, I peered into a set of inflatable clear plastic domes. The urban igloos contained office furniture, a desk and a big armchair, along with a couch and some plants. They were temporary offices for therapists, and they were housed in clear plastic domes to send a message: "There's nothing to be ashamed of." Passersby could pop in and have a chat session with a therapist.

In another such installation in the park, Talkspace marketers employed a row of fun-house mirrors, lining the sidewalk at the park's edge. One mirror was concave and pinched people's features into small beady points, while another was convex, enlarging viewers' features. Other mirrors were bent in order to contort and distort people's faces and limbs. Placards, placed on top of each mirror, displayed statements such as "This is what Instagram makes me feel like." Beside the mirrors were billboards, displaying an array of actual Instagram posts, such as a selfie of a man grinning in front of a burning building with the caption "The roof! The roof! The roof is on fire!" At the top of the billboards, messages were written to mimic a surgeon general's notice: "Warning: Excessive social media use can result in a lack of empathy toward others" and "Warning: Social media is highly addictive and can lead to psychological withdrawal symptoms." The display was provocative, meant to encourage passersby to consider their dependence on technology, status, and image. The placards made people think, and the mirrors made people reflect. At a nearby table, where Talkspace staff handed out information about the company to passersby, stood a flat mirror, with no distortions, above which a sign read, "This is what you really look like (and you look awesome!)."

All the way back in 1992, in his book *Turn Signals Are the Facial Expressions of Automobiles,* Donald Norman commented that the new photographic technology of that day—video-recording devices in particular—distracted people from fully engaging in their daily experiences. "Whenever I travel," he wrote, "I watch with awe and amazement people overloaded with recording devices . . . Once upon a time there was an age in which people went to enjoy themselves, unencumbered by technology, with the memory of the event retained within their own heads. Today we . . . record the event, and the act of recording then becomes the event. Days later we review the event, peering at the tape, film, video in order to see what we would have seen had we been looking. We then show the recorded event to others so they too can experience what we would have seen had we been looking. Even if they don't care to experience it, thank you."

Given the state of our attention-grabbing economy and the host of variable rewards baked into this era of technological wonders, it's evident we need to further the cause of design ethics. This requires innovating products that engage us all in more meaningful, more therapeutic, and more life-enhancing ways. This work could not be a more vital challenge for fuzzies and techies to tackle. Remember, product design is a form of storytelling, and a form of translation from an analog world to the digital universe. Products built with insights from the study of human nature, informed by both fuzzy and techie, tell the most compelling stories.

SIX

Enhancing the Ways We Learn

One of the remarkable ironies regarding the raging debate over the need for our schools to focus more on teaching science, technology, engineering, and math (STEM) is that many of the technology experts in Silicon Valley are sending their children to "soft" schools. These are schools that emphasize building the precise skills that a liberal arts college education seeks to foster, chief among those being intellectual curiosity and confidence, creativity, strong interpersonal communication, empathy for others, and a love of learning and problem solving.

In 2011, the *New York Times* ran an article entitled "A Silicon Valley School That Doesn't Compute," highlighting how the chief technology officer of eBay, along with employees of Google, Apple, Yahoo, and Hewlett-Packard, send their children to the Waldorf School of the Peninsula in Los Altos, California, one of some 160 private schools around the United States that follow the Waldorf method of instruction. Also known as Steiner education, because it was originally based on the educational philosophy of Rudolf Steiner, the Waldorf moniker derives from 1919, when the Waldorf-Astoria Cigarette Company in Stuttgart, Germany, first instituted the program to teach the children of its employees. The method focuses on physical activity and hands-on creative learning, including play, for the early childhood years, and in the elementary years, a key emphasis is on building social skills and artistic ability. At the secondary school level, there is particular focus on critical thinking as well as instilling understanding and empathy toward others. Perhaps most surprising for a school in the heart of Silicon Valley is that in the classrooms of the Waldorf School of the Peninsula there are no screens at all.

The technology company executives who send their children there understand that, as education researcher Michael Horn argues, "machines are automating a whole bunch of these things [work tasks], so having the softer skills, knowing the human touch and how to complement technology, is critical, and our education system is not set up for that." Harvard economist David Deming has done research that provides strong backup for the value of the human touch in today's job market, and for the future. In a paper entitled "The Growing Importance of Social Skills in the Labor Market," published in 2015, he shows that the market for science, technology, and engineering jobs has been contracting, while the fastest growth in high-skilled jobs is in those professions that require strong interpersonal skills, such as law, nursing, and business management. Yet, as Horn notes, the stress on STEM skills has drowned out attention to the critical need to build better soft skills. With the implementation in the United States of the Common Core curriculum in K–12 public education, which puts a heavy focus on teaching and measuring specific skills, time for instruction of any kind beyond that rigid core is becoming increasingly squeezed. In addition, with the added stress on proving the efficacy of instruction through standardized tests, making the case for the value of teaching the soft skills has become more difficult, as they're not easily evaluated by standardized tests. The soft skills have quietly become our educational "dark matter," like the enormous amount of matter in the universe that can't be measured by astronomers but that they know profoundly shapes the nature of the solar system.

So how do we foster the soft skills, the creative confidence, a sense of adventure in learning, and a wide-ranging curiosity in our children that are so important while also equipping them with the necessary knowledge of technology as well as the other STEM disciplines? How do we give students the right skills, the so-called "right stuff," namely those qualities like character, leadership, and confidence? How do we achieve a fuzzy-techie balance in education that will give them the best opportunity for success?

The good news is that a recent innovation boom in education is producing numerous promising approaches and tools, with much of this work focusing on combining technology tools with human wisdom about how we learn. Educational tech startups are being hotly pursued; since 2010, venture capitalists have plowed more than $2.3 billion into companies seeking to address K–12 education. In short, great strides are being made, moving beyond outdated and largely ineffective approaches in combining technology and education.

Finding the Right Balance in Teaching

The effort to integrate technology tools into education stretches back a few decades, albeit with mostly disappointing results. Distance learning programs, for example, which offer all classes remotely by computer, have been the subject of much controversy, with critics asserting that the lack of person-to-person classroom time undermines teaching quality.

To consider just one case in point, the outcomes for students of the Electronic Classroom of Tomorrow (ECOT), an online, publicly funded charter school operating out of Columbus, Ohio, are troubling. The school, which serves more than seventeen thousand students across the state, boasts of having some of the largest graduating classes in America. But upon closer investigation, their numbers are—in the parlance of Silicon Valley—referred to as "vanity metrics," seemingly impressive results that really aren't true indicators of success. In a 2016 story entitled "Online School Enriches Affiliated Companies If Not Its Students," the *New York Times* pointed out that according to federal data on ECOT, eighty students drop out for every one hundred students who graduate.

The students who ECOT is primarily catering to have special needs, such as medical issues, or have had a history of behavioral problems in school. Plus, the lack of one-on-one classroom supervision and personal engagement with teachers seems to exacerbate the drop-out problem. By the way, the drop-out issue is by no means isolated to this one school. Drop-out rates of other online-only schools are also much higher than the national average. The national high school graduation average is 82 percent. But a report by America's Promise Alliance, a consortium of education advocacy organizations, reveals that the average graduation rate for online schools hovers around 40 percent, less than half that of physical schools. In 2014, the ECOT graduated less than 39 percent of its senior class. The *New York Times* went so far as to say that "publicly funded online schools like the Electronic Classroom have become the new dropout factories."

More promising is the explosion of online self-teaching tools in recent years, most notably those courses provided by the nonprofit Khan Academy and the advent of massive open online courses—or MOOCs, as they're known—offered both by traditional universities, including many of the Ivy League colleges, and by private firms such as Coursera and Udacity. Salman Khan, the founder of Khan Academy, recognized the need for tutorials to augment students' learning in school when he began helping his cousin with her math homework. He created hundreds of short videos that broke lessons down into extremely easy-to-follow instructions, and the Khan Academy library of tutorials has now grown to cover the full school curriculum, as well as offering practice exercises and tools for teachers.

At the college level, MOOCs are now available across a wide swath of university education, and many are taught by leading experts in their fields. These services are bringing high-quality instruction to the masses, making it available at either no cost or at a much-reduced cost, and they are certainly to be applauded. But the truth is, this kind of self-guided instruction online also has limits. The completion rates for most MOOCs are, for example, quite low. The bottom line is that these tools are wonderful augmentations to traditional person-to-person education but should not be considered as ultimate replacements for person-to-person instruction.

Educational innovators looking for new approaches have been exploring how we can pair the amazing capabilities of technology —its broad reach, its ability to deliver vast amounts of information at lightning speed, and its potential for innovative forms of interactive instruction—with the vital human touch of personal engagement with both teachers and other students. One of those individuals leading the way is Esther Wojcicki, a fuzzy and a journalism teacher at Palo Alto High School known as "Paly," who has for decades advocated a style of teaching known as "blended learning." This approach, in which she has been a pioneer, harnesses the power of technology in order to facilitate it.

Innovating to Improve Blended Learning

Different experts define blended learning in their own unique ways, but in essence, it involves incorporating technology tools into hands-on, largely self-directed and project-based instruction. A May 2011 report by the Innosight Institute identified forty different organizations that support forty-eight models for blended learning. Some prescribe mostly classroom-based learning, with a teacher lecturing and only relatively small doses of self-guided learning by students on computers. At the other end of the spectrum, all courses are viewed online, and the teacher becomes a coach or tutor, roaming the classroom to observe, answer questions, and advise, as students work on projects during class time. Some schools use technology in the classroom to personalize instruction, meaning that students are allowed to move through course material at their own pace. Still other schools use technology to add hours to the school day outside their walls. Overall, students are said to find blended learning a more engaging style of instruction than the traditional lecture-based model.

Since 1984, Esther Wojcicki has taught at Palo Alto High School, a public high school. There, she has been a pioneer in the field of blended learning. At Palo Alto High School, she's an institution, known affectionately as "Woj," the favorite teacher of many students both past and present. She is also the mother of three high-profile women in Silicon Valley: Janet, who is a professor of pediatrics at UCSF Medical School; Susan, who is the CEO of YouTube; and Anne, who is the founder of the genomics testing company 23andMe and who was married to Google cofounder Sergey Brin. Google was created in her daughter's garage, so Woj clearly has direct lines to the vanguard of innovation.

Woj was an English major at UC Berkeley and also studied French history at the Sorbonne, but she's no Luddite. She was, in fact, one of the first to bring computers into the classroom. She was so excited by her first encounter with a Macintosh in 1987 that she immediately applied for a grant and secured funds to buy a number of Macs for her students to use. She's never stopped exploring ways to enhance her teaching with technology. Recently she helped lead the Google Teacher Academy, which runs free seminars for teachers from all around the world that introduce them to technology tools for use in teaching and the latest methods being developed. She also coauthored the 2015 book *Moonshots in Education: Launching Blended Learning in the Classroom,* which offers a wealth of advice and inspiration to educators about the potential of the approach. Recognizing her trailblazing influence, the Rhode Island School of Design awarded her an honorary degree in 2016. I've been fortunate to know Woj for nearly twenty years, having met her when I joined the founding team of *Verde*, a feature magazine I helped launch and edit while I was one of her students at Palo Alto High School.

Being in her class was indeed memorable. From the very first day, Woj put her blended-learning philosophy into practice, immediately having us vote for who would play which roles in publishing *Verde*, with some of us becoming editors and others working on page design, using the then-newfangled Adobe PageMaker and Photoshop programs. We even sold advertising, charging a then-fledgling startup called Google $800 (we should have asked for stock) for the back page while the company was still running out of Woj's daughter's garage. Woj then told us our production schedule and wished us good luck. She has joked that blended learning is the laziest form of teaching, because as a teacher, you delegate everything to your students.

But in truth, as Woj did with us, the teacher carefully observes the students as they work on their projects, always available to offer insights and to help steer them. Vital, however, is that teachers relinquish the strict control of the traditional lecturing style of classroom teaching. This is essential so that students are not subject to a command-and-control hierarchy in the classroom, but rather learn how to independently self-manage and how to interact thoughtfully with their peers, assisting one another, asking one another for help, and collaborating on projects, just as is so important for colleagues in work life to do.

In 2009, Woj and her team began pursuing a Career Technical Education grant from the State of California to create the New Media Arts Center, a teeming state-of-the-art space of innovation at the high school level, where largely self-directed students now produce live television and radio programming, content-rich newspapers, and multiple magazines. Among the high-profile public figures attending the 2014 ribbon cutting were Google founders Larry Page and Sergey Brin, *Huffington Post* founder Arianna Huffington, and actor James Franco, an alumnus of the program who's even painted murals around the building. When I visited the arts center I was reminded of the hyberbusy Bloomberg TV headquarters in New York City; it was a comparable hive of activity. The light-filled atrium is littered with beanbags, but I didn't see any students lounging. They were buzzing with purpose — some working on the center's daily newscast, others monitoring live streaming of video stories from soundproof studios.

The atrium is designed to host regular public events, such as lectures, and featured onstage that day was a startup founder, who I was to learn had received funding from Benchmark Capital, the venture capital firm that invested in Stitch Fix and Uber. He was giving a presentation about his company's technology architecture, speaking to the Android Developers Club. The center doesn't just simulate cutting-edge tech journalism, with *New Yorker* quotes indelibly scrawled into tiles in the bathrooms, and benches elegantly constructed out of retired Apple computers, such as those we used when I was editor; it is truly both a digital hub and a place of interpersonal exchange and community. As Jack Brock, the editor of *Verde,* put it, "There's a lot of investment in the STEM fields because it's Silicon Valley . . . Paly invests in the arts." Indeed, next door to the New Media Arts Center is a $29 million Center for the Performing Arts.

Over lunch, Woj explained that blended learning fosters creative confidence and complex problem solving in students. The learning-by-doing philosophy allows students not only to struggle with projects but also to fail, teaching that such failures are inevitable and that perseverance is vital to success. It teaches that learning and accomplishment are not simply a matter of memorizing information and reciting it in tests. It encourages students to be creative and work out their own solutions, rather than expecting to be given the answers.

In the last few years, a handful of studies have shown students making impressive gains with the help of blended-learning tools and techniques. In 2010, SRI International conducted a study on blended learning entitled "Evaluation of Evidence-Based Practices in Online Learning" for the U.S. Department of Education. It looked at blended-learning studies from 1996 through 2008 and found that students in these kinds of environments generally outperformed their peers in classes that take place fully in person— and also outperformed classes that took place fully online. In sum, students in blended environments outperformed both fully fuzzy and fully techie approaches.

A series of case studies released in September 2015 by the Evergreen Education Group and the Clayton Christensen Institute for Disruptive Innovation also showed great gains in some school districts that have adopted blended-learning models. In Middletown, New York, students in blended-learning classrooms rotated through stations for math, reading, and other subjects, sometimes working on a computer, other times with a teacher or small group. Those students scored 18 percent higher in reading and 7 percent higher in math on the state tests. In Spokane, Washington, the educational district saw its graduation rate climb from 60 percent in 2007 to 83 percent in 2014, after instituting blended-learning curricula across multiple programs.

In April 2016, MIT's Online Education Policy Initiative issued a report entitled *Online Education: A Catalyst for Higher Education Reforms,* examining where online education fits into higher education. Created in 2013 to focus on a radical proposal for blended learning at MIT that included freshman and senior years that were conducted almost entirely online, the task force recommended that schools focus on people and processes, *not* on technology. Specifically, it stated that "online learning will not replace teachers, just as the fly-by-wire system has not replaced aircraft pilots. But just as a fly-by-wire aircraft control system enables a human pilot to operate her aircraft more effectively, through dynamic digital scaffolding, a human teacher could affect differentiated instruction to a large number of students and achieve overall class learning objectives. Aided by technology, teachers can refocus their efforts on the aspects of learning that online tools cannot provide, including coaching and fostering reflection and creative thinking."

Legions of educators are working to enhance the practice of blended learning. Esther Wojcicki helped organize the Google-sponsored Moonshot Summit in order to showcase their innovations and to spur sharing of ideas and results; the summit has spawned an avid community bursting with recommendations about apps for education and other tools and approaches. There is far too much happening to cover more than a sliver in this chapter, but I did feel compelled to share a few examples of a few pioneers who are achieving particularly exciting results.

Escape Rooms Inspire Student-Led Learning

James Sanders has had a number of light-bulb moments in his life. The most recent came while he was playing an escape room game in Edmonton, Canada. Escape games are problem-solving situations where participants must solve a series of clues and puzzles to escape from a physical room within a specific timeframe. Similar to whodunit games like Clue, escape room games leap into real life. For video game aficionados, they are analog role-playing games. For theater buffs, they're immersive theater, similar to performance installations such as *Sleep No More*, an adaptation of Shakespeare's *Macbeth* performed by London's Punchdrunk theater group and brought to life in a multistory mansion in Manhattan. But in Canada, James Sanders was there to attend the Google Education Summit with a group of high school students and teachers, and they had decided that playing an escape game would be a great way to spend their evening. Sanders was struck that a group of students would willingly choose to spend their night off playing a game that required them to do some intensive critical thinking. He saw an engagement and enthusiasm in their collaboration that he knew could be magical in the classroom.

Sanders, a classic liberal arts undergraduate, studied social studies and history at Western Washington University, where he developed a strong interest in education. He became involved in a revamping of the educational requirements at the school, a component of which was finding ways for the university to leverage technology tools better. Upon graduating, he won a coveted spot in the Teach for America program and then took a teaching job in South Los Angeles, eventually earning his master of arts in education at Loyola Marymount University and becoming a sixth-grade English and social studies teacher at Carnegie Middle School in Carson, California.

Sanders saw that his students didn't have great access to the new tools of learning, but he was undaunted. In 2009, he decided to take his entire classroom online and was the first teacher in America to go paperless, having his students work via Google Chromebooks instead. As an early adopter of the technology, he was able to get the devices directly from Google. His students loved it, and Google was so impressed, it asked him to come on board as a part-time contractor to advise on the development of its marketing strategy for the Chromebook.

Sanders took a further plunge into tech-based education when he decided to join the video-streaming service YouTube, leading several education initiatives for the company, including YouTube for Teachers. "When I joined," he recalls, "YouTube was where you found cat videos, not educational videos." Though he loved his work at YouTube, by mid-2012, he had met Esther Wojcicki and the two came up with an idea for a technology-enabled educational tool—digital badges, or customizable digital accolades that teachers could use to reward their students for mastery of a certain subject. Similar to a Girl Scout or Boy Scout badge, it was a way to create digital waypoints for student academic achievement, and a way to introduce online game mechanics into offline classrooms. Digital badges were as much a behavioral product as they were tech, but they had roots in online gaming. Game mechanics are tools that incentivize engagement through things like playing levels and earning points. They cofounded a company called ClassBadges, which provided these free digital badging services for teachers, and they sold the company two years later to an educational platform called EdStart.

It was a quick win, but Sanders wasn't done innovating in education. After the sale to EdStart, he decided to take a position as innovation manager at KIPP Bay Area Schools, where he collaborated with Salman Khan and his team to help incorporate Khan Academy videos into classroom teaching in KIPP's schools. From that role, Sanders moved on to become presidential innovation fellow at the White House, helping to develop the ConnectED plan to bring Wi-Fi Internet connectivity to 99 percent of American schools by 2018.

His latest innovation, inspired by that night playing the escape room game in Edmonton, is Breakout EDU, a toolkit for engaging students in critical thinking exercises by requiring them to figure out how to open a box. He had originally thought of simply bringing the escape room idea into teaching with games that locked students in the classroom, but, as he recalls, when the team he assembled started researching the idea, "we learned quickly that it might be illegal to lock kids in a classroom." He then pivoted to the idea of a game that would give students clues and a set of items with which they would have to figure out how to open a locked box. To accomplish the task, they would encounter all sorts of puzzles that would force them to collaborate.

In the summer of 2015, James went to Target to buy a big plastic box and he ordered hundreds of dollars of different kinds of locks online. He experimented every weekend for three months with combinations of different items and different challenges, and ultimately ended up with a kit that was made up of a small lock box, six locks, a black light, an invisible ink pen, a UV light, a USB drive, and two "hint cards."

One teacher at Gravelly Hill Middle School in Efland, North Carolina, created a poetry Breakout game where students pretend to be Langston Hughes in Harlem in May 1936. They receive an urgent telegram that *Esquire* magazine is about to publish their poem "Let America Be America Again" but without giving them credit. They must call the publisher to remedy the situation, but the magazine goes to print in forty-five minutes. Students must solve a number of puzzles related to Langston Hughes and his poetry to crack codes, open the locks, and ultimately get *Esquire*'s phone number out of the lock box. If they fail, they won't get credit for having written one of their greatest works of poetry. While the first Breakout lock boxes were made of wood, and decidedly nontechie, the learning style is blended, as students solve physical challenges, collaborate as teams, and use the Internet to find answers.

Just one year after launching, the company was selling thousands of kits per month and teachers were inventing a wealth of new games, with 98 percent of those that are featured on the company's website being designed by teachers, not by Breakout EDU employees. All of the games must be solved with the same basic kit of items, but the ways in which they can be reassembled are endless. There are games designed for kindergarten-level literacy all the way to Advanced Placement physics and environmental science. In one designed for computer coding, students input the right code to reveal a Quick Response (QR) barcode they use to navigate to a hidden website. From there, they solve a number of logic puzzles that help them open physical locks.

Mitchel Resnick, a professor of learning research and the head of the Lifelong Kindergarten group at the MIT Media Lab, has compared these new technology-enabled tools to "Froebel's gifts," named after the German educator Friedrich Froebel, the inventor of kindergarten. Froebel created play materials, such as a set of wood blocks and a wooden ball, and balls of yarn with a string attached, with which his kindergartners learned through playing. Sanders's Breakout EDU kits are play materials that facilitate collaborative learning and the joy of problem solving in older children. They inspire children to take the failures and frustrations they encounter in solving the puzzles in stride, plus the game approach motivates them to stretch their minds to be creative and discover solutions, rather than merely looking for answers. Whereas failure on a problem set might engender frustration, in a game it's simply part of the challenge of winning.

Engaging Students with Self-Learning

Another researcher who is pushing the boundaries of online education platforms, investing them with more fuzzy awareness of how children can best be inspired to deeply engage with learning, is Sugata Mitra, a professor of educational technology at Newcastle University. His unorthodox experiments in the slums of New Delhi captivated people around the world and became part of the inspiration for the movie *Slumdog Millionaire*. In 1999, Mitra chopped a hole in the wall of his office building on the edge of a slum in New Delhi and placed a computer inside. Kids flocked to the device and within hours had taught themselves how to browse without any instruction from adults. Soon, they were watching videos and had taught themselves enough English that they could email and use the search function to read articles.

Mitra proceeded to conduct a series of what he calls Hole in the Wall experiments, in which children used computers to teach themselves math and science. Mitra was pushing past the blended-learning model, in which the teacher acts as a coach, and developing methods in which no teachers are involved. To him, the key staples of learning are the Internet and fellow students, and he wants to radically reinvent school instruction. He stresses that forcing humans to memorize a bunch of facts is outdated in the age of the Internet. And even scholars such as Mitchel Resnick agree with Mitra on the point that for questions with clear right answers, teachers are less necessary. Instead of teaching kids a bunch of facts, it's better to teach them to be creative thinkers and good communicators—to him, what will matter in the digital age is an ability to ask questions, to think critically, and to utilize tools to solve problems.

In 2013, Mitra was awarded the TED Prize, which came with $1 million in prize money, to put his ideas into practice. He used the money to build learning laboratories to connect children to information through what he calls Self-Organized Learning Environments, or SOLEs, and to build an online platform to connect and support those environments. He calls his system the School in the Cloud, and his first School in the Cloud laboratory opened inside a traditional high school in Killingsworth, England, in December 2013.

In Mitra's approach, children receive a complex question that is designed to stimulate thoughtful conversations, and they are then given a period of time to research it. Questions are open-ended and don't have answers that they can simply look up. For example, a sample question might be: What would happen to the earth if all the insects disappeared? The point of providing students an imponderable question, or a question for which there are many approaches, is to teach them that the world is not black-and-white; it is not about memorizing facts, but it is about learning to grapple with challenges that cannot be pinned down. These kinds

of questions teach investigatory approaches and comfort in ambiguity. Gray-area questions require courage in their approach.

Secondarily, they also teach about the various types of sources
and how to navigate among them. Are all sources created equal?
Or do some require greater rigor, greater accuracy, or accountabil-
ity? Indeed, these are the very questions we all need to ask as we
open the newspaper or turn on the television.

Students divide into small groups, each armed with a computer,
and using whatever tools they can marshal—Google, Wikipedia,
YouTube, or other resources they think up—they try to answer
the question they've been presented. They're encouraged to check
out what other groups are doing, even to share answers with them.
In this paradigm, collaboration is not cheating; it's an effective
way to share insights and to problem solve. The competitive spirit
drives learning.

This model can also be adapted to include teachers, though it's
important that teachers not insert themselves into the situation,
but rather wait for the students to seek their input. The role of the
teacher is less about passing on knowledge and more about being
the listener in chief. Kids like to show and tell adults what they've
learned, something in which every parent becomes well schooled.
Teachers, or in the case of Mitra's application of his model other
adults, can play an important role in strengthening children's
sense of accomplishment. For this reason, Mitra employs what he
calls his "grandmother method," with some seventy-five adults
mentoring and acting as sounding boards for all of the children in
the faraway school, all done over Skype.

In preparing our kids for working life, and for jobs that don't
yet exist and so can't be trained for, Mitra believes that it's best
to teach them how to solve problems. "Knowing," as he says, "is
going obsolete." Providing students with open-ended questions

teaches them how to operate in ambiguity, how to compartmentalize a problem, and how to manipulate different tools to achieve different ends. It also spurs them to engage in a depth of inquiry, in which it is as much learning the process of acquiring information as it is the specific knowledge gained that truly matters.

Mitra's method may seem extreme, and in fact, it has drawn criticism for the suggestion of leaving children so entirely to themselves in the learning process. Michał Paradowski, a professor of applied linguistics at the University of Warsaw in Poland, challenged the wisdom of this model in an article entitled "Classrooms in the Cloud or Castles in the Air?," arguing that "we need to show them at least some of the possible paths and open the doors, so they can look beyond their immediate concerns." But Mitra's TED Prize shined a spotlight on his experiments, and some teachers have tested them closer to home in ways that don't entirely leave educators out of the equation. According to this line of thinking, the teacher's role ought to be in proposing good questions and helping students learn how to use technology tools for finding answers. The goal is to pair the fuzzy and techie optimally, teaching humans to ask better questions and helping them learn how to make machines provide better answers.

One of the teachers adapting Mitra's methods is Dora Bechtel, who has introduced SOLEs to her second-grade students at the Campus International School, housed at Cleveland State University in Ohio. Similar to Mitra, she asks her students a "messy question" that doesn't have a black-and-white correct answer. In a unit about cities, she designed a SOLE around the question, "Why do cities change?" Designing a SOLE requires not just devising a broad, ponderable question without a simple answer, but it also involves critical thinking on the part of the teacher to consider some of the guardrails or potentialities. Bechtel worried that her cities question might frustrate her lowest achievers, but when she paired them together, they used videos to learn hard-to-understand concepts, and when they encountered text that was difficult for them to read, they found apps that read the text for them. After a second grader asked, "Could we hear if our ears were square?" his class did a SOLE around how hearing works, looking into both the physics and the biology of what makes our ears function. Any such question can serve as fodder to explore knowledge using our digital tools.

The MC2 STEM High School in Cleveland, Ohio, has also adopted SOLEs. In ninth grade, the capstone project is called "rockets and robots," and students are tasked with building one of each. In addition, they are instructed to answer the question, "Just because we can make the technology, should we?" What a fruitful application of technology to inspire engagement with the issues, as well as the liberal arts and the soft skills, children will need in working life.

Teacher as Coach

Diane Tavenner is the founder and CEO of Summit Public Schools (SPS), a nonprofit organization based in Silicon Valley. In 2003, Tavenner opened Summit Preparatory Charter High School in Redwood City, California, which *U.S. News and World Report* has called a "school of the future." While Redwood City sits at the heart of Silicon Valley, it's a working-class city. The idea behind Summit was to bring *all* of the area's public school kids, rich or poor, brilliant or underperforming, into the same building, and to teach them in an inclusive environment that was focused on producing well-rounded graduates who were ready for college. Almost half of Summit students are Hispanic, and 42 percent are low income. In its first decade in operation, 96 percent of its graduates were accepted into four-year colleges.

Summit uses blended learning to focus on four things: cognitive skills, content knowledge, real-life experiences, and healthy habits of success. The school contends these four skills are the most important in enabling students to excel in college and beyond. The school also seeks to foster the soft skills, such as self-awareness, self-management, social awareness, interpersonal skills, and responsible behavior. The emphasis in developing thinking skills is on improving decision-making abilities. "Look at the economy," Tavenner says. "It's not about concrete knowledge, it's about higher order thinking skills, and the ability to perpetually learn and grow."

Rather than focus on the rote drills so often leaned upon in schools seeking to improve test scores, Summit provides instruction through video presentations, seminars, and hands-on learning. That doesn't mean kids aren't learning facts and figures; it just means that teachers don't waste their most precious resource—time and attention—delivering content. Students have mentors, and all students—not just creative ones—annually partake in four two-week-long learning "expeditions" into subjects such as art, yoga, film, and music. These experiences are meant to match those of more affluent students.

To teach kids content, Summit banks heavily on technology, which is quite innovative. Tavenner wanted to provide students with a deeply personalized form of education, allowing teachers to give each student the particular type of instruction that will help them learn at their own pace to study engaging topics that will help them reach their long-term goals. So Tavenner and her team created what they call their Personalized Learning Platform, which is a Common Core–aligned program that students log into to see all their projects and learning goals for the year. A progress bar shows them whether they're on track, ahead of schedule, or falling behind in each class. Their progress is visible motivation, but can also serve as a reminder of all that they have to do. By allowing students to take charge of directing their own learning and work at their own pace, Summit is equipping them with the time management skills they'll need in college and later in life. They also learn independence, another skill needed in college, and increasingly in our self-directed gig economy.

At the beginning of the school year, students are presented with a list of content knowledge standards they're expected to learn. Summit teachers don't create lesson plans; they're called playlists. Playlists allow students to work at their own pace and teachers to observe how their students are doing. When students click on each concept, the tool launches a playlist that includes a diagnostic assessment so students can see how much they already know about the topic and how much they still have to learn. These playlists include resources like videos and websites, practice materials, and a final assessment to be taken under teacher supervision. Students can also give their feedback on lessons by voting up or voting down resources that are or are not helpful. Plus content within playlists can be substituted easily. Students spend around sixteen hours a week on computers, working their way through lessons in all the traditional content areas. About half of that computer work takes place during school hours, with the rest of it done at home.

Teachers become coaches rather than lecturers. They are in the classrooms with students and they monitor students' progress in real time as the day progresses, offering special assistance when a student gets stuck. Students are thus encouraged to do something that's a vital skill for thriving in college and work life: asking for help when you can't figure something out alone. The Summit approach is not about replacing the classroom and teacher; it's about bringing the best of technology into the classroom and reinventing the role of teachers. To date, Summit has created over 700 playlists that don't automate, but supplement teachers.

Summit received a big boost of support in 2014 from Facebook founder Mark Zuckerberg and his wife, Priscilla Chan, after they toured the school. They liked what they saw and asked Tavenner what they could do to help. Tavenner's team was short on programming expertise, and Zuckerberg offered up a team of engineers to help troubleshoot the glitches in the technology system that the school's team had built. The goal is to make an improved version of Summit's Personalized Learning platform available for free to schools nationwide. Today, it's offering free tools to help one hundred public schools across America build their own playlists.

Although not all are sold on the model of "standardized personalization," calling it somewhat of an oxymoron, the bottom line is that many students arrive at Summit with lower-than-average scores, and yet Summit consistently outperforms other schools in the area. In spring 2016, 93 percent of Summit's entering freshmen graduated, and 99 percent of its graduates were admitted to four-year colleges. Once Summit graduates are in college, their completion rate is double the national average. Although the program is still small, with around two thousand five hundred students, this fresh and innovative approach of in-person, self-directed blended learning is showing early signs of promise.

Better Involving Parents

Rachel Lockett is a fuzzy, one who realized that she could play a vital role in helping to improve education by working to develop better communication technology to schools and parents. She joined startup Remind, which has built a platform, much like Slack for K–12 education, that facilitates easy and accountable communication among teachers, students, and parents.

Rachel had no experience in technology when she decided to go work at Remind. What she had was a classic liberal arts experience in discovering unexpected ways to apply her talents. After earning her BA in human biology at Stanford, she moved to Baltimore to work at the Annie Casey Foundation, focusing on helping to find foster care for children and to improve juvenile justice. That work got her interested in education because she realized that schools are the first gateway in many children's lives that provide hope. Even if a child grows up in the foster care system, if they go to a good school, they can overcome the difficulties of their upbringing. She decided that education was where she wanted to have a real impact.

Rachel's journey in education began when she moved to Boston and joined the Center for Effective Philanthropy, where she met with hundreds of schools and educators who were Gates Foundation grant beneficiaries. She built survey tools and tried to figure out what was really working in education and what wasn't. This experience inspired her to become a teacher. In short, she wanted to get into the trenches.

Heading back to California, she received her teacher training through the Aspire Charter Schools, which has a residency program; she taught at Aspire schools in the San Francisco East Bay area for three years. The exposure to the innovative energy of Silicon Valley she received from living in San Francisco inspired her to think about how she could use technology to enhance education. What she liked about Remind is that it solves a problem that is one of the most vexing for schools. "Parents and teachers are two of the most valuable contributors to society," she explains, "and they're often also the most overwhelmed. What we enable through technology is faster, easier, safer communication between parents, teachers, students, and administrators." Rachel understood that she had a comparative advantage as a teacher in helping to develop technology to improve education, and today she's the head of user experience.

The Remind offices must have made her feel right at home when she started. Giant paper airplanes hang from the arched wood beams crossing the ceiling. There are hopscotch squares in the entryway, and the front desk is made entirely of wooden twelve-inch school rulers. I take a seat on a couch where the pillows are covered in letters and numbers, and then make my way into a conference room where the back wall has a texture that I can't quite make out until I sit down. Upon closer look, the entire wall is covered in No. 2 pencils lined up side by side and end to end, a tight mosaic of wood, eraser, and graphite. The office is modeled as a classroom, but one with transparency and with open, relaxed spaces.

Historically, schools have communicated with parents and students by email blasts and robocalls—prerecorded messages left on voice mail systems. But in an era where most people don't have home phones, many people don't check voice mail, and email directories are outdated, Remind decided that communication had to be done differently. Their idea is to reach people where they are, through the method of an individual's choice.

Rachel explains: "If your class is math, you tell your students to text '@math' to a short code such as 81010, or download the app. Then everyone in the room is on your group messenger, and you can reach them directly." She joined as a community manager, where she spoke the language of education to teachers and administrators. In her year at the company, she's already running all its user experience research, driving product development. Business is going well. The company has raised nearly $60 million from some of the top investors in Silicon Valley, and more than thirty-five million teachers, parents, and students use it.

Remind is putting into practice insights from academic research into how important parental involvement in school can really be in a child's performance. Peter Bergman, a professor of economics and education at Columbia University's Teachers College, is one of the researchers who have contributed to these findings. He teamed up with a school in a poor neighborhood in Los Angeles to test the effect small interventions could have on student performance. The parents of 242 students in grades six through eleven were randomly selected to receive additional information about their children's progress at school. A few times each month, a student's family would get an email, text message, or phone call with information on the child's grades and missing assignments. The messages were detailed, including the name of the class, assignment, problems, and page numbers of the missing work.

Not surprisingly, with this kind of improved communication, parents became far more involved in their children's education. Those who received additional information contacted the school to talk about their children's progress a stunning 83 percent more often than those who didn't get the extra information. Attendance at parent-teacher conferences increased by 53 percent. In response, students got on top of their schoolwork, completing 25 percent more of their assignments, missing 28 percent fewer classes, and becoming 24 percent less likely to display unsatisfactory work habits. These very simple interventions were having a significant impact on parent engagement with teachers, and with their children.

When students started working harder, they got better results. High school students whose parents were kept well apprised of their performance had GPAs 0.19 standard deviations higher than those whose parents were given only the standard information. Test scores in math increased by 0.21 standard deviations. By comparison, when children began attending the lauded KIPP Academy Lynn charter school in Massachusetts, test scores improved by 0.35 standard deviations in math and 0.12 in English.

Basic text message intervention offers tangible promise, at least in the high schools where it has been tried. These small interventions aren't going to fix the current education system all alone, but they do pack a lot of bang for the buck. Bergman calculated that in this experiment, it cost roughly $156 to increase one child's GPA or math score by 0.10 standard deviations—and that's if teachers are doing all of the work manually. Automating parts of the process would likely drop the cost far further.

A 2014 study by Ben York and Susanna Loeb, two Stanford University education researchers, corroborated Bergman's work. They examined whether text-messaging interventions like those that Bergman used with the parents of high school kids could be used to encourage parents with preschool children to help their kids develop literacy skills.

Research has consistently shown that there are huge language gaps between rich kids and those who come from low-income homes, and that those gaps begin to emerge while children are young. In fact, before age four, wealthier children hear roughly thirty million more words than poorer children. The best way to help close these gaps is to get parents to read to their children often, talk aloud to them, sound out words, point out rhyming words —that kind of thing. But getting parents to consistently do those things is tricky. The most common interventions are regular home visits, which are too expensive to scale, or hours-long workshops that deliver a barrage of parenting advice and then leave parents to remember and use the information at the right time.

Instead, York and Loeb decided to try to use simple technology—text messages—to deliver advice to parents when they need it most. They followed 440 families, most of them with low incomes, who had preschool students enrolled in a public school in San Francisco. Half of the families got text messages three times a week that had action items that would help develop the children's literacy skills. Here's a sampling of texts that might be sent in a week: "FACT: Kids need to know that letters make up words. Kids with good letter knowledge become strong readers," "TIP: Point out the first letter in your child's name in magazines, on signs & at the store. Have your child try. Make it a game. Who can find the most?"; "GROWTH: Keep pointing out letters. You're preparing your child 4K! Now when you point out a letter ask: What sound does it make?" In contrast, the parents in the control group got one message every two weeks with basic information about vaccines or enrolling their child in kindergarten.

Parents who got the detailed text messages reported that they were much more likely to do the kinds of literacy activities prescribed in the messages, and more likely to contact their children's teacher to discuss their kids' schooling. And here's the kicker: when students were given literacy tests at the end of the year, those whose parents got the texts were two to three months ahead of their peers. Plus, the intervention was cheap: less than $1 per child. Home visit programs, by contrast, can cost as much as $10,000 per child and require substantial time.

Remind is making this kind of tech communication, which research shows is so important, simple for teachers, students, and parents. It's a communications platform that allows one-to-one, or one-to-many, communication that is tracked and cannot be deleted. Unlike text messages that are sent via teacher or student phones and can be deleted, the Remind channel offers a safe place for all to engage professionally and accountably.

Remind public announcement can also deliver messages in the preferred format for each individual, and it can even be translated using Google Translate if the parent's or student's first language isn't English. It engages parents and students who might otherwise be isolated.

"I was recently speaking with a sixth-grade English teacher," Rachel Lockett told me. "He talks to the parents of struggling students every other day using Remind. When I asked him how he felt about this, as it was obviously increasing his workload, he said, 'No, this is alleviating the hardest part of teaching, which is knowing you have a student who's struggling and not knowing how to help them, or how to communicate with their family to help them improve.'" Remind is using technology to help build connections and deeper relationships.

Paul-Andre White, known to his students simply as "P. A.," is the principal of Leal Elementary School in Cerritos, California, and a big fan of Remind. Leal was an early adopter of the technology. When asked about Remind, he gushes with enthusiasm. "It's just awesome." He laughs. "It's amazing how much it has impacted my school culture. Parents are feeling really connected to the school, and their kids. Even if it's not about their child, they like to see what's happening at their child's school. If my kid's a kinder, but I'm getting this text about a fifth-grade class, my kid's going to be there one day, and it's great to see the innovative things that they're doing, the types of things that they're learning, the ways they're being asked to think. It's really engaged the whole community."

Prior to Remind, finding a way to connect with parents was one of the most challenging aspects of teaching. "You're relying on a kindergartner to relay a message to a parent," P. A. remembers. Now he has seven hundred parents available in his pocket, whom he can text on a moment's notice. "I use it to broadcast important messages. It could be a reminder about it being a minimum day, or it could be a classroom spotlight. My teachers use it for homework reminders, or to tell a parent, 'Hey, your kid learned about this today, so ask them this question.' My son is in first grade, so I know the drill. 'What was your favorite part of today?' 'Recess.' 'What did you learn today?' 'I don't know.' Instead you can say, 'Hey, I heard you learned about lizards today. How many facts can you remember about them?' It's a way to engage the child and reinforce learning at home."

Bottom line: With kindergartners around the age of five years old, many of the parents P. A. is communicating with are under the age of thirty. For the parents, this is their reality: text messaging and Internet-based communication are the norm, and by creating a dedicated channel through which to communicate, Remind has shown its ability to nudge behavior.

One day, when the power went out, the school went dark for three hours. "Parents couldn't call us because all of our phones are IP based, and the Internet was down," P. A. recalls. "My cell phone worked, so I just sent out a Remind, and 90 percent of my parents knew within minutes that everything was fine, and that the power outage was being addressed." When there was a general bomb threat within the LA Unified School District, LAUSD shut down all the schools. Leal is in Los Angeles County but is in a different school district. "I came in early, and our phone was ringing off the hook. As soon as I got the clearance that our district wasn't shut down, I sent out a Remind. We had the highest attendance in the district that day. I sent out the Remind, the phone calls stopped immediately, and the kids all got to school."

P. A. uses the tool as a broadcast mechanism, but his teachers primarily engage the chat feature to communicate one-to-one with parents. "There's a chat feature, so we don't get a parent's number, and they don't get ours. You can set up shop hours, so there are boundaries. Messages can't be deleted. They can't be falsified, so teachers feel very protected by that," P. A. explains. Today he's helping roll Remind out across the other twenty-eight schools in his district. His superintendent is setting up a channel to communicate with all the district principals, a channel for all staff, and then one that's community-wide. "It's more effective than Twitter or Facebook," P. A. opines. "To me going into that realm never seemed like a good fit because of the public nature. This protects the kids' privacy."

Says P. A.: "Technology is an enhancer of what we're trying to do. It doesn't matter what the application is; it's meant to improve things." When he had a site council election to solicit parental volunteers to represent the school on budgetary issues, he figured it'd be a pain as usual. "In the past it was like pulling teeth to get people to even know about it. But I sent out a Remind saying 'any parent who would like to be considered, please add your name to the Google doc.' I had fifteen parents volunteer for six positions, and I had to run an election. I'd never had to do that before."

Technology is being used to reshape so many aspects of the educational landscape; this introduction to a handful of the innovators just scratches the surface of important developments. Looking across the broad landscape of innovations, what's clear is that it's not the technology-only approach that some technologists have advocated, but human-computer symbiosis that is leading to the most effective, and the most humane, solutions.

The Best of Both Fuzzy and Techie

In the various blended approaches, from Esther Wojcicki's journalism classrooms to James Sanders's Breakout EDU games, from Sugata Mitra's concept of self-organized learning environments to Diane Tavenner's playlist approach, the teacher is increasingly becoming the coach, one aided by technology.

At Summit, teachers monitor a dashboard displaying how students are progressing in real time, who's getting stuck, and who needs more help. The teacher is in the same physical space as the students; the students leverage technology to access their daily playlists. This approach is not about replacing the school with all technology and no walls. It's not about online education. It's about bringing the best of technology into the classroom and reinventing the roles of teachers.

Kelly Hogan, a biologist and director of Instructional Innovation for the College of Arts and Sciences at the University of North Carolina at Chapel Hill (UNC), found that active learning in the classroom raised average test scores by 3 percent, and double that for first-generation college students and African American students. In her study, "Getting Under the Hood: How and for Whom Does Increasing Course Structure Work?," published in *CBE—Life Sciences Education* in 2014, she looked at data from six semesters of her four-hundred-person Intro to Biology class at UNC, comparing student achievement in classes with "low course structure" and "higher course structure." Low course structure was defined as traditional lecture-hall approaches, whereas high course structure had preparatory homework and in-class activities such as using classroom-response software on laptops and mobile phones.

Hogan deduced that by giving students online assignments to complete before class, she could provide more team-based, in-class exercises. As these team-based exercises were more active, there was less in-class lecturing, or command-and-control teaching. It helped students get more out of their reading and had a dramatic impact on those students who might otherwise have been less inclined to speak out during class or communicate their preparedness. Overall, her students performed well in "moderately structured" sessions that struck a balance, where the teacher played the role of coach. By using technology to help provide shorter-form engagements followed by interruption for memory consolidation, these "moderately structured" environments can likely help students learn more effectively.

Jeffrey Karpicke is a psychologist at Purdue University who studies human learning and memory. Through his research he's found that it's imperative to practice information retrieval—that is, the recovery of information from your long-term memory. In a 2011 study, "Retrieval Practice Produces More Learning Than Elaborative Studying with Concept Mapping," published in *Science*, Karpicke sorted college students into four random groups and gave each of them several scientific paragraphs to memorize. The experiment pitted a variety of study methods against one another. Some students read the material repeatedly, as many times as they could. Others read the material in several short bursts, and still others drew elaborative concept maps of the material.

The last group of students took a "retrieval practice test" in which they wrote everything they could remember about the material in a free-form essay. When all the groups were tested on the paragraphs a week later, the students who did the retrieval practice test outperformed every other group. Karpicke found that "retrieval is not merely a read-out of the knowledge stored in one's mind; the act of reconstructing knowledge itself enhances learning."

Karpicke believes that when we practice retrieving information, we are creating a set of cues that our brains can use later on. We're laying down bread crumbs in our mind, ways to find our way back. Ironically, students using other techniques felt overconfident about how prepared they were, while students using retrieval techniques felt somewhat underprepared but then outperformed the rest of the students. The results were clear: practicing retrieval of information has measurable impact on performance.

When technology is used to help self-directed students learn at their own pace while leveraging teacher coaching with efficient interruptions for memory consolidation and information retrieval, it can be an immense asset. Technology alone cannot be seen as a panacea for all the problems that besiege the world of education, but by blending these approaches—by bringing together the best of both fuzzies and techies—we have a chance to improve it.

SEVEN

Building a Better World

Gabo Arora studied philosophy and film at New York University. While he is no technology dystopian, he is concerned about how our always-on devices may be affecting us. He turns his Wi-Fi router off at night to unplug from the barrage of the web. "I feel like it's doing something bad for my brain," he says, laughing in self-deprecation, given his line of work. He is a virtual reality (VR) filmmaker, working with the newest breed of technology expected to compete for our attention. "My son is in a Waldorf School. He's five and has no idea what an iPad is. I consider that a badge of pride," Arora says. "But at the same time, I don't find it to be a contradiction to try to understand how our technology can do good for humanity." He is a leader in exploring that potential for VR.

Arora is the award-winning creator of the United Nations Virtual Reality film series. He has directed half a dozen award-winning VR films, which have graced screens at the Sundance Film Festival and Cannes Film Festival. He's also shown them to the business and political leaders who gather for the annual World Economic Forum in Davos, Switzerland, as well as to the United Nations General Assembly. The films are about some of humanity's gravest recent challenges—the Syrian refugee crisis, Ebola in Liberia, the 2015 earthquake in Nepal, pollution in China, Amazon deforestation, the rights of women in the Democratic Republic of Congo. Arora had never worked with VR film until he met pioneering VR director Chris Milk, who runs a production studio called Within and has now collaborated with Arora on a number of his films. The two met at a party thrown by rock band U2, for which Milk had made music videos, while Arora had worked with the band's lead singer, Bono, on antipoverty campaigns. Milk has helped Arora to use the power of VR to give viewers an immersive experience that simulates actually traveling to tragedy-stricken locations that they would not otherwise be able to visit, enveloping the viewer in their sights and sounds.

He has introduced viewers to Syrian refugees in Jordan, survivors of Ebola in Liberia, and mothers of sons and daughters lost in Palestine. In *Clouds Over Sidra*, the VR headset puts you in the middle of a classroom in the Zaatari refugee camp in Jordan, and as you turn around to survey the scene, you might lock eyes with a child who, momentarily, looks up from her notebook. The experience is truly visceral. You are there, just as in the film *Waves of Grace* you are on the roof of an abandoned hotel in war-torn Monrovia, Liberia, listening to the joyous voice of a woman accompanied by a man playing an olive oil can guitar, looking over at a sunset with the breeze on your face, and feeling admiration for the resilience of this pair of survivors.

Arora's mission is to instill not only a better understanding of these problems but also empathy for the people enduring them. His official day job is as a senior advisor to the UN secretary-general, making recommendations about which issues the UN should focus on. He never expected to go into humanitarian policy work, but as with so many of the liberal arts graduates we've met in earlier chapters, the insights, skills, and concerns he developed through his education have helped him excel in the work. He's becoming a trailblazer in finding a socially valuable application for a new kind of technology that some tech analysts have viewed with trepidation, if not outright scorn. For example, writing in the *New York Times* about a new VR headset being developed by Microsoft, the paper's longtime Media Equation columnist David Carr posited, "The amount of actual, unencumbered reality we experience seems endangered . . . What is it about our current reality that is so insufficient that we feel compelled to augment or improve it?"

Arora was inspired to go into humanitarian work after experiencing the horror of the 9/11 attacks on New York's World Trade Center. Having attempted, but failed, to start a career as a feature filmmaker in Hollywood, he returned to his hometown, the New York City borough of Queens. After 9/11, he says, he "wanted to help reshape American foreign policy, and America's image." He also says, "If 9/11 hadn't happened, there's no way I would work at the UN." He has succeeded in his effort to move people with his films, and they have become a powerful tool in the UN's fundraising for relief programs. The UN-run UNICEF has shown Arora's films in forty countries around the world, to both public audiences and individuals being solicited for large donations, and the films have cut the number of conversations needed to convince a donor to contribute in half. According to UNICEF data, VR has helped double the propensity to donate from one in twelve to roughly one in every six people. It makes outreach twice as effective.

When Arora first pitched virtual reality films to the top brass at the UN, most of them scoffed. With access to headsets being limited, they argued, no one would watch the movies. But Arora stuck to his convictions. He was confident that VR would be going mainstream, and he thought his films could set an important precedent for using the cinematic technology in meaningful ways, rather than as just a way to escape into fantasies or to experience thrills, like simulations of skydiving or of rollercoaster rides.

While the 9/11 attacks inspired him to pursue humanitarian work, he says his undergraduate training in philosophy instilled in him the belief that his film talents could, and should, be applied to advance the social good. "I am very influenced by the existentialists," he says, and he's a particular fan of Jean-Paul Sartre and Albert Camus. "Paradoxically, while you'd think the message you might learn from them would be 'Life is meaningless, so do nothing,' for Sartre and Camus, the only way you can develop some sense of inner freedom is through your own volition and your own actions. Sartre was politically engaged, as was Camus." Arora notes that when Camus asked his teachers what was the best way for him to make a difference in the world, they told him to write novels, which he did to wide acclaim. Arora is also a believer in the power of art to influence minds and change lives. "What I do is not VR," he says, "it's storytelling. Novels are great empathy machines. VR now offers the ability to bring telepresence to storytelling," which makes it more intensely immersive. He is an artist and a philosopher with a deep dedication to the liberal arts mission of enhancing the quality of human life, and he is leading the way in making VR technology serve that purpose.

Virtual reality is one of the technologies, along with machine-learning and natural language processing, that has developed rapidly in recent years. The concept dates back at least to 1985, when Jaron Lanier began pioneering the development of the technology at VPL Research. But VR was far from ready for prime time, and it's taken more than thirty years for commercially viable headsets to be produced. The titans of technology business are competing furiously to become the market leaders. Microsoft is developing a headset it calls HoloLens, which can project holographic images on surfaces such as a living room wall. Facebook founder Mark Zuckerberg is so impressed by VR's prospects that in 2014, Facebook purchased device maker Oculus, which got its start on crowd-funding site Kickstarter, for $2 billion. Google has invested heavily in the VR startup Magic Leap and made its own foray into creating hardware with its Daydream VR headset.

But in counterpoint to the enthusiasm, VR has drawn fire due to worries that, as David Carr has pondered, it will hook people even further into spending time interacting with technology rather than with friends and family. Some visions of how it might shape our lives in the future are extreme. As writer Monica Kim highlighted in an article in the *Atlantic* titled "The Good and the Bad of Escaping to Virtual Reality," futurist Ray Kurzweil imagined that "by the 2030s, virtual reality will be totally realistic and compelling and we will spend most of our time in virtual environments . . . We will all become virtual humans." Though such a result seems highly unlikely, other predictions, and concerns expressed, are more sobering.

In 1992, Donald Norman, the futurist who wrote *Turn Signals Are the Facial Expressions of Automobiles,* wrote about VR as an Event Fanatic of the Future (EFF), who "views the real world through a TV lens . . . TV goggles are securely strapped to his head, electronics are strapped to his waist, lenses and microphones are mounted on his head . . . Pity the poor professor lecturing to EFF's class." He concludes with the thought-provoking comment, "Maybe the professor is replaced by a computer-generated television image. Artificial images teaching artificial minds." More recently, Sherry Turkle, a professor of social studies of science and technology at MIT, has raised concerns about VR. She is the director of MIT's Initiative on Technology and Self and has spent the past three decades observing how technology impacts the quality of our social lives. She wrote the books *Alone Together: Why We Expect More from Technology and Less from Each Other* and *Reclaiming Conversation: The Power of Talk in a Digital Age* to raise the public's consciousness about how the time we spend online may be diminishing our ability to engage in authentic human connection. She warns that digital communication allows us to airbrush our imperfections, to engage when convenient, and to craft new versions of ourselves, and that ironically it distances us from one another even as we're spending so much time digitally connecting. She asks, "Are we on a diet of social media that's hurting face-to-face conversation?"

Turkle challenges the view of Gabo Arora and his filmmaking collaborator Chris Milk that VR is, as Milk said in a 2015 TED Talk, "the ultimate empathy machine," through which "we become more connected, and ultimately, we become more human." In a speech of her own in San Francisco in 2016 Turkle argued, "In virtual reality, we're given the idea that we can dispense with the contingencies, the difficulties, the trouble of having to be with each other face to face with all of the imperfection . . . It encourages us to . . . think that we can find empathy without conversation, without being present."

Speaking specifically about Arora's film *Clouds Over Sidra* and Milk's TED Talk, in which he showed video footage of suit-clad men sitting in a climate-controlled room in Davos, Switzerland, watching the film through virtual reality goggles, Turkle noted that "these men aren't cold or tired or hungry. They're not meeting any refugees." She makes it clear that she enjoyed the film, but also warns that when "technology goes from better than nothing, to better than something, to better than anything," we can lose appreciation for the special rewards of face-to-face interaction.

These sharply contrasting views about the value of VR are indicative of the complexity of crafting technology innovations so that they enhance the quality of our lives rather than diminish it. The potential of the new breed of technologies to change our lives is a double-edged sword. While they can be applied to achieve a great deal of good in the world, they also have the potential to cause great harm, or, as with Turkle's caution about VR, to change our behavior in ways that, if we were more aware of the ensuing changes, we might opt out of. With some of the applications of the new technologies, the potential positives and negatives are more obvious than with others. For example, it's clear that autonomous-vehicle technology offers the potential to make our roads safer, to free us from the drudgery of long-distance driving trips, and to provide more efficient point-to-point transit, which might obviate the need for costly forms of public transportation that place heavy burdens on government coffers. But it's also clear that it has the potential to cause havoc if vehicles aren't designed with a deep understanding of the complexities of human behavior.

With VR, the situation is more muddied. Gabo Arora is arguably harnessing the technology to do a great deal of good. At the same time, Sherry Turkle must be applauded for cautioning about the technology's limits and possible revenge effects. One thing is sure: making the best use of the technology will require more of exactly the kind of creativity, human-centered concern, and critical thinking that both Arora and Turkle, with their liberal arts training, are bringing to the task.

Probably no one understands the double-edged nature of the new technologies quite as acutely as those who are working to defend our national security. This is one area in which fuzzies partnering with techies is unquestionably helping to do a world of good.

Pairing Up to Make Our World Secure

As our technology has gotten more complex beneath its veneer of simple interfaces, so too has our world. Theaters of warfare are no longer confined to the air, land, and sea. Today war is also waged in cyberspace.

The amorphous bands of individuals who call themselves the "Islamic State" (ISIS) have ruthlessly demonstrated the asymmetric risks of nonstate actors attacking traditional nation-states. The fuzzy pairing with the techie is not always a force for good. ISIS has brought the new tech tools to the ages-old enterprise of psychological warfare, marketing its suite of evil ideas with the same kind of precision targeting and persuasive techniques that are used to lure us into spending too much money on the latest shiny gadget or tantalizing gourmet coffee drink.

As technology continues to evolve, unfortunately so will the nature of threats. With the development of the Internet of Things, any connected device will become vulnerable to hijacking, from home thermostats and medical devices to self-driving cars and, even, more ominously, the computer systems that monitor and control our critical infrastructure, such as the electrical power grid. As we network more and more of our devices, more and more sophisticated attacks on our security will become possible.

Consider the case of the Stuxnet computer virus, brought to the public's attention in 2010. Stuxnet is a cyberweapon reportedly built by Israel and the United States to target Iranian nuclear centrifuges, but the code could be repurposed by our enemies and turned against our own infrastructure—factories, airports, pipelines, and power plants. Unlike conventional weapons, which can only be used once, cyberweapons offer the potential for dangerous concurrence, use and reuse.

Harnessing the power of the new technologies to combat escalating threats is essential, and to do so, collaboration between
techies and those with the skills and perspectives of both the humanities and social sciences is critical. Fuzzy skills and perspectives can help in many ways, such as providing insight into the
nature of political alliances, the psychology of combat and terrorism, and the nature of social networks (both online and offline),
as well as sharing expertise about the dynamics of teams that can
improve teamwork in the field. Training in these disciplines can
additionally help develop moral rigor and the awareness of cultural factors in conflicts.

When Drew Faust, the president of Harvard University, delivered a 2016 lecture to 800 cadets and faculty at the U.S. Military
Academy at West Point, she spoke of the essential role that the humanities have to play in training effective and empathetic leaders.
The nature of inquiry that the humanities foster, she said, "teaches
us how to scrutinize the thing at hand, even in the thick dust of
danger or drama or disorienting strangeness . . . It imparts skills
that slow us down—the habit of deliberation, the critical eye,
skills that give us capacity to interpret and judge human problems;
the concentration that yields meaning in a world that is noisy
with information, confusion, and change. The humanities teach us
many things, not the least of which is empathy—how to see ourselves inside another person's experience." Attempting to do this
myself, I visited West Point on a stone-cold October day. Inside
Washington Hall, where all four thousand four hundred cadets as-
semble and dine daily, I was reminded by a "firstie," as seniors
are known, that unlike other branches of the military, which "man
equipment," the army endeavors to "equip the man."

We can see this in the wisdom with which retired U.S. Army
lieutenant general Karl Eikenberry, the U.S. ambassador to Af-

ghanistan from 2009 to 2011, worked to help restore the devastated culture of that country, advocating for projects such as the restoration of the Citadel of Herat. Dating to 330 BC, the Citadel has an illustrious history as a bastion of national defense and was used by a string of empires as their military headquarters. Eikenberry argues that by restoring the monument, which now houses the National Museum of Herat, it "offered the people of Afghanistan, traumatized by decades of conflict and chaos, evidence of a rich culture and prior days of glory."

One of the stars on Eikenberry's team was archaeologist Laura Tedesco, the State Department's "Monument Woman," whose job it was to excavate Afghanistan's ancient treasures, preserving its history as a tolerant and inclusive country. When the State Department asked for her service, the then-forty-year-old mother of two dropped everything and moved to Afghanistan for sixteen months. Her work demonstrates what Eikenberry has called the "intrinsic value of the humanities" in how we wage war and rebuild tattered states.

Another firm believer in this cause is Professor Elizabeth Samet, who for nearly twenty years has taught popular literature classes at West Point. Every one of the one thousand one hundred incoming cadets each year since 1997 has taken a class with her. She says that lessons from traditional literature train soldiers "to follow lawful orders and never surrender their moral judgment." One of Samet's West Point students, who earned a degree in art, philosophy, and literature, and went on to become a captain in the army, serving in Iraq and Afghanistan, is Emily Miller. She was one of the few women who would gear up and go on night raids with the Seventy-Fifth Ranger Regiment, an elite Special Forces team that targeted top-level Taliban and al-Qaeda commanders. When the Chinook helicopters delivering the team for missions dropped them behind enemy lines, Miller's job was to ensure the safety of the women and children in the area. She was the leader of a nineteen-woman Joint Special Operations Task Force that aimed to build rapport with the Afghan female population. "Every night we'd go out on night raids," she recalls. "Our job was to work with the women and children, so we learned everything we could about the history and culture of Afghanistan." She earned a Bronze Star and Combat Action Badge for her work in Afghanistan, bringing the heart to join the fist on the front lines of war.

Miller developed such a compassion for the plight of the Afghani people that after her deployment, she cofounded Rumi Spice, a company she launched on Kickstarter, which exports saffron, the most expensive spice in the world, acquired directly from those women she met behind enemy lines on night raids in Afghanistan. Today, Rumi Spice, based at The Plant, a workspace on the South Side of Chicago, sells Rumi saffron to some of the best restaurants across America, enabling those Afghani women to provide their families with financial security.

The social sciences bring much-needed perspective about the complexities of conflicts and their causes, as well as important insights into the limits of technology in the fog of war. The blowback effects of the use of unmanned aerial vehicles, more popularly known as drones, in the pursuit of terrorists illustrate this need. While these high-tech precision weapons have effectively targeted many terrorist leaders, they can also bring a strike capability well over the horizon, where a soldier has more distance from potential unintended victims and consequences. Technological weapons may seem a solid route to taking fallible human judgment out of the equation of battlefield conflict, and to protecting soldiers from direct engagement, but the truth is that fuzzy prowess is, and will be, critical to waging war. That is why the practice of "war gaming" is still very much alive at the Naval War College in Newport, Rhode Island. When I visited the college, founded in 1884 to help foster character among the navy's top performers, leaders explained to me that their curriculum is equal parts timeless and timely, striking a balance between classic texts by Thucydides and Carl von Clausewitz and the evolving challenges of cyberwarfare. A centerpiece of the training is the repetition of multiday adversarial war games, because battlefield situations are so fraught with complexities that no current-day technology tool can navigate them without human decision-making.

The good news is that an inventive force of both public and private organizations is leveraging every man-plus-machine advantage to help make our lives more secure. New fuzzy-techie partnerships are devising brilliant means to identify threats earlier, to monitor them more rigorously, and to deploy a new array of precision tools to defuse them. One important initiative is bringing together fuzzies and techies to collaborate in applying the methods developed by Silicon Valley technology innovators for the U.S. military.

Bringing Lean Startup Tactics to Military Defense

The Defense Department has long worked to lure technologists from Silicon Valley into the military. But in 2015, Secretary of Defense Ashton Carter flipped the model around and decided to take the military to Silicon Valley, creating the Defense Innovation Unit Experimental (DIUx). One of the ancillary results of this security push into technology has been the establishment of a class called Hacking 4 Defense (H4D) at Stanford University, spearheaded by two U.S. Army colonels, Joe Felter and Pete Newell, who understood that the incredible demands on today's military personnel and policymakers call for real collaboration across the fuzzy-techie divide.

Felter, retired from the U.S. Army Special Forces and a former director of West Point's Combating Terrorism Center, runs the Empirical Studies of Conflict Project at Stanford. He applied his expertise from getting a PhD in political science to developing more effective approaches to tackling the terrorist threat. Newell spent thirty-two years in uniform and earned a Silver Star for leading a combat battalion into Fallujah, Iraq. He led the creation of an innovation team for the army, the Rapid Equipping Force, which brought together military personnel and academics across many disciplines to find solutions to emerging problems. Felter and Newell joined forces with professor and serial entrepreneur Steve Blank to develop the course, and they are three of the course's instructors.

Blank is the innovator of a methodology known as customer discovery, which creates new products that are more attuned to people's needs and desires by soliciting feedback from them on the basis of prototypes and then iterating improvements according to that feedback. Central to the method is developing an understanding of the main problems that customers are facing. This method was drawn upon by one of Blank's students, Eric Ries, to create the well-known Lean Startup approach to launching a company, which was subsequently popularized in Ries's book *The Lean Startup*.

The Hacking 4 Defense class brings this same kind of Lean Startup approach to finding solutions to actual problems submitted to the course website by military groups and the intelligence community. Students develop an understanding of the challenges military personnel face by putting themselves in the military's shoes, whether by crawling in the dirt at a training camp, donning dry suits to understand the scuba diving needs of Navy SEALs, or visiting an air force base to better understand the bomb suit specs of ordnance disposal units. The class is open to students from all departments, and the goal is to facilitate creative collaboration.

When one surveys the problems posted for the class to tackle, the need for fuzzy insights about how to better develop and deploy technologies is pronounced. For example, one challenge, posted by U.S. Air Force Fifteenth Operations Support Squadron, is to "develop an organic, team, or network centered structure that enhances the squadron's communication, adaptability, resilience, and specialty skills." The description goes on to explain, "We need a structure that shows every member their valued place in the organization and their ability to communicate freely with any other member in the squadron . . . This challenge is focused on organizational change; technology can help but should not be a primary focus."

Another challenge, posted by the U.S. Army Cyber Command, is to "determine how to use emerging data mining, machine learning, and data science capabilities to understand, disrupt, and counter our adversaries' use of social media." The description highlights that "current tools do not provide users with a way to understand the meaning within adversary social media content . . . Current tools and methods monitor social media streams and can provide quantitative measures (volume, relevance, search). These tools fall short by failing to capture the content from the sites where most of the actual meaning is transmitted."

The course has garnered so much attention that in the fall of 2016 the instructors hosted seventy-five attendees for an educators class. In 2017, thirteen other colleges, such as Georgia Tech, the University of Pittsburgh, the University of Southern California, and Georgetown, will begin offering their own Hacking 4 Defense courses, also with problem sets provided by the defense and intelligence communities. In 2016, Blank and Felter also helped create Hacking 4 Diplomacy, a course aimed at building technology solutions for the State Department. Co-taught with Jeremy Weinstein, a political scientist and former director for development and democracy on the White House National Security Council, the class offers students opportunities, for example, to work on building tools to combat violent extremists such as ISIS. Solutions will likely combine the power of machine-learning algorithms with data pulled from a number of online sources, and with the fuzzy understanding of the culture and psychology of adversaries.

Solving the World's Most Intractable Problems

A great irony of the development of today's high-powered technologies is that so many people on the planet are still afflicted by the most basic of problems that have plagued humanity through the ages: in addition to the tragedies of political and military conflict, they suffer from hunger and disease, lack of education, and stalled economic development. But these days, armed with an awareness of the new breed of tech tools, and working with techie partners, legions of those trained in the liberal arts, with a real passion for working to improve our world, are creating remarkable innovations that address some of these challenges.

Many of these creators are founding private sector startups, such as Nate Morris, who founded the billion-dollar Lexington, Kentucky–based Rubicon Global, the "Uber for trash," a company helping cities manage waste. Morris has degrees in government and public policy. In Austin, Texas, Evan Baehr, founder of Able Lending, wants to give loans to "the Fortune 5 million" and has raised over $100 million to do so. He studied international affairs, and earned a master of arts in religion, with a focus on ethics and law. Others are spearheading nonprofit social entrepreneurship solutions, such as Casey Gerald, founder of MBAs Across America, a program that pairs MBA students with small businesses. Gerald, a student of political science and entrepreneurship, believes we need a "new field manual for business," and "humble doubt" when it comes to accepting the status quo. Leila Janah, the founder of Sama, which means "equal" in Sanskrit, is helping match workers in the developing world with digital work. Janah studied African economic development.

What is perhaps less publicized is that so many others are working within long-established relief organizations, helping to bring a new tech-savvy approach to their missions. This is a sign of great promise to direct the power and experience of these major players on the world stage of humanitarian relief toward more innovative solutions. One need look no further than down the hallways of the United Nations, often described as a bloated and ineffectual bureaucracy, to see the potential for transformation. While there is still work to be done, Gabo Arora is but one of the innovators at the vanguard of the UN applying the new technology tools to global problems.

Another fuzzy at the vanguard of technology within the UN is Massimiliano "Max" Costa, who earned a degree in literature from the University of Turin and another degree in violin and music from the renowned Ghedini Conservatory in Cuneo, Italy. He played in a number of orchestras across Northern Italy, and he was on his way to becoming a professional violinist when he made a detour into policy, and then into tech. "As a musician, you sleep with genius. You play Bach and Brahms, and you dream with them. Music taught me perseverance. I spent thousands of hours with my violin. But you learn, and then you want to build," he recalls. A posting to Baku, Azerbaijan, as an energy policy attaché, then led him to a master's degree in international affairs at Columbia University and a job at the Boston Consulting Group. Today, now based in Berlin, Germany, he works for the World Food Program (WFP), a United Nations organization focused on eradicating world hunger. There he's helped launch Share the Meal, a WFP-sponsored Apple iOS app that allows global citizens to donate money to help provide meals. He joined forces with Sebastian Stricker, who received a PhD in international relations at the University of Vienna and was working as a business innovation advisor at the World Food Program in Rome, Italy.

Stricker had an idea for harnessing the power of smartphones to combat hunger, and teamed up with WFP Innovation Accelerator lead Bernhard Kowatsch. Together they concluded that today there are twenty smartphone users for every one hungry person on the planet, and with just a fifty-cent contribution per day per smartphone user, hunger could be completely eradicated. Stricker, Costa, and team thus decided to develop the app. They approached a number of funders of early-stage tech companies in Silicon Valley for support, but they were told their idea was flawed and they should instead focus on redistributing underutilized food through vast supply chains and logistics systems. Undaunted, they were confident in their understanding of the problem, having spent years in international aid and food security, and they knew they could hire engineers to build the app without big venture backing.

Sure enough, in the first month after the app was launched, users made 120,000 donations and paid for over 1.7 million daily rations for schoolchildren in Lesotho. As of this writing, the app has been downloaded more than five hundred thousand times, and the funds raised have provided more than 5.7 million meals. What's more, the app is only a first step in how they believe technology can bring them scale. The goal is to grow the impact by incorporating the Share the Meal technology into other platforms. For example, by working with a company like Square, the small-business iPad-based point-of-sale system, they could enable consumers to share a meal when they purchase their own food at their local café.

Two other fuzzy UN staffers who are notable pioneers in harnessing the new technologies are Erica Kochi and Christopher Fabian, who colead UNICEF's Innovation Unit. Among the many other ways they've innovated with tech, in collaboration with a team of engineers, in rural Uganda, they figured out how to convert oil drums into durable, rugged solar-powered educational computer kiosks, which are referred to as Digital Drums. *Time* called it the "best invention of 2011," and the Smithsonian featured it in its Cooper Hewitt, Smithsonian Design Museum in New York.

Neither Kochi nor Fabian is a techie by training. She studied economics and Japanese at the School of Oriental and African Studies (SOAS) in London, and he majored in philosophy at the American University in Cairo, Egypt, and media studies at the New School in New York City. Having both made their way into humanitarian work, they have acted as superb translators between the United Nations and the technology world, creating "a bridge between the practice of social development and the disciplines of technology and design," as Kochi said in a 2011 *Forbes* interview. Among the other innovations they've spearheaded is an open-source framework called RapidSMS that allows people in the field to collect and consolidate data, turning every smartphone into a data collection tool and a last-mile delivery mechanism. For example, in Zambia and Malawi they use mobile devices to deliver HIV test results so even those in remote areas can have an instant understanding of their test results and then pursue treatment. Today, Fabian is exploring how frontier technologies such as the blockchain public ledger system might be harnessed to help register the two hundred million children under the age of five who were born in territories of conflict, and who lack any form of birth registration, often locking them out of access to health care and education.

There are real questions to be asked of innovation units popping up within every organization, whether this is the most efficient way to create change, or if, like Steve Blank's courses, organizations ought to help provide clarity around the problems society faces. But such innovative solutions also offer real hope of making substantial new headway in tackling the many long-standing problems that still afflict so many people of the world. The truth is, for efforts like these to solve large-scale social problems and to have maximal impact, innovation is needed not only regarding specific solutions to particular problems, but also in making governments more willing and effective agents of change. Governments must become more agile problem solvers, more responsive to citizen needs and rights, and in order to drive that change, they must become more transparent. Fortunately, that was the mission of a government major turned lawyer who was inspired to bring more transparency to U.S. governance after witnessing the lack of it in war-torn Afghanistan.

Opening Up Government

Many technology startups have been founded in garages, like Woj's daughter renting hers out to the Google founders. For Zachary Bookman, his story was a little different: he was living in a shipping container in Kabul, Afghanistan, when he conceived of OpenGov, a software startup that builds tools to help state and local governments have better access to, and better analyze, their financial data and then make it all transparent to their citizens.

Bookman got his BA from the Government and Politics Department of the University of Maryland, and then received a JD from Yale Law School, while also studying diplomacy and governance at Harvard's Kennedy School of Government. As part of his studies at the Kennedy School, he traveled to Pakistan with a U.S. diplomatic delegation that met with tribal chiefs and governors of provinces. He developed further expertise in governance issues when he won a Fulbright scholarship to work in Mexico City at the Federal Institute for Access to Information.

There he studied how a new law establishing unprecedented transparency in the workings of the Mexican government, the Federal Law of Transparency and Access to Public Government Information, was being implemented. Passed in 2002, the law was a landmark in what Bookman described, in a law review article about his findings in Mexico, as "a growing international movement, both at the supra-national level and within sovereign nations, to give citizens more knowledge about, and by extension more participation in, the workings of the institutions that govern their lives." A little background: For years, the Mexican government was ruled by the tight fist of the Institutional Revolutionary Party, known as the PRI, which had restricted press access to information and controlled elections through a corrupt political patronage system. Bookman found that though the law was leading to some important gains in transparency, many government officials were pushing back, obstructing its implementation, and the law was not having a substantial impact on reducing corruption. He concluded that "the transparency community must fight on and fight harder for its freedoms."

After he returned from Mexico, Bookman took a position as a law clerk at the U.S. Court of Appeals for the Ninth Circuit, which piqued his interest in practicing litigation. He then headed to the hotbed of Silicon Valley, taking a job as a litigator at the Keker & Van Nest law firm in San Francisco, where he represented clients in disputes over contracts and trade secrets, and took on white-collar crime cases. The work was satisfying, but it didn't allow him to apply the expertise he had developed in governance issues, and he found himself wanting to have more of the impact he'd experienced in Pakistan and Mexico.

He decided that he wanted to realign his career around his passion for greater governance and transparency. He applied and was selected for a position as an advisor to U.S. Army general H. R. McMaster on the Combined Joint Interagency Task Force–Shafafiyat ("Transparency"), an anticorruption task force at the International Security Assistance Force headquarters in Kabul, Afghanistan. He walked away from his cushy life in San Francisco and moved across the world.

Immediately, Bookman began to experience the inefficiencies that plagued even an organization as sophisticated in operational logistics as the U.S. Army. His actual deployment took months because the contract for his job, which was issued by CENTCOM, aka Central Command, relied on the approval of the congressional budget, which dragged on and on due to wrangling between the political parties. When Bookman finally arrived in Afghanistan, he encountered a series of snafus. No one seemed to have prepared for his arrival, and his hosts scrambled to figure out who could get him where he needed to go and to equip him with the proper safety apparatus. Soldiers trying to assist him asked all sorts of questions in confusion: "Who can drive Bookman? Does he have a holster for his weapon? Does he have a belt for the holster? Does he have a Leatherman to connect the holster to the belt holder? Where's the guard for the machine shop that holds the Leatherman?"

He was supposed to report to the International Security Assistance Force's compound, but no one seemed to know the procedure for entering the compound, asking, "Which gate will we use? How do we enter the gate, and what happens if it is locked? Where is his billet? Where is the memo authorizing his billet? Where is the key to his room? How do we obtain a blanket for the bed?" His billet, it turned out, was totally improvised and he ended up sleeping on a bunk in a storage container in the parking lot of the compound. Nonetheless, he reflects on it fondly.

Bookman's job was to press Afghani authorities on major issues of corruption, and to work with the military to observe justice in the four-fifths of the country that is rural. There, despite major coalition pressures for Afghanistan to adopt a formal but foreign system of justice, he saw a proud people who fiercely guarded their way of life. In 80 percent of the country, justice was still predominately carried out by local elders, on a simple consensus basis. He witnessed corruption of the Afghani government and a lack of protections of the most basic citizens' rights that were supposedly put in place by the new government. He also observed shadow justice being carried out everywhere the coalition tried to push an outside model on the local people. "The challenge to Afghanistan's stability appeared self-evident: How can the state project justice where it can't reach?" he reflected in a 2012 piece he wrote for the *New York Times*.

He'd board a Chinook helicopter and ferry out over craggy peaks and brown rivers to remote villages, observing installations of the coalition's imposed judicial system, but he struggled to see what was best for Afghans. He realized the fundamental challenges of transparency in all systems of government, and perhaps the same need to question the way things were done at home.

Bookman's experiences in Afghanistan fueled his determination to come up with an innovative solution for holding governments more accountable through transparency. As he considered approaches, while still in Afghanistan, he contacted friends who had technical expertise, to help him understand the potential of technology to make data more understandable. Basically, he wanted to make government data more accessible to the public. As soon as he got home, he approached the mayor's office in the city of Palo Alto and asked if he and a team he had assembled could experiment with creating a visualization program that would show trends in the city's budget data, allowing the government to analyze it better and also to communicate better to the public about issues such as the impact of any shortfalls or clarifying exactly how taxpayer money was being spent.

He assumed that because Palo Alto was the de facto capital of Silicon Valley, it must have its data and technology in order. Bookman recalls that the city officials were happy to hand over the data they were requesting, but asked, "How do we give you our budget data?" Bookman realized then that not only did governments need better ways to visualize data; they also needed the basic means to extract it from their systems. The budget office was using a thirty-year-old accounting system, predating the Internet. Bookman recalls, "We thought to ourselves, Wow, we can solve this, so we started OpenGov."

That was in 2012. Today, OpenGov is a cloud-based software service for governments to use in managing their finances and also for providing easy access to the public to information about spending and budget issues. Over one thousand state and local governments are now improving their transparency by using OpenGov, including major cities like Santa Fe, Miami, Pittsburgh, Washington, DC, and Minneapolis. The service has evolved to offer a host of tools not only for data visualization, which was the original vision, but also for facilitating more efficient work processes and easier planning. A key goal is to make the work of city officials more efficient by helping them design better budgets while also making governments more accountable to the public about their budgeting decisions. The mission and scope are grand. "We want to sign on every government in the country," Bookman says.

He's being greatly supported in that mission by one longtime government finance specialist, Charlie Francis, who is a testament to the fact that driving technological innovation today is still wide-open terrain for anyone willing to embrace the new tools. Francis is in his late sixties and more than free to retire, but having dropped out of retirement to join the OpenGov team, he has never been more invigorated by his work. The story of his career speaks volumes about how pressing the need is for better data collection, analysis, and transparency.

OpenGov in Action

When Francis heard about OpenGov, he pounced, becoming one of the technology's early adopters. He knew all too well about the need for better data analytics and reporting for governmental departments, despite all the computing tools that had become available since he'd begun his career. In fact, when he took his first job in municipal finance in Denver in 1971, the office he worked for didn't even have a calculator. They were too expensive at the time. Instead, he'd tape six pieces of ledger paper together, displaying the figures in thirty-five accounts of the Denver Urban Renewal Authority across the top of a picnic table, and then would calculate the totals of rows and columns manually. The task took him three days. So when Texas Instruments came out with a $250 calculator a few years later, he begged his boss to invest in one. He agreed, and Francis memorized the seventeen-page Texas Instruments manual. The calculations that had once taken him three days only took him half a day. As a reward, his boss gave him the next two and a half days off.

Francis became a technology enthusiast, and he welcomed each big new computing innovation. Shortly after he left Denver to take a job as a finance director in a small town in coastal Florida, the first desktop computers were rolled out. The computer that his office purchased came loaded with a program called VisiCalc, the forerunner of Lotus 1-2-3 and Excel. Now Francis found that he no longer needed ledger paper and a calculator. He seized the opportunity to input every bit of municipal financial data he could find. When he started, the city hadn't had an audit in years, and checks were constantly bouncing. But thanks to his efforts, within one year he earned the highest award a government finance specialist could receive from the Government Finance Officers Administration (GFOA), a certificate of achievement for excellence in financial reporting. "I was the darling of the city," he says, laughing.

In 1983, when Lotus 1-2-3 came out, Francis realized the program, which included the ability to create graphics from data, would allow him to do a better job of visualizing the city's financial information, which led him to many more money-saving discoveries. Having entered ten years of weekly revenue numbers from the city's five beach parking lots, and then creating a graph tracking the revenue through the course of each year, Francis noticed that each year, there was a significant dip in the line displaying earnings for one week every year—always the same week—from parking meters in those lots. He wracked his brain trying to figure out what could be causing the dip in earnings. "Then, I was reading Sherlock Holmes one night," Francis recalls, "and Sherlock Holmes says, 'Watson, if you've eliminated all of the possible, the impossible must be true.' The next day I went to my police chief, and I said, 'Cliff, this week next year, we're going to go sit out in that parking lot, and do a stakeout.'" Francis's hunch proved right. "The first night of that week, a group of parking meter bandits showed up. They were paying for their summer vacations by stealing from the meters, aided by an accomplice who worked at the meter company and provided them with a master key."

Years later, Francis took a job as the administrative services director and treasurer for the city of Sausalito, a maritime paradise just north of San Francisco. "I had just come to Sausalito as a new finance director and the 2008 recession was settling in," he recalls. "Cities were opening up their labor agreements, implementing furloughs, and cutting pay and benefits." His counterparts in most cities and towns were recommending spending cuts, and his boss asked him to do the same. But when he examined the data, he realized that Sausalito had the resources to last through the recession without making cuts. He suggested that instead of taking those drastic measures, the town carry out an economic stimulus program. But in working to make the case to his skeptical higher-ups, Francis struggled mightily with exporting the data from various systems and trying to make it accessible to nonspecialists.

After all his time in municipal finance, he still didn't have the tools he needed to bring clarity about the data to officials, let alone to the public. He recalls that he was thrilled when in 2009 he first got a look at the OpenGov software. "As soon as I saw the demo, I fell in love." At the time, Zachary Bookman (yep, the same Bookman from earlier) was personally showing the demo to government officials, and when Francis pulled out his personal credit card to pay for the service, Bookman told him, "Sign the contract, Charlie, we trust that the City of Sausalito can pay us." Sausalito signed up, and Francis turned its municipal data into a thing of beauty and transparency, with reports for everything.

By 2012, Charlie had worked with OpenGov to incorporate all

of Sausalito's public information, making it visually navigable. He then organized the city's budget data into eight reports spanning twenty-three years of budget history, allowing fellow administrators, and the public, to view trends as far back as 2002, and looking forward through projections to 2026. "That helped me build trust with the public," he recalls, "by showing that we were doing the right things." For example, when he noted that fire department expenses were driving a rise in the budget that would cause a crunch in future years, he was able to convince the union representing the firefighters to negotiate a new employment contract and to explain to the public why the new settlement was needed. He was also able to build support for more funding for capital projects to improve the city. While much of the public supported a small tax increase to fund the projects, a vocal minority was opposed. "I used OpenGov to show exactly how the revenues would be used and that we weren't going to use it for pensions or operating expenses; that it would be entirely devoted to the capital projects," he explains. In the end, the ballot measure passed by 63 percent of the vote. "OpenGov totally reinvigorated my passion for local government and finance," Francis says. "At sixty-five years old, I was getting a little jaded. This came along and totally changed me."

In August 2015, at Zachary Bookman's invitation, Francis put in his resignation and moved an hour south to Redwood City to join OpenGov as a director and subject matter expert. Today his role is to get municipal leaders and local officials as excited about OpenGov as he is. Traveling all over the United States, he leads workshops to help other finance directors like him understand the power of data. "This is revolutionary," he says. "I want to evangelize the old baby boomers like me who are getting close to retirement. You don't get rewarded much in local government, but you do get punished. In order for this kind of revolutionary tool to be widely accepted, we need to be able to convince a lot of people to use it in a power-user kind of way. I just met a woman in a little town called Burnet, Texas. She's as old as me, and she's as excited as I am about using OpenGov." Today Francis is a product evangelist who calls upon his forty years of municipal experience to question how things have been done, working with techies to build the products that can make tens of thousands of government employees' lives easier, and to improve transparency across North America.

In sum, there's no question that the opportunities to apply the new technology tools to advance the social good are unbounded, for both the young and for those with long experience in careers. Concerns about how the new technological advances will shape our lives are well-founded; the technologies can be wielded to inflict great harm, and even when they are intended to enhance our lives, they can have many unforeseen and unfortunate consequences. The best way to ensure that their potential to strengthen our security, to solve social problems, and to alleviate suffering all around the globe is realized is to make sure that more creative collaboration, such as that being spearhead by the Hacking 4 Defense class at Stanford and UNICEF's Innovation Center, is actively facilitated. Any one of us with the will and the creative confidence is empowered, by the remarkable tech toolkit now at our disposal, to play a significant part in making our world a better place. But as leaders of organizations, cities, and governments, we must consider not only how we can create more techies, but also how we can conjoin both the techie and the fuzzy to address some of the most persistent problems.

EIGHT

The Future of Jobs

Silicon Valley is known as the hub of innovation, but some of the most advanced work in applying new tech tools is being done far, far across the globe, in the remote Australian Outback.

The city of Perth, on the coast of southwestern Australia, is one of the most isolated urban centers in the world, surrounded by hundreds of thousands of square miles of the parched Outback desert, where a deep blue sky touches the caked red-dirt horizon in every direction. Perth is connected to Sydney on the Australian east coast by the Indian Pacific railway, doing exactly what its name suggests, connecting one ocean to another. Looking west from Perth is a stretch of five thousand miles of uninterrupted water, finally lapping up on the shores of southeast Africa.

Reminiscent of San Diego, California, with a breezy tranquility and elegant skyline, Perth has become a thriving metropolis despite being so remote, for much the same reason the cities of California's coast were settled—the surrounding territory is rich in precious metals. Mining companies, including BIS Industries and Rio Tinto, do a booming business in Perth.

The prospect of earning big money—an average of over $160,000 per year—mining for iron ore and gold has attracted thousands of young men and women from across Australia for well over a hundred years. But during the past decade, mining companies have implemented machine automation to improve the safety and efficiency of their operations, becoming among the most automated of all industries. Self-driving Volvo trucks manufactured in Sweden are being pressed into service in large open-pit mines all across Australia. Scania, another Swedish vehicle company, has pioneered trucks that use GPS and LIDAR (light detection and arranging) sensors to operate with optimal efficiency, minimizing fuel consumption. The trucks are said to have improved efficiency by 15 to 20 percent. Mining conglomerate Rio Tinto reports a 12 percent efficiency gain through its own automations, saving millions not only in oil and gas costs, but also in reduced rubber consumption.

Before automated trucks, humans drove vehicles like the CAT 797, a bright-yellow, four-thousand-horsepower truck capable of carrying four hundred tons, or eight hundred thousand pounds, of load. Each CAT 797 truck costs around $5.5 million, and the tires cost more than $40,000 each. If that sounds like a lot of money for a tire, consider how massive and strong they must be. Each truck requires six Bridgestone 59/80R63 XDR tires, which stand thirteen feet tall and weigh nearly twelve thousand pounds. Each tire is supported by two thousand pounds of steel—enough to build two small cars—and wrapped in enough rubber to make six hundred standard automobile tires.

How has Rio Tinto been saving on the cost to procure that rubber? Humans driving at variable speeds up and down circular ramps brake more than they need to, resulting in greater tire turnover. In fact, one of the reasons Rio Tinto and others moved to automated trucks was because of rubber savings—automated trucks apply brakes only when necessary, increasing the life span of those pricey tires.

In the remote northeastern corner of Australia, in a thinly populated, arid region known as Pilbara, Rio Tinto has also been pioneering autonomous haulage and drilling systems since 2008. The company operates over sixty autonomous trucks, and those trucks have covered 3.9 million kilometers since 2012, loading extracted iron ore onto Rio Tinto's AutoHaul system, the world's first fully autonomous, heavy-haul long-distance railway. Rio Tinto calls this its "Mine of the Future." It is run from a location that is hundreds of miles away, in Perth, by a four-hundred-person operations staff, who manage fifteen mines in total, as well as thirty-one iron ore mining pits, four port terminals, and one thousand six hundred kilometers of railroad. The remote operation is made possible by data visualization software that interprets masses of data coming in from sensors on the autonomous vehicles and installed at the mines, and produces easy-to-read displays for the pit controllers, geologists, drill-and-blast teams, and other personnel who supervise the activity. The automation technology allows machines to work autonomously in the dangerous mining pits so humans don't have to.

Such triumphs of automation, which are being achieved in an increasing number of industries, have fueled concerns about the massive job loss that Martin Ford predicts in *Rise of the Robots*. Academic research has also raised alarms. In the often-cited 2013 study conducted by Oxford University economists Carl Frey and Michael Osborne, entitled "The Future of Employment: How Susceptible Are Jobs to Computerisation?," the authors concluded that "47 percent of total U.S. employment is in the high risk category" for machine automation over the next one to two decades.

What's more, how so many jobs will be replaced by new jobs for humans to do is very much unclear.

Job displacement by machines is commonly referred to as "technological unemployment." The argument that masses of human workers would lose their jobs—jobs that would not be replaced by other kinds of work—has been made many times in the past, including at the dawn of the Industrial Revolution and during the Great Depression in the early twentieth century. Economist John Maynard Keynes contended that job losses during the Depression due to technological advances were leading to "means of economizing the use of labor outrunning the pace at which we can find new uses for labor."

But history contradicts that thesis: As prior waves of technological innovation led to great job displacement, thousands of new and different jobs eventually popped up and offset the losses. In the Industrial Revolution, the vast majority of farm jobs were replaced by factory jobs, so that whereas in 1900 approximately 50 percent of all American workers were employed on farms, today that number is just 2 percent. Then, from the middle to late twentieth century, much of the new manufacturing work in the United States and other developed nations was either automated—by the introduction of robotics technology to the factory floor—or shipped abroad to the less developed nations. But again, plentiful new jobs in the service industries emerged.

Conceding this point, Martin Ford argues, however, that the current wave of technological innovation will lead to even more severe job displacement than occurred in the past. In other words, this time is different. Fewer new jobs will be created because machines are now able to perform not only many manual tasks as well as humans do, but also some cognitive tasks, and they will be getting better at mimicking human intelligence. This is why he predicts that machines will take over many high-level white-collar jobs as well as manual ones.

The counterintuitive truth we will explore in this chapter is that as our technology continues to improve—and there can be no doubt that it will—cultivating our humanity, in particular the softer skills that the liberal arts foster, will be the best way to ensure job security.

The Strong Demand for Soft Skills

Harvard economist David Deming's research on how the soft social skills regularly lead to business teams performing more efficiently was mentioned in Chapter 2. Deming has conducted pathbreaking research on the value of soft skills in the labor market, and he has discovered that "the fastest growing cognitive occupations—managers, teachers, nurses and therapists, physicians, lawyers, even economists—all require significant interpersonal interaction," which means that performing them well requires real proficiency in the fuzzy skills involved in both understanding human nature and accounting for it in interactions. In his 2015 NBER working paper entitled "The Growing Importance of Social Skills in the Labor Market," Deming reported that jobs with a high importance of social skills have grown by roughly 10 percent as a share of labor since 1980. Ironically, he also found that the market for jobs in many of the STEM fields, by contrast, have declined by 3 percent over the same period. In fact, Deming has argued that "the slowdown in high-skilled job growth is driven by science, technology, engineering and math (STEM) occupations," and that among these occupations, "engineers," "programmers and technical support," and "engineering and science technicians" are the jobs that are shrinking the fastest. While other jobs in STEM fields, such as computer science, mathematics, and statistics, are growing, they're actually growing at far slower rates than jobs that require strong social skills. What's more, 92 percent of nine hundred executives polled by the *Wall Street Journal* in 2016 stated that soft skills were "equally important or more important than technical skills," and 89 percent of those executives further stated that they had a "very or somewhat difficult" time finding candidates with those requisite skills.

This trend of the growing need for soft skill talent, and of job losses in the STEM fields, is likely to pick up pace in the coming years due to further democratization of increasingly intuitive technical tools, and to the training of large populations of more technologically proficient workers in the developing world. Just as in the past several decades globalization led to the outsourcing of masses of manufacturing jobs, followed by the outsourcing of many knowledge workers' jobs, many technology jobs that have been performed by U.S. workers will be shipped abroad. Consider the case of Andela, the New York–based company that we heard about in Chapter 1. It runs a Technical Leadership Program in Lagos, Nigeria, and Nairobi, Kenya, that trains burgeoning techies. There is such demand to be admitted into the program that it has an acceptance rate under 1 percent, making it "harder to get into than Harvard," according to CNN. Andela received 40,000 applications for just 280 places in 2016, and already has 200 programmers based in Nigeria and Kenya. The program teaches high-level programming skills and offers the services of technology teams for hire. Indeed, leading technology employers such as Microsoft and IBM have worked with the service. While Andela is only scratching the surface of what will become a huge workforce of overseas technologists, it's already caught the attention of Mark Zuckerberg and Google Ventures, which invested in its $24 million round in 2016.

As education reporter Valerie Strauss wrote in the *Washington*

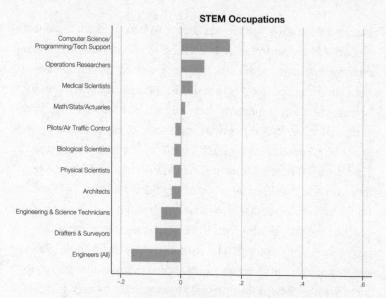

Change in Relative Employment for Cognitive Occupations, 2000–2012
(100x Change in Employment Share)
Source: 2000 Census and 2011–2013 ACS.

Post, "Trashing the liberal arts seems to have become practically a sport." Marc Andreessen and Vinod Khosla, whose disparaging comments about the liberal arts were quoted earlier, are part of the clamoring chorus. And as Strauss points out, criticisms have been particularly popular among politicians, no doubt singing the song that many of their constituents want to hear. Kentucky governor Matthew Bevin suggested Kentucky cut state college tuition funding for French literature majors. Former Florida governor and onetime presidential hopeful Jeb Bush said that universities ought to warn students, "Hey that psych major deal, that philosophy major thing, that's great, it's important to have liberal arts . . . but realize, you're going to be working [at] a Chick-fil-A." Florida senator Marco Rubio erroneously argued that welders make more money than philosophy majors, "because the market for Greek philosophers is tight."

Yet the great irony of all this criticism is that it's the liberal arts and their cultivation of distinctively human abilities—which machines can't yet even approximate—that are paving the way to the most reliable employment today and will continue to do in the coming years. Harvard labor economist Lawrence Katz, with whom David Deming has studied and collaborated, makes this point. "I actually think it may be that a really strong liberal arts education is going to be more valuable in the future," he says. Success, he argues, will be determined by one's "ability to deal with what can't be turned into an algorithm; how well do you deal with unstructured problems and how well do you deal with new situations."

The Potential Displacement of Soft Skills Has Been Greatly Exaggerated

Some might object that Deming's research is drawn on data from the past, from 1980 to 2012, just when the latest in machine learning began taking off. With the amazing feats being accomplished these days by machines, such as Google's DeepMind creating a program to defeat the world champion of Go, might it not be that the technology is advancing so far now—and will improve so much in the future—that, as Martin Ford asserts, many of the jobs for which the liberal arts soft skills are so important will in fact soon be taken over by machines?

In summer 2016, the *McKinsey Quarterly* published an analysis of eight hundred occupations that delved into this question. The researchers evaluated which of the over two thousand tasks comprised within those occupations were susceptible to machine automation. They concluded that "while automation will eliminate very few occupations entirely in the next decade, it will affect portions of almost all jobs to a greater or lesser degree, depending on the type of work they entail." Researchers at the McKinsey Global Institute make a vital point that has not received appropriate attention in the debate over future technological unemployment—that while machines will take over many of the *tasks* performed as parts of *jobs*, they will not be able to take over many jobs entirely, or at least not for the foreseeable future. In fact, they will merely enhance the quality of jobs by taking over the most rote, mind-numbing tasks. Of course, there are categories of jobs where the short-run technical feasibility of automation will be higher than rates of change in previous decades. McKinsey researchers estimate that only 5 percent of whole jobs will be automated. This is in stark contrast to the Oxford study citing 47 percent of U.S. jobs are "in the high risk category" for machine automation. Authors of the McKinsey Global Institute study found that roughly 30 percent of activities, or tasks, in 60 percent of U.S. jobs will change, but this only points to a changing environment in which worker flexibility will be a preeminent skill.

To get a better understanding of what kinds of work machines will be taking over in the foreseeable future and what types of jobs humans will keep for themselves—and therefore why those soft skills nourished by the liberal arts will continue to give humans a competitive edge—it's valuable to draw on the analysis of MIT economists Daron Acemoglu and David Autor. They analyze the impact of new technologies on the labor market and which jobs are in jeopardy of being taken over by machines. Building upon Autor's prior work with Frank Levy and Richard Murnane, they use a simple framework for making that evaluation. All work can be classified as either cognitive or manual, and as either routine or nonroutine. They assert that routine tasks, whether they are of a cognitive or manual nature, are ripe for automation, while nonroutine manual tasks and abstract cognitive tasks are relatively safe from automation, at least for quite some time.

Acemoglu and Autor define routine tasks as those that are so well understood by humans that a specific set of instructions can be written as a computer program and executed by a machine. "For a task to be autonomously performed by a computer," they write, "it must be sufficiently well defined (i.e., scripted) that a machine lacking flexibility or judgment can execute the task successfully by following the steps set down by the programmer. Accordingly, computers and computer-controlled equipment are highly productive and reliable at performing the tasks that programmers can script—and relatively inept at everything else." Nonroutine tasks are those that cannot be broken down into such a set of instructions. These tasks are not just high-end skills; they can be manual or highly abstract, requiring creative and original thinking: true problem solving, intuition, persuasion, and creativity.

Routine tasks are the cornerstones of many jobs, especially

middle-skilled jobs, and that includes both many manual and cognitive tasks. The same study by the McKinsey Global Institute estimates that upwards of 78 percent of routine physical work—tasks such as welding, soldering on an assembly line, packing goods, or preparing food—could already be done by machines, and that in specific categories, 90 percent of such tasks could eventually be automated. A company called Momentum Machines has invented a hamburger-cooking robot that can churn out six burgers a minute. We already have automated hotel check-in and even some cafeterias, and the McKinsey analysis suggests that 73 percent of food services and accommodation work is technically capable of automation. In the retail sector, it is estimated that as much as 53 percent of all activities could be automated, activities such as stock management, logistics, and packing and shipping merchandise.

Technical feasibility is, of course, only one determinant of when automation can and will occur. In other words, technology and labor are not perfect substitutes. The costs of investing in technology will also determine the timing, as will the cost of labor that serves as technology's alternative. Norms and regulations around such substitution will also matter significantly. For example, in China, where labor is much cheaper, factories feature 36 robots per 10,000 manufacturing workers, whereas in Germany there are 292, in Japan 314, and in Korea 478 robots, because the cost of labor is significantly higher there. But as the cost of assimilating these technologies into work environments inevitably decreases, a threshold will be crossed, whereby the economics of the substitution of human labor by machines may make it eventually inevitable.

Acemoglu and Autor highlight that, by contrast, nonroutine tasks, both manual and cognitive, will remain the province of humans. While most cognitive jobs require higher levels of education and many manual jobs require less education, Acemoglu and Autor argue that all these nonroutine tasks have one thing in common: they're far less susceptible to technological automation.

The Situation Matters

While the framework Daron Acemoglu and David Autor provide for discerning which jobs are likely to be taken over by machines is very powerful, what's missing from their discussion is a characterization of the various types of situations in which people must perform their work. A job is not only about the tasks of which it's comprised; it's also about the work environment in which it is done. The characteristics of the workplace also matter.

This brings us back to Andreas Xenachis, from Chapter 2, aboard the USS *Blue Ridge* monitoring a flood of data about movements of all kinds in the South China Sea. The situation he's operating in is highly complex. He's got to factor into his judgments what advice to send to his commander, which reveals not only what the data is showing, but a host of other factors, such as the various relationships among the parties with territorial claims, which are by no means fixed but are ever-evolving, as well as what is in each of their strategic interests. He's also got to account for the foibles of human behavior, which often lead us to act against what is actually in our strategic interests. In addition, he's got to be alert about the possibilities of misinterpretation by various parties and of accidental incidents. A Chinese Coast Guard vessel might not have intended to plow into the path of a Vietnamese fishing boat that merely miscalculated the speed of the vessel and failed to get out of the way. This is why so many highly trained and deeply knowledgeable humans are manning the C4I monitors and chatting vigorously with one another to make their assessments on a moment-to-moment basis. There are many concurrent and emerging properties, and the various behaviors impact the potential chain of events.

A powerful method for taking into account the nature of each situation and how it determines the skill set needed to do a job well was developed by researcher David J. Snowden and management consultant Mary E. Boone. They have proposed what they call the Cynefin Framework, which was developed specifically regarding the work of high-level business executives, but also applies to work in general. Snowden and Boone contend that, too often, leaders take a one-size-fits-all approach to managing when the range of situations they must deal with actually varies greatly. Leaders should instead adjust their approach to management according to a number of factors. Snowden and Boone's delineation of these factors helps greatly to clarify the lines between the jobs that machines will be able to do on their own and those that for the foreseeable future will still be done by humans.

Cynefin (say "ku-nev-in") is a Welsh word, selected by Snowden, who is Welsh. It's one of those words expressing a concept that in other languages requires a whole phrase to describe. The meaning, as Snowden translates it, is "the multiple factors in our environment and our experience that influence us in ways we can never understand." The framework breaks down management situations into five categories: simple, complicated, complex, chaotic, and disorder. Leaders have to first evaluate the situation they're in and sort it into one of those categories in order to determine the best strategy for managing it. Each category requires a different approach. For example, in both simple and complicated situations, cause-and-effect relationships are perceptible, and leaders can then assess the facts and decide what to do. But in complex and chaotic contexts, there's no apparent relationship between cause and effect; emerging patterns and properties, of both data and be-havior, determine how we should act.

There's also a fifth category, disorder, in which even simple situations are managed poorly, perhaps because there are dueling factions within an organization, or an array of differing perspec-tives about the best course of action, that lead to no clear-cut way to decide which should take precedent. There may also be so many issues that need immediate action that none of them truly get the attention they deserve.

Combining this framework with Daron Acemoglu and David Autor's distinction between routine and nonroutine jobs, we can come to a more refined assessment of why the fuzzy liberal arts grad will remain invaluable for so many kinds of work. Both routine manual and routine cognitive jobs that are performed in simple situations can be strictly broken down into a set of best practices, and they will increasingly be automated. For example, in logistics work, the tasks that are taken over might include the packing and shipping of items, or assembling goods on pallets. At German express logistics company DHL, 20 percent of logistics facilities are already automated, and they're piloting collabora-tions with Rethink Robotics, maker of a robot named Baxter. As mentioned, in hospitality, automated tasks will include checking people in and delivering room service within the highly controlled environment of elevators and hotel hallways. But additionally in other industries such as health care, nursing assistants spend two-thirds of their time manually collecting health information, some-thing that is already being made possible through passive sensor technology. All of these jobs contain a high proportion of manual tasks that can be codified into rules, and they are done in relatively simple, predictable environments.

Many cognitive tasks are also largely routine and no more insu-

THE CYNEFIN FRAMEWORK

Simple: The relationship between cause and effect is fairly easily discerned by everyone, and the best approach is to assess the situation, categorize it, and respond using a "best practice," a script that is codified. This is the realm of "known knowns."

Complicated: Cause and effect can be discerned, but they require expert analysis or investigation. Here, the best approach is to sense the problem, analyze it, and then respond to it. The leader's role is to get as much input as possible from a wide variety of experts, and then to take decisive action. Best practices are not codified as in simple situations, but the environment is fact-based. This is the realm of "known unknowns."

Complex: This is where the relationship between cause and effect can be seen — but only in retrospect. Unlike in the first two contexts, where right answers definitely do exist, in the complex context there is no definitive right answer. Instead of trying to impose order on the situation, the leader first needs to let patterns emerge, and then use that information to make best bets for moving forward. This is the realm of "unknown unknowns."

Chaotic: The relationship between cause and effect is impossible to determine because all of the variables are shifting so quickly. Trying to determine what's causing what in these situations is nearly impossible and therefore becomes less important than triage; it's better just to try to stop the bleeding, taking action to establish basic order, see where order is still absent, and then work to take the situation from chaotic to complex, where there are tools for extracting patterns from data.

Disorder: The best approach is to break the situation into individual parts, sort each part into one of the other four contexts, and deal with it according to the aforementioned methods of management.

lated from technology. They are highly uniform and can be carried out programmatically. Many cognitive jobs contain a high proportion of tasks that involve best practices, where employees are required to respond in predetermined ways. This is true, for example, in responding to customer service inquiries, for which many companies actually provide employees with prewritten scripts. Such cognitive jobs are also highly susceptible to automation, as we're seeing with a rapidly growing population of customer service "bots," that is, computer programs that can decipher text through natural language processing or speak in a humanoid voice and automatically listen to customers' questions (and, often, their frustrations, given that the technology still has a way to go before it's up to human proficiency). It's also not only low-end cognitive jobs that are susceptible. While in retail, 47 percent of a floor salesperson's activities might be automated, according to McKinsey, upwards of 86 percent of auditing, bookkeeping, and accounting could be done through technology. In other words, there is greater risk of automation for higher-skilled cognitive, rather than manual, labor. In other fields such as wealth management, where advisors take into account allocation preferences and risk tolerance, and operate on best-practice principles, aspects of the job are also tenuous. So-called robo-advisors already help optimize portfolios, nudging the role of financial planner toward a need for softer relationship management and interpersonal skills.

Manufacturing largely follows strict rules and is performed in a relatively straightforward environment—i.e., the factory assembly space, which is highly controlled. For this reason, the automation that has already taken over so much of manufacturing will inevitably take over more and more of it. Indoor hydroponic farming, or other types of work in structured environments, will be more susceptible to automation than work such as livestock farming, where there is more variability. However, it's important to note that even in these highly structured environments, it's still early days for robotics. At Amazon, one of the most advanced warehouse systems in the world, where there are thirty thousand little orange Kiva robots lifting and carrying goods from place to place, the capabilities are limited. According to robotics scientist Andreas Koller, "It's easier to build an autonomous car than a robot for a warehouse . . . Warehouses, because of their variety, are less structured than highways and freeways." In other words, even these highly controlled environments pose significant challenge.

For work performed in complex situations, the ability of machines to take over for humans is even more limited. Machine learning seems to suggest that some tasks, routine and nonroutine, cognitive and manual, that are performed in these environments may be able to be automated. Self-driving cars, for example, are performing cognitive as well as manual tasks that are in many ways nonroutine. But the various environments in which self-driving cars are most successful might still be classified as more complicated on closer inspection. For example, highway driving, while more predictable than urban driving, is not done in a controlled environment like a factory. The reason automation has taken hold in mining is precisely because the environment, while dangerous for humans, is complicated rather than complex. The issues yet to be fully addressed before self-driving vehicles can be safely unleashed in all scenarios suggest that, although Google's self-driving cars hum around Mountain View and Uber's self-driving cars navigate the streets of Pittsburgh's Strip District, much more R&D is needed and the deployment of self-driving cars will proceed in stages, with thresholds established for safety. Rather than the all-or-nothing "serial automation" being pursued by Google and Tesla, Daniela Rus, director of MIT's Computer Science and

Artificial Intelligence Lab, argues for "parallel automation," or a "guardian angel system" that observes human drivers and helps intervene if and when onboard sensors can prevent an accident. Given the challenges of full autonomy in both high-speed and high-complexity environments, this driver assist "intelligent," rather than autonomous, approach, being pioneered by Toyota in partnership with MIT, shows promise.

This is because in complex, and even more so in chaotic and disordered, situations, full automation is still a long way off, and it may never be able to take over fully for humans. These situations require dynamic, nonroutine, highly agile interpretation and subsequent improvisation of analysis and action. While within each of these kinds of situations there are certainly repetitive tasks, both manual and cognitive, that will be handed over to machines, these environments require *in situ* learning by doing, learning that cannot be preprogrammed or taught in advance of getting your hands dirty. Flying an airplane is an example of a job in which much of the work has long been automated, and yet we haven't done away with pilots. Technological "scaffolding" can take care of nearly all of the *best*, and even *good*, practices in flight, but planes still require human input to supplement them in complexity. In fact, in spite of highly automated aeronautics and glass cockpit avionics, Boeing sees a need for the industry to hire 30,850 pilots every year for the next twenty years. The reason is that the art of flying a plane can quickly change from complicated to complex, and sometimes to chaotic, situations in which even pilots and their human judgment and experience are often not able to respond adequately.

When both engines of the Airbus A320 being piloted by Captain Chesley B. "Sully" Sullenberger III were knocked out shortly after takeoff from LaGuardia Airport, with the plane soaring three thousand feet above the Bronx, Sully drew on his extensive flight experience to courageously land the plane on New York's Hudson River. Having been a superb air force pilot who had spent years in the cockpit of the heavy, supersonic F-4 Phantom fighter jet, he knew the theory of how to slow a powerless descent. In just seconds, he was able to triage the situation and take decisive action. Ironically, the extraordinarily difficult feat was made even harder by the plane's automated flight control system. As Sullenberger later explained, one of the features of the system, which is meant to avert disaster, is that at low flight speeds, "regardless of how hard the pilot pulls back on the sidestick, the flight control computers will not allow him to stall the wings and lose lift," which is exactly what he had to do to land on the Hudson. As he attempted to pitch the nose of the plane to slow his airspeed over the water, computer overrides nearly made that impossible. There is good reason that when a flight hits turbulence over the North Atlantic, those on board hope and pray that there is an experienced pilot up front who can draw upon expertise potentially broader and more comprehensive than what system designers can imagine.

Is Deep Learning a Different Story?

The greatly increased power of machine learning, which is sometimes referred to as deep learning, has led to predictions that further breakthroughs in artificial intelligence are right around the corner. This suggests that machines will actually become capable of artificial general intelligence (AGI), a form of intelligence that is truly humanlike in all its forms. What does this bode for the fuzzy role in innovation?

Well, the likelihood of machines ever attaining this capability is hotly debated, and if it is possible, that achievement is years and years in the future. To appreciate how far from general intelligence machines are, it's instructive to consider the limits of even the most impressive recent feats in AI. DeepMind, a company that was developed out of University College London's Computational Neuroscience Unit and was acquired by Google for $500 million in 2014, developed a program called AlphaGo. DeepMind used a combination of machine learning, decision trees, and algorithms—tools that together comprise what we call "artificial intelligence"—and all of the AI trained AlphaGo to play the ancient Chinese game Go, with the aim of the machine defeating the game's human world champion.

Computers have conquered many board games, including tic-tac-toe, checkers, Monopoly, Clue, and chess, but the AlphaGo victory marks a significant departure from these other feats in that it was not accomplished by straightforward brute-force computational power. To win at these other games, the computers were programmed with the rules of the game, and given sufficient computational power and speed so that they could calculate all possible next moves and evaluate the best one given the human player's move. The machines prevailed in these other games due to sheer computing power and memory, not because of anything that could be characterized as approximating human intelligence. Because in these preprogrammed approaches, every move was a "known known," the computer's greatest feat was not in attaining intelligence so much as it was in reducing each game to a simple situation that could be scripted.

DeepMind, however, prevailed at Go using a different approach, which is the reason that it garnered so much international attention. South African entrepreneur Elon Musk, founder of Tesla and SpaceX, heralded it as a ten-year jump in AI. Others called it the dawn of artificial general intelligence. To understand how remarkable the computer's victory was, it's important to know a little about the game of Go. The board features nineteen horizontal and nineteen vertical lines. Players place small white and black stones at the intersections of the lines. Once a stone is placed on the board it cannot be moved. If the stone is surrounded by an opponent's stones, then that stone is "captured." The reason many found DeepMind's win so profound was because Go has too many possible moves and combinations for a machine, even an extraordinarily powerful one, to be able to run through and evaluate all possibilities for a next move.

AlphaGo engineers taught the program to play Go not by pre-programming a vast storehouse of moves, but by writing machine-learning algorithms. They trained AlphaGo using historical game data from thousands of past matches, and then allowed it to "learn" patterns by playing a human adversary. They even built other deep-learning machines similar to AlphaGo so it could compete against them using its own intelligence. All of this was done to give the program exposure to as many potential situations as possible, in other words, to give it "experience."

Because the potential game paths and combinations are too numerous to be preprogrammed, AlphaGo had to make reasonably informed decisions under conditions of ambiguity, just as we humans must often do. To facilitate this process, the programmers constrained the "search depth," the extent to which the machine would sort through possible solutions, so that the computer would make the best *relative* move based on the information available rather than trying to find the best *possible* move. In other words, while the brilliant programmers weren't able to reduce the complexity—or the "dimensionality" as they might say—of the game enough to codify "best practices," they were able to give the machine the ability to recognize patterns, and then use "good practices."

Let's look at this subtle difference. As humans, we think

through a set of possibilities as rigorously as possible, and then we act. We measure and analyze what we can, but when analysis can't definitively tell us what to do, we rely on intuition, or faith, or sometimes blind luck. Hungarian-British philosopher Michael Polanyi commented about this ability, which he said relies on "tacit knowledge" that humans "can know more than we can tell." AlphaGo's search depth allowed the machine to make moves that *appeared* to be the result of a decision-making process—remarkably similar to human intuitive thinking. Other moves seemed the result of original thought rather than rote evaluation of past moves. But was AlphaGo tacitly aware of its decisions, or was it merely calculating probabilities faster than a human?

AlphaGo also seemed to develop a distinctive style of play, as human players of the game do. Skilled human players develop preferences for certain tactics as they gain experience. Spectators who watched AlphaGo play champion Lee Sedol in Seoul, South Korea, reported there was a beauty revealed by a surprising set of choices that the machine made. But in actuality, they were surprising moves only because the machine acted on probabilities in areas of the board beyond the computational abilities of a human player. The irony of AlphaGo's win was that the engineers helped a machine beat a human by constraining its options so that it had to act more like a human, but after all, it was one enabled with prodigious real-time computational power.

There is no question that AlphaGo's achievement is a landmark in the process of developing smarter artificial intelligence. But there are obvious distinctions between the human "wetware" —a term used to describe the human brain as compared with computer software and hardware—which develops its own capabilities, and a program such as AlphaGo, which—don't forget—required sophisticated programming by some of the most capable human minds. AlphaGo is still essentially *reproducing* intelligence, though perhaps creative machine intelligence will become a *new* form of intelligence.

Fan Hui, the three-time European Go champion, who lost five straight matches to AlphaGo, called the defeating move "not a human move." But then again, the machine is entirely dependent on humans to create its internal logic, monitor it from a "control room," and point it toward data to learn from, whereas the human mind teaches itself a great deal of what it knows. It is a brilliant technological advance when compared with our own abilities completing an isolated task such as playing Go.

One more thought. Here's a twist on an old conundrum: If AlphaGo were alone and no one were around to watch it, would it be considered independently intelligent? Based on the current evidence, I think the breakthrough of true artificial general intelligence is yet to come. In fact, even David Silver, one of AlphaGo's creators, says that while this technology can be repurposed to help society in many profound ways, true AGI is "decades away."

Machines Can't Intuit, Create, or Feel

A whole set of human abilities still haven't been even approximated by artificial intelligence. For example, machines are still incapable of true idea origination. Russian programmers behind the Prisma app have figured out how to use neural networks to turn your latest photograph into a work of art in the style of Van Gogh or Picasso, which is certainly impressive and loads of fun, but there's no originality involved in doing so. Walk slowly with a student of contemporary art history through the Andy Warhol Museum in Pittsburgh, stand in front of Picasso's *Guernica* at Madrid's Reina Sofía, or drag your fingers along the cold, undulating steel of a Richard Serra to know art. Machines are also incapable of anything resembling human emotion, and therefore utterly lack empathy. Google can feed its AI engine 2,865 romance novels in order to make it more fluent in emotional language and situations, but will that really make it empathetic, capable of understanding love or desire? Will our machines laugh with Jane Austen and feel the *pathos* of Tolstoy? These are just two of the key characteristics of the mysterious phenomenon known as human consciousness, which even today's smartest machines don't possess.

Anyone who saw the movie *The Imitation Game*, about how Alan Turing, the inventor of the Computer Age, cracked the Germans' Enigma code during World War II, can recall that context and human intuition played a central role in his machine's success. And more than four decades ago, Hubert Dreyfus, a philosopher at UC Berkeley, outlined the conceptual limits of artificial intelligence in his 1972 book, *What Computers Can't Do*. Those limits revolve around the difference between computation, which machines do very well, and consciousness, which machines don't possess. Many in the high-tech community ignored or mocked Dreyfus's argument at the time, but even today the debate continues. In 2011, along with Harvard philosophy chair Sean Dorrance Kelly, Dreyfus said, "The greatest danger . . . is not that it proves machines could be better versions of us, but that it tempts us to misunderstand ourselves as poorer versions of them." Leading experts in AI today generally agree that the advent of more powerful machine-learning algorithms and more capable natural language processing cannot yet approximate human intelligence and are still in the "in vitro phase."

Even Netscape founder and billionaire venture capitalist Marc Andreessen, who was quoted in Chapter 1 as having once warned liberal arts students that they "likely will end up working in shoe stores," argued in the *Financial Times* in 2014 that he doesn't believe robots will eat all the jobs. "There is still an enormous gap between what many people do in jobs today, and what robots and AI can replace," he said. "And there will be for decades . . . even when robots and AI are far more powerful, there will still be many things that people can do that robots and AI can't. For example: creativity, innovation, exploration, art, science, entertainment, and caring for others. We have no idea how to make machines do these."

Today, Fei-Fei Li is the director of the Artificial Intelligence Lab at Stanford, and also a proponent of going beyond data-driven deep learning, embracing the fuzzy emotional and social components of intelligence. "We [humans] are terrible at computing with huge data," she says, "but we're great at abstraction and creativity." We need diversity of thought and the curiosity to ask the right questions, two characteristics nurtured through the liberal arts. And we need people passionate in all disciplines to bring that expertise to bear on our newest tools. There ought to be anthropologists, sociologists, and psychologists in every cutting-edge AI lab.

"Keep your own *Iliad* under your pillow," Harvard president Drew Faust advised the hundreds of cadets in her lecture at West Point in 2016. "Lead, also, on behalf of the liberal arts—of the traditions of human experience and humane insight that they represent. Recognize the importance of the attributes they have given you, mark their presence in your lives, advocate for them in the lives of others . . . Be the world's best force for the humanities—and thus for human possibility."

Technology's promise is great, but it requires our liberal arts in equal measure, the fuzzy and the techie working together in pursuit of shared human goals.

Conclusion: Partnership Goes Both Ways

This book has focused on the role that those with liberal arts degrees can play in applying such emerging technologies to the creation of breakthrough innovations. Techies are their equal and vital partners, and they, too, can and must drive the process of bridge building between the fuzzy and techie. Techies are crucial to this process, and will continue to drive groundbreaking new innovations that haven't yet even been conceived. Techies continue to spearhead the development of many of the most exciting new products and services. South African entrepreneur Elon Musk has pushed the frontiers of both electric vehicle adoption and the democratization of access to space travel; Larry Page and Sergey Brin have made the world's information available and are today on to new challenges such as bringing about universal access to the Internet; Rodney Brooks, founder of Rethink Robotics, has forged new frontiers in what our robots can help us manufacture.

Other techies are behind pioneering the natural language processing that is improving how we command our technology with our own voice, making it what we say, rather than what we see, that counts. Amazon, for example, is offering its voice command technology, which powers the voice of Alexa in the Amazon Echo, to any innovator who wants to make use of it through its Alexa Skills Kit. The software toolkit is available for free, and to further spur adoption, the company created a $100 million investment fund to support entrepreneurs in developing ideas. Companies such as PullString, founded by the techie folks behind Pixar and named after the pull-string *Toy Story* character Woody, are packaging up the functionality to easily create chat bots that can respond to queries in Slack or Facebook Messenger and perform basic conversations. Even Google's deep learning, such as that used by AlphaGo, is being made available through its TensorFlow machine-learning library and is being put to use in incredible ways. Makoto Koike, an automotive designer in Japan, for example, used TensorFlow to make his parents' lives easier through machine learning. By assembling Arduino hardware, a Google Raspberry Pi Internet-connected computer board that costs around thirty-five dollars, and off-the-shelf cameras, he built a machine that helped his father, a Japanese cucumber farmer, classify and sort cucumbers by quality, with 70 percent accuracy. Koike first manually photographed and classified thousands of cucumbers, and then used those images as training data to teach TensorFlow what specific features in cucumbers represent quality, and what to try to identify in future photographs. Techies may often be stereotypically characterized as "geeks" with little interest or aptitude in fuzzy concerns, but this is as untrue as the arguments denigrating the value of the liberal arts in our technological world. The fact is that techies have driven many partnerships across the fuzzy-techie divide, and they can be highly effective bridge builders.

Take the case of Doug Ricket, the cofounder and CEO of Pay-Joy. He's a former Google software engineer who teamed up with a fuzzy named Mark Heynen, a history and immigration studies major from Amherst College, to found their company. They met while working on the Google Maps team, where they were mapping Africa. After working at Google, Ricket augmented his expertise in technology by getting out from behind a computer screen and traveling to villages in the small West African country of Gambia, working for a social enterprise called d.light that is trying to bring solar energy devices to poverty-stricken communities.

Though still a director of engineering based out of Hong Kong, Ricket turned himself, in effect, into an anthropological researcher, spending months in African villages with potential customers, who he realized had no access to credit. Without credit, the high upfront cost of solar panels proved prohibitive. He further observed that many of these same people purchased prepay cell phone plans from local kiosks. Why couldn't they purchase solar panels in the same way? he wondered. Ricket devised a software solution for d.light that enabled customers to purchase their new solar panels over time, only a few dollars at a time.

Returning to the United States, Ricket decided to apply the same basic model to helping the roughly 45 million Americans without credit gain access to today's greatest tool: a smartphone. Teaming up with Heynen, the chief business officer, Ricket launched PayJoy in 2015, enabling consumers to buy phones over time at much lower interest rates than the alternatives. After only one year in business, PayJoy had raised over $18 million from venture capitalists, and the company's ultimate goal is to move beyond the U.S. market and to empower anyone on the planet to purchase a smartphone, or indeed any new type of device.

The point of emphasizing the role of fuzzies is not to say they have an exclusive on the opportunities opening up; it is to say that the fuzzy combined with the techie is the formula for the most transformative, and most successful, innovations—the ones that will most effectively solve the many vexing problems to be tackled and will most humanely enhance our lives. Just as techies like Doug Ricket stand to benefit a great deal in their efforts to drive innovation by learning about fuzzy perspectives and methods of inquiry, the ability of fuzzies to partner with techies will be greatly enhanced if they develop their own technological literacy. As we progress into an ever more technological future, the goal must be to bridge the divide between the fuzzy and techie in our educational systems, all the way from children's earliest learning experiences through college and graduate study, and to make them reflect this necessary duality in society.

Two Cultures Conjoined

In a famous lecture at Cambridge University in 1959 titled "The Two Cultures," British politician Charles Percy (C. P.) Snow, who was both a physicist by training and a novelist, lamented a growing divide between the sciences and humanities, speaking of the "mutual incomprehension[,] . . . hostility, and dislike" that had taken hold. As the twentieth century progressed and the computer revolution unfolded, information technology joined the hard sciences on their side of this chasm. It is time to build more bridges across the divide. C. P. Snow also said in his lecture that "the clashing point of two subjects, two disciplines, two cultures—of two galaxies, so far as that goes—ought to produce creative chances."

That is precisely the case with the merging of the fuzzy and the techie. The creative breakthroughs to be achieved by facilitating more appreciation and fluency across the chasm demand that we innovate in education with the same kind of vigor that so many entrepreneurs are bringing to innovation in products and services. This is the best way to ensure not only that the potential of the new technologies is realized, but also, just as important, that people are prepared to perform the jobs of the future.

As with the new work being created in helping to make self-driving cars safe and with the two thousand five hundred new jobs as fashion stylists that Stitch Fix has created, many new types of work and specific jobs will likely emerge. Just as economist John Maynard Keynes couldn't predict the many new jobs that would emerge in the post–Great Depression economy, it's not possible to accurately forecast which new jobs might develop. Some analysts surmise that the number of new types of jobs will be substantial. In fact, the U.S. Department of Labor predicted in a report that as many as 65 percent of children in school today will work in jobs that have not yet been created. Considering someone born today could be working well into the 2080s, the expectation that we can forecast any of their needs beyond self-reliance and creativity reveals our own hubris.

While we cannot know what they will be, we can safely conjecture that many if not most of them will require technological literacy. Motivated learners can sufficiently master the technology with a wealth of resources now available, as Katelyn Gleason did before launching her innovative health-care technology business Eligible and as Katrina Lake has done in collaborating with data scientist Eric Colson and building Stitch Fix. But if learning about the nature of the tech tools and the underlying principles of their operation were a standard part of a liberal arts education, included in the syllabus of *how* we learn and question, perhaps that would truly empower legions more fuzzies to collaborate with techies.

One need look no further to see the benefits of bridging the divide in educational programs than the symbolic systems major at Stanford, launched by a group of professors that included Tom Wasow, who was the dean of undergraduate students at Stanford

University from 1987 to 1991. "I spent a lot of time thinking about what undergraduate education should be," he recounts. Wasow himself combined tech and fuzzy expertise in his own education, getting an undergraduate degree in mathematics from Reed College and then a PhD in linguistics from MIT.

Working at the interface of language and computing, Wasow was one of the pioneers who contributed insights that have made natural language processing possible today. He could see the writing on the wall about the enormous benefits of combining techie and fuzzy skills, and the symbolic systems program brought together courses in computing with ones in philosophy, logic, linguistics, and psychology. It was a major that didn't want to play by the traditional STEM versus liberal arts rules, and neither have its prolific cast of entrepreneurial graduates, who include Reid Hoffman, founder of LinkedIn; Mike Krieger, cofounder of Instagram; Scott Forestall, software creator of the iPhone and iPad; and Marissa Mayer, early Google executive and CEO of Yahoo. Google's VP of product management for Android, who also helped launch the Chrome web browser, got a degree in symbolic systems along with a master's in psychology, and Facebook's chief product officer, Chris Cox, also graduated from the program. Even Mark Zuckerberg admits that the program churns out "among the most talented people in the world." Wasow is a quiet and discerning fuzzy-techie figure at the very heart of our technological world.

Other bridge-building fields of study have been created already, of course. Psychology, linguistics, and neuroscience come together to make cognitive science. Sociology and civil engineering have been combined in urban policy, computing and design have been combined in data visualization, and psychology and computing have been combined in usability research. More such explicitly fuzzy-techie majors should be fostered, such as combining philosophy and engineering into "design ethics," anthropology and data science into "data literacy," sociology and statistics into "human analytics," literature and computer science into "narrative science," and law and data science into "predictive regulation." Momentum behind doing so is building. One academic institution answering the call is the Rhode Island School of Design (RISD), where the Airbnb founders studied and Esther Wojcicki delivered a 2016 commencement address.

RISD advocates what it calls STEAM education, the blending of technical fluency (STEM) with art and design (A), and it's catching on. The Andover, Massachusetts, public school system has made STEAM education a primary goal. In DeSoto, Texas, the DeSoto West Middle School offers the iSTEAM3D Magnet Academy, where students learn about urban planning by using Minecraft to engineer the city, and then a MakerBot 2 3-D printer to bring their city to life by printing physical buildings and roads. Students use Foldit, a game where players fold proteins in new ways, and in the process crowd-source new combinations for scientists to potentially cure diseases, to learn about chemistry. In 2013, then-president of RISD John Maeda helped kick off the bipartisan Congressional STEAM Caucus, focused on making this a national priority.

We must no longer quarrel over a false dichotomy between STEM and liberal arts education. As we collect more data, we require great consideration as to what we ought to do with it. As we build devices, we must interrogate their design. As we construct algorithms, we must ask what assumptions they are based on and consider the protections against biases. As we create more data scientists, we require more data literacy. Fuzzies and techies should not be considered as oppositional; they are concurrently vital. As the new tools allow greater access to the power of technology, advances in our machines will require greater engagement of our humanity.

"First the muscle work, then the routine work, then, maybe, the real brainwork," author Kurt Vonnegut wrote of machine automation in his 1952 book, *Player Piano*. We have been fascinated by technological change for decades, and indeed today's fears shouldn't be blindly whitewashed with optimism. But as we look to the timeless skills that will keep us relevant in a dynamic world we cannot forecast, one way we will develop these very real skills from within our communities is by nurturing, rather than shunning, the liberal arts inquisition of who we are, what we want, and why we matter. By pairing fuzzy with techie, techie with fuzzy, we can manage the accelerating changes facing our world.

Our education, products, and institutions should ideally all be one part fuzzy and one part techie in order to capitalize on the untold opportunities of our fast-evolving tech-driven future.

Acknowledgments

Just as there are many fuzzies behind the scenes of our technology-led world, there are many hidden influences and contributors behind a published book. This work certainly would not have been possible without the immense support of Emily Loose, whose superb intellect and sharp eye helped me refine my arguments over many months of work. Thank you, Emily. To Shay Maunz and Barbara Richter, thank you for your brilliant additions. Sharam Mercer and Rebekah Iliff, without your many influences, I would not have met Bill Tancer, who made the very kind introduction to my agent, Mel Flashman, at Trident Media. Mel, your boundless energy over the past three years have brought this book to life.

To Rick Wolff and his wonderful editorial staff at Houghton Mifflin, thanks for taking a big swing on a first-time author, and pushing me to bring this book to fruition on a timeline faster than anyone thought possible. To my friends around the world, thanks for helping me set up shop in San Francisco and Pittsburgh, London and Berlin, on a train across the western United States, and in countless West Village and Williamsburg cafés, where the bulk of this book was written. To Tommy Dyer, Pratap Ranade, Sam Cervantes, Aaron Levenstadt, and Petar Maymounkov, thank you for your patience and guidance, helping me hash out the latest in big data, AI, and machine learning.

To all those in the book who shared their time, story, and passion, and to all those no longer in the book, thank you for contributing to this hard but deeply rewarding process of posing an idea and chasing it down. Much like a startup, books are iterated one word, paragraph, and page at a time. They are refined and changed, always organic, never complete. They become a time capsule, not a finished work. Getting to know you all better and trying my best to represent your courage and fortitude in creation has been both a challenge and a tremendous honor.

To Ambassador Richard N. Gardner, my mentor, who helped shepherd me into the Council on Foreign Relations, and Bill Draper, thank you for your friendship and guidance. Thanks to Jonathan Zittrain, who told me that having a multitude of passions is better than one, and to Sheryl Sandberg, who told me that I didn't have to choose between the public and private sectors.

Thanks to Katherine Barr, Allen Morgan, Ed Zimmerman, and Will Porteous, who helped give me my start as a venture capitalist, and to Abhas Gupta for making Sand Hill Road a lot more fun. Thanks to Scott Sawyer for your friendship and encouragement when I embarked on this project years ago in the green room, and to Clare Ros and little Pippy, curled at my feet for much of the writing process, for your love and support throughout. You made these months endlessly more enjoyable.

Thanks most of all to my family, my little sister Anna who's the real writer of the bunch, and my parents, Craig and Susan. You guys gave me the gift of your energy, curiosity, and confidence to believe that absolutely anything is possible if—as Steve Jobs said—you're hungry and foolish enough chase it.

Notes

AUTHOR'S NOTE

page

x   *"software eats the world"*: Marc Andreessen, "Why Software Is Eating the World," *Wall Street Journal*, August 20, 2011, http://www.wsj.com/articles /SB10001424053111903480904576512250915629460.

1. THE ROLE OF THE FUZZY IN A TECHIE WORLD

1   *$25 million in venture capital*: "Eligible," Crunchbase, August 2016, https://www.crunchbase.com/organization/eligible-api#/entity.

4   *"take off like a rocket ship"*: Katelyn Gleason, interview by author, May 29, 2016.

      one hundred most creative people: "Most Creative People 2013," *Fast Company*, May 13, 2013, https://www.fastcompany.com/3009150/most -creative-people-2013/73-katelyn-gleason.

      she was named one of Forbes's *30 Under 30*: "2015 Forbes 30 Under 30: Healthcare," *Forbes*, September 2015, http://www.forbes.com/pictures /eidg45hdkg/katelyn-gleason-29/#75b1c02369f1.

5   *eligibility claims per month*: Eligible, accessed June 2016, https://eligible .com/.

      Butterfield studied philosophy: George Anders, "That 'Useless' Liberal Arts Degree Has Become Tech's Hottest Ticket," *Forbes*, August 17, 2015, ac- cessed June 2016, http://www.forbes.com/sites/georgeanders/2015/07/29 /liberal-arts-degree-tech/#263a3e6c5a75.

      neoclassical social theory: "Company Overview of Palantir Technologies

Inc.," Alexander C. Karp, Bloomberg.com, http://www.bloomberg
.com/research/stocks/private/person.asp?personId=455286685&
privcapId=43580005.

6 *bought for $390 million:* Neal Ungerleider, "RelateIQ, Salesforce's $390
Million 'Siri for Business,' Grows Up," *Fast Company,* September 15,
2015, https://www.fastcompany.com/3051088/elasticity/relateiq
-salesforces-390-million-siri-for-business-grows-up.

literature at Harvard: Eugene Kim, "Not Every Silicon Valley Leader Is
an Engineer, Including These 9 Super Successful Liberal Arts Majors,"
Business Insider, August 1, 2015, http://www.businessinsider.com
/9-silicon-valley-leaders-that-didnt-study-engineering-2015-7/#ben
-silbermann-is-the-cofounder-of-pinterest-the-11-billion-photo-sharing
-and-social-media-service-but-silbermann-studied-political-science
-at-yale-and-went-on-to-work-in-online-advertising-before-coming
-up-with-the-idea-for-pinterest-8.

7 *"Stay hungry. Stay foolish":* Stanford University, "Steve Jobs' 2005 Stanford Commencement Address," YouTube video, 2008, https://www
.youtube.com/watch?v=UF8uR6Z6KLc.

"make our heart sing": Jonah Lehrer, "Steve Jobs: 'Technology Alone Is
Not Enough,'" *The New Yorker,* October 7, 2011, http://www.newyorker
.com/news/news-desk/steve-jobs-technology-alone-is-not-enough.

"Second Machine Age": Erik Brynjolfsson and Andrew McAfee, *The Second
Machine Age: Work, Progress, and Prosperity in a Time of Brilliant Technologies* (New York: W. W. Norton, 2014).

8 *caused a stir:* Vivek Wadhwa, "Engineering vs. Liberal Arts: Who's Right
—Bill or Steve?," TechCrunch, March 21, 2011, https://techcrunch
.com/2011/03/21/engineering-vs-liberal-arts-who's-right—bill-or-steve/.

well-paying jobs: Steve Kolowich, "How to Train Your Draconian,"
Inside Higher Ed, March 1, 2011, https://www.insidehighered.com
/news/2011/03/01/gates_tells_governors_they_might_determine
_public_university_program_funding_based_on_job_creation.

"relevant to the future": Vinod Khosla, "Is Majoring in Liberal Arts a Mistake for Students?," *Medium* (blog), February 10, 2016, https://medium
.com/@vkhosla/is-majoring-in-liberal-arts-a-mistake-for-students
-fd9d20c8532e#.85j9edu5q.

"working in shoe stores": Jay Yarow, "Marc Andreessen at the DealBook
Conference," Business Insider, December 12, 2012, http://www
.businessinsider.com/marc-andreessen-at-the-dealbook
-conference-2012-12.

9   *"Can Robots Be Lawyers?":* Dana Remus and Frank S. Levy, "Can Robots Be Lawyers? Computers, Lawyers, and the Practice of Law," *SSRN Electronic Journal,* December 30, 2015, doi:10.2139/ssrn.2701092.

10 *one hundred thousand African programmers:* Etelka Lehoczky, "This Startup Trains African Programmers for the Best Software Developer Jobs in the World," Inc.com, March 2016, http://www.inc.com/magazine/201603/etelka-lehoczky/andela-training-african-programmers-tech-workers.html.

    $10,000 to train each fellow: Allie Bidwell, "African Company Pays People to Learn Computer Science," *U.S. News and World Report,* May 14, 2015, http://www.usnews.com/news/stem-solutions/articles/2015/05/14/andela-an-african-company-paying-people-to-learn-computer-science.

    fewer than one in ten: Charles Kenny, "Why Factory Jobs Are Shrinking Everywhere," Bloomberg.com, April 28, 2014, http://www.bloomberg.com/news/articles/2014-04-28/why-factory-jobs-are-shrinking-everywhere.

11 *first graders learn to code:* Klint Finley, "Estonia Reprograms First Graders as Web Coders," *Wired,* September 4, 2012, https://www.wired.com/2012/09/estonia-reprograms-first-graders-as-web-coders/.

    "the teaching of philosophy": Charlotte Blease, "Philosophy Can Teach Children What Google Can't—and Ireland Knows It," *Guardian,* January 9, 2017, https://www.theguardian.com/commentisfree/2017/jan/09/philosophy-teach-children-schools-ireland.

14 *player-ranking iPhone application:* Scott Hartley, "Startups for Retirees, Not Just Drop-Outs," *Medium* (blog), August 5, 2014, https://medium.com/@scotthartley/startups-for-retirees-not-just-drop-outs-6ee007b6584f#.ddnmb3iuv.

    skills taught in the liberal arts: Fareed Zakaria, *In Defense of a Liberal Education* (New York: W. W. Norton, 2015).

16 *"science can't capture":* Stanford University, "Steve Jobs' 2005 Stanford Commencement Address."

17 *crowd-sourced study platform:* Christina Farr, "Zuckerberg Admits: If I Wasn't the CEO of Facebook, I'd Be at Microsoft," VentureBeat, October 20, 2012, http://venturebeat.com/2012/10/20/zuck-startup-school/.

    "money to create jobs": Nicholas Kristof, "Starving for Wisdom," *New York Times,* April 16, 2015, http://www.nytimes.com/2015/04/16/opinion/nicholas-kristof-starving-for-wisdom.html.

    U.S. Department of Labor: John O'Connor, "Explaining Florida Gov. Rick Scott's War on Anthropology (And Why Anthropologists May Win),"

StateImpact NPR, October 20, 2011, https://stateimpact.npr.org/florida
/2011/10/20/explaining-florida-gov-scott-war-on-anthropology-why
-anthropologists-win/.

Melissa Cefkin: Brett Berk, "How Nissan's Using Anthropology to Make
Autonomous Cars Safe," The Drive, November 24, 2015, http://www
.thedrive.com/tech/999/how-nissans-using-anthropology-to-make
-autonomous-cars-safe.

18   *accounting for all dangers:* Danny Yadron and Dan Tynan, "Tesla Driver
Dies in First Fatal Crash While Using Autopilot Mode," *Guardian,* June
30, 2016, https://www.theguardian.com/technology/2016/jun/30/tesla
-autopilot-death-self-driving-car-elon-musk.

a Harry Potter movie: Mahita Gajanan, "Tesla Driver May Have Been
Watching *Harry Potter* Before Fatal Crash," *Vanity Fair*—Hive, July 2,
2016, http://www.vanityfair.com/news/2016/07/tesla-driver-may-have
-been-watching-harry-potter-before-fatal-crash.

19   *system of gestures:* Anjana Ahuja, "Hail the Algorithms That Decode
Human Gestures," *Financial Times,* September 6, 2016, https://www
.ft.com/content/6b23399a-743c-11e6-bf48-b372cdb1043a.

"beefing up their skillset": Andy Sharman, "Driverless Cars Pose Worrying
Questions of Life and Death," *Financial Times,* January 20, 2016,
https://www.ft.com/content/b1894960-a25a-11e5-8d70-42b68cfae6e4.

20   *"trolley problem":* J.-F. Bonnefon, A. Shariff, and I. Rahwan, "The Social
Dilemma of Autonomous Vehicles," *Science* 352, no. 6293 (2016):
1573–76, doi:10.1126/science.aaf2654.

21   *"Our Driverless Dilemma":* J. D. Greene, "Our Driverless Dilemma,"
Science 352, no. 6293 (2016): 1514–15, accessed August 2016, doi:10.1126
/science.aaf9534.

"Connected and Self-Driving Car Practice": "Elliot Katz—Overview,
People," DLA Piper Global Law Firm, https://www.dlapiper.com/en/us
/people/k/katz-elliot/.

22   *patterns in matching:* Fiona Ng, "Tinder Has an In-House Sociologist and
Her Job Is to Figure Out What You Want," *Los Angeles Magazine,* May 25,
2016, http://www.lamag.com/longform/tinder-sociologist/.

"digital dualism": Nathan Jurgenson, "Digital Dualism Versus Augmented Reality," *Society Pages,* February 24, 2011, https://thesocietypages
.org/cyborgology/2011/02/24/digital-dualism-versus-augmented
-reality/.

23   *it created scarcity:* Felix Gillette, "Flirty Frat App Goes Philosophical:
Snapchat Has Its Own Sociologist," Bloomberg.com, October 03, 2013,

https://www.bloomberg.com/news/articles/2013-10-03/flirty-frat-app
-goes-philosophical-snapchat-has-its-own-sociologist.

Snap's online magazine called Real Life: Jordan Novet, "Snapchat Is
Starting Real Life, an Online Magazine About Technology," Venture-
Beat, June 16, 2016, http://venturebeat.com/2016/06/16/snapchat-is
-starting-real-life-an-online-magazine-about-technology/.

"surprise and delight": Anders, "That 'Useless' Liberal Arts Degree."

24 *being taught to liberal arts majors*: Khosla, "Is Majoring in Liberal Arts a
Mistake?"

25 *"Croatian folk dance"*: Charles McGrath, "What Every Student Should
Know," *New York Times,* January 8, 2006, http://www.nytimes
.com/2006/01/08/education/edlife/what-every-student-should
-know.html.

he explained in 2013: Linsey Fryatt, "Zach Sims from Codecademy—the
22-Year-Old CEO," *HEUREKA*, January 22, 2013, http://theheureka.com
/zach-sims-codecademy.

26 *"adaptable to changing circumstances"*: Elizabeth Segran, "Why Top Tech
CEOs Want Employees with Liberal Arts Degrees," *Fast Company,* August 28, 2014, http://www.fastcompany.com/3034947/the-future-of-work
/why-top-tech-ceos-want-employees-with-liberal-arts-degrees?utm
_campaign=home.

27 *"modes of thought"*: S. Georgia Nugent, "The Liberal Arts in Action: Past,
Present, and Future," The Council of Independent Colleges, August
2015, http://www.cic.edu/meetings-and-events/Other-Events
/Liberal-Arts-Symposium/Documents/Symposium-Essay.pdf, 28.

28 *"that it wasn't true," he recalled*: Anders, "That 'Useless' Liberal Arts
Degree."

"today's global economy": Hart Research Associates, "It Takes More Than
a Major: Employer Priorities for College Learning and Student Success,"
Liberal Education 99, no. 2 (Spring 2013), https://www.aacu.org
/publications-research/periodicals/it-takes-more-major-employer
-priorities-college-learning-and.

"engineering majors by 10 percent": Alice Ma, "You Don't Need to Know
How to Code to Make It in Silicon Valley," Official LinkedIn Blog,
August 25, 2015, https://blog.linkedin.com/2015/08/25/you-dont-need
-to-know-how-to-code-to-make-it-in-silicon-valley.

29 *"zero to one"*: Peter A. Thiel and Blake Masters, *Zero to One: Notes on
Startups, or How to Build the Future* (New York: Crown Business, 2014).

"some kind of social change": Sam Altman and Mark Zuckerberg, "Mark

Zuckerberg: How to Build the Future," YouTube video, August 16, 2016, https://www.youtube.com/watch?v=Lb4IcGF5iTQ.

30 *tech and nontech functions:* Michael E. Porter and James E. Heppelmann, "How Smart, Connected Products Are Transforming Companies," *Harvard Business Review,* October 2015, https://hbr.org/2015/10 /how-smart-connected-products-are-transforming-companies.

2. ADDING THE HUMAN FACTOR TO BIG DATA

31 *Vietnamese exclusive economic zone (EEZ):* Erica S. Downs, "Business and Politics in the South China Sea: Explaining HYSY 981's Foray into Disputed Waters," Brookings, June 24, 2014, https://www.brookings .edu/articles/business-and-politics-in-the-south-china-sea-explaining -hysy-981s-foray-into-disputed-waters/.
under his command: Andreas Xenachis, telephone interview by author, May 25, 2016.

32 *layers of defense:* Zack Cooper, email interview by author, September 21, 2016.
projected to go to Asia: Shen Dingli, Elizabeth Economy, Richard Haass, Joshua Kurlantzick, Sheila A. Smith, and Simon Tay, "China's Maritime Disputes," A CFR InfoGuide Presentation, 2016, http://www.cfr.org /asia-and-pacific/chinas-maritime-disputes/p31345#!/?cid=otrmarketing _use-china_sea_InfoGuide.

33 *designed for fighter jets:* Jane Perlez, "China Building Aircraft Runway in Disputed Spratly Islands," *New York Times,* April 16, 2015, http://www .nytimes.com/2015/04/17/world/asia/china-building-airstrip-in -disputed-spratly-islands-satellite-images-show.html.
can be claimed by many: Mike Ives, "Vietnam Objects to Chinese Oil Rig in Disputed Waters," *New York Times,* January 20, 2016, http://www .nytimes.com/2016/01/21/world/asia/south-china-sea-vietnam-china.html.
under international law: "A Freedom of Navigation Primer for the Spratly Islands," Asia Maritime Transparency Initiative (AMTI), 2015, https:// amti.csis.org/fonops-primer/.
U.S. sonar array: Andrew S. Erickson, "The Pentagon's 2016 China Mil- itary Report: What You Need to Know," *National Interest,* May 14, 2016, http://nationalinterest.org/feature/the-pentagons-2016-china-military -report-what-you-need-know-16209.
near the Philippines: Alexander Neill, "The Submarines and Rivalries Underneath the South China Sea," BBC News, July 11, 2016, http:// www.bbc.com/news/world-asia-36574590.

major international crisis: David Pilling, "US v China: Is This the New Cold War?," *Financial Times,* June 10, 2015, https://www.ft.com/content /a301aa60-0dcf-11e5-aa7b-00144feabdc0.

34 *security of the rig:* Ernest Z. Bower and Gregory B. Poling, "China-Vietnam Tensions High over Drilling Rig in Disputed Waters," Center for Strategic and International Studies, May 7, 2014, https://www.csis .org/analysis/china-vietnam-tensions-high-over-drilling-rig-disputed -waters.

"challenge Chinese coercion": Zack Cooper, email interview by author, September 21, 2016.

35 *honing his analytical skills:* "Andreas Xenachis," Truman National Security Project, 2016, http://trumanproject.org/home/team-view/andreas -xenachis/.

36 *prone to break down:* Tim Harford, "How to See into the Future," *Financial Times,* September 5, 2014, https://www.ft.com/content/3950604a -33bc-11e4-ba62-00144feabdc0.

in the South China Sea: "Aggregative Contingent Estimation (ACE)," Office of the Director of National Intelligence (IARPA), https://www.iarpa .gov/index.php/research-programs/ace.

37 *the next secretary-general of the United Nations:* Stephen J. Dubner and Philip Tetlock, "How to Be Less Terrible at Predicting the Future," *Freakonomics* (podcast), January 14, 2016, http://freakonomics.com /podcast/how-to-be-less-terrible-at-predicting-the-future-a-new -freakonomics-radio-podcast/.

38 *results of the competition were astounding:* "The Good Judgment Project," *CHIPS,* January–March 2015, http://www.doncio.navy.mil/CHIPS /ArticleDetails.aspx?ID=5976.

"Humans are more important than hardware": "SOF Truths," U.S. Army Special Operations Command, http://www.soc.mil/USASOCHQ /SOFTruths.html.

ever read on prediction: Cass R. Sunstein, "Prophets, Psychics and Phools: The Year in Behavioral Science," Bloomberg.com, December 14, 2015, https://www.bloomberg.com/view/articles/2015-12-14/prophets-psychics -and-phools-the-year-in-behavioral-science.

39 *on his desk:* David Brooks, "Forecasting Fox," *New York Times,* March 21, 2013, http://www.nytimes.com/2013/03/22/opinion/brooks -forecasting-fox.html.

human smarts and data: Ibid.

need to be prepared: Philip E. Tetlock and Paul J. H. Shoemaker,

"Superforecasting: How to Upgrade Your Company's Judgment," *Harvard Business Review,* May 2016, https://hbr.org/2016/05/superforecasting-how-to-upgrade-your-companys-judgment.

electric vehicle adoption in China: Michelle Eckert, "Help Wharton Forecast the Future of Electric Vehicles," Mack Institute for Innovation Management, April 21, 2016, https://mackinstitute.wharton.upenn.edu/2016/electric-vehicles-forecasting-challenge/.

40   *"is becoming obsolete":* Chris Anderson, "The End of Theory: The Data Deluge Makes the Scientific Method Obsolete," *Wired,* June 23, 2008, http://www.wired.com/2008/06/pb-theory/.

"we need smart questioners": Luciano Floridi, *The Fourth Revolution: How the Infosphere Is Reshaping Human Reality* (Oxford: Oxford University Press, 2014), 129–130.

41   *called "the cloud":* Gary Marcus and Ernest Davis, "Eight (No, Nine!) Problems with Big Data," *New York Times,* April 6, 2014, http://www.nytimes.com/2014/04/07/opinion/eight-no-nine-problems-with-big-data.html.

improve crop yields: Dan Charles, "Should Farmers Give John Deere and Monsanto Their Data?," NPR, January 22, 2014, http://www.npr.org/sections/thesalt/2014/01/21/264577744/should-farmers-give-john-deere-and-monsanto-their-data.

human role in analyzing data: Anderson, "The End of Theory."

42   *match human ability:* Jeremy Bernstein, "A.I.," *The New Yorker,* December 14, 1981, http://www.newyorker.com/magazine/1981/12/14/a-i.

today's technology: M. Mitchell Waldrop, "Computing's Johnny Appleseed," *MIT Technology Review,* January 1, 2000, https://www.technologyreview.com/s/400633/computings-johnny-appleseed/.

43   *Anthony Goldbloom:* Anthony Goldbloom, telephone interview by author, April 4, 2016.

44   *a midsize airline:* Tomio Geron, "GE Uses Crowdsourcing to Solve Air Travel Delays and Healthcare," *Forbes,* November 29, 2012, http://www.forbes.com/sites/tomiogeron/2012/11/29/ge-launches-crowdsourcing-quests-to-solve-air-travel-delays-and-healthcare/#14cd4dfe87b2.

85 percent of the time: "Now There's an App for That," *Economist,* September 19, 2015, http://www.economist.com/news/science-and-technology/21664943-computers-can-recognise-complication-diabetes-can-lead-blindness-now.

45   *skills required in the market:* The Hewlett Foundation, "Hewlett Foundation Sponsors Prize to Improve Automated Scoring of Student Essays: Prize to Drive Better Tests, Deeper Learning," news release, January 9,

2012, http://www.hewlett.org/newsroom/press-release/hewlett
-foundation-sponsors-prize-improve-automated-scoring-student
-essays.

"faster and less expensively": "Hewlett Foundation Awards $100K to Win-
ners of Short Answer Scoring Competition," Getting Smart, October 4,
2012, http://gettingsmart.com/2012/10/the-hewlett-foundation
-announces-asap-competition-winners-automated-essay-scoring/.

$20 billion company: Sarah Buhr, "Palantir Has Raised $880 Million at a
$20 Billion Valuation," TechCrunch, December 23, 2015, https://
techcrunch.com/2015/12/23/palantir-has-raised-880-million-at-a-20
-billion-valuation/.

46 *secretive three-letter agencies*: Andrea Peterson, "Can You Really Use
Anti-Terrorist Technology to Choose Better Wine?," *Washington Post*,
September 13, 2013, https://www.washingtonpost.com/news/the-switch
/wp/2013/09/03/can-you-really-use-anti-terrorist-technology-to
-choose-better-wine/.

U.S. Special Operations Command: Hannah Lang, "Palantir Wins $222M
Contract to Provide Software Licenses to SOCOM," Washington Technology, May 26, 2016, https://washingtontechnology.com/articles/2016
/05/26/palantir-socom.aspx.

47 *"partnership with various technologies"*: Shyam Sankar, "The Rise of
Human-Computer Cooperation," speech, TEDGlobal 2012, Glasgow,
Scotland, June 2012, https://www.ted.com/talks/shyam_sankar_the
_rise_of_human_computer_cooperation.

48 *warned in 2016*: Megan Smith, D. J. Patil, and Cecilia Muñoz, "Big Risks,
Big Opportunities: The Intersection of Big Data and Civil Rights," *White
House Blog*, May 4, 2016, https://www.whitehouse.gov/blog/2016/05/04
/big-risks-big-opportunities-intersection-big-data-and-civil-rights.

distorted by many factors: "Predictive Policing," interview with Kristian
Lum, *Data Skeptic* (podcast), June 24, 2016, http://dataskeptic.com
/epnotes/predictive-policing.php.

49 *reported crime data*: Bureau of Justice Statistics, "Nearly 3.4 Million Violent Crimes per Year Went Unreported to Police from 2006 to 2010,"
news release, August 9, 2012, http://www.bjs.gov/content/pub/press
/vnrp0610pr.cfm.

response of police departments: "Predictive Policing," interview with
Kristian Lum; "Policing," Human Rights Data Analysis Group, https://
hrdag.org/policing/. See: "Kristian [Lum] and William Isaac have
collaborated on a statistical model that demonstrates how bias works
in predictive policing. They reimplemented the algorithm used by

one of the more popular vendors who sell this technology to police departments. The analysis shows how the predictive models reinforce existing police practices because they are based on databases of crimes known to police . . . As William [Isaac] said at a recent Stanford Law symposium, predictive policing tells us about patterns of police records, not patterns of crime. And as Patrick [Ball] said recently at a talk at the Data and Society Research Institute, technology and massive samples tend to amplify, not ameliorate, selection bias."

National Survey on Drug Use and Health: Kristian Lum and William Isaac, "To Predict and Serve?," *Significance* 13, no. 5 (2016): 14–19, doi:10.1111 /j.1740-9713.2016.00960.x.

drug use is roughly even across all ethnic groups: Ibid.

quotas for the discrepancy: The War on Marijuana in Black and White, report, American Civil Liberties Union (ACLU), June 2013, https://www .aclu.org/files/assets/aclu-thewaronmarijuana-rel2.pdf.

50   *"and mask opportunity":* Smith, Patil, and Muñoz, "Big Risks, Big Opportunities."

beyond traditional law enforcement: Vivian Ho, "Seeking a Better Bail System, SF Turns to Computer Algorithm," *San Francisco Chronicle,* August 1, 2016, http://www.sfchronicle.com/crime/article/Seeking-a -better-bail-system-SF-turns-to-8899654.php.

your gateway to access: Om Malik, "Uber, Data Darwinism and the Future of Work," Gigaom, March 17, 2013, https://gigaom.com/2013/03/17/uber -data-darwinism-and-the-future-of-work/.

"I'm not one of them": Cathy O'Neil, *Weapons of Math Destruction* (New York: Allen Lane, 2016).

51   *pernicious feedback loops:* Cathy O'Neil, "Weapons of Math Destruction," YouTube video, speech, Personal Democracy Forum, New York, June 7, 2015, https://www.youtube.com/watch?v=gdCJYsKlX_Y.

illustrates O'Neil's point: "Predictive Models on Random Data," interview, *Data Skeptic* (podcast), July 22, 2016, http://dataskeptic.com/epnotes /predictive-models-on-random-data.php.

Knowledge Discovery and Data Mining Cup: Claudia Perlich, "All the Data and Still Not Enough," YouTube video, lecture, Data Skeptics, New York, March 18, 2015, https://www.youtube.com/watch?v =dSOrc5kWGe8.

ultimately the patient: Claudia Perlich, Prem Melville, Yan Liu, Grzegorz Swirszcz, Richard Lawrence, and Saharon Rosset, *Winner's Report: KDD CUP Breast Cancer Identification,* report, 2008, http://www .prem-melville.com/publications/cup-kdd08.pdf.

53 *"They are fundamentally moral"*: O'Neil, *Weapons of Math Destruction*, 218.

"making data science cool": Jeff Chu, "Most Creative People 2013: 99–100. Hilary Mason, Leslie Bradshaw," *Fast Company*, May 13, 2013, http:// www.fastcompany.com/3009220/most-creative-people-2013/99-100 -hilary-mason-leslie-bradshaw.

"data literacy": Leslie Bradshaw, Beyond Data Science: Advancing Data Literacy," *Medium* (blog), December 17, 2014, https://medium.com /the-many/moving-from-data-science-to-data-literacy-a2f181ba4167# .bwiz7hc1g.

"Just Do It": Jeremy W. Peters, "The Birth of 'Just Do It' and Other Magic Words," *New York Times*, August 19, 2009, http://www.nytimes .com/2009/08/20/business/media/20adco.html?_r=0.

"analysis to presentation": Bradshaw, "Beyond Data Science."

55 *analytical, and quantitative skills:* National Association of Colleges and Employers (NACE), "Employers Seek for Evidence of Leadership, Teamwork Skills on Resumes," news release, November 6, 2015, http:// www.naceweb.org/about-us/press/employers-seek-leadership -teamwork-skills.aspx.

(A *striking 15 percent*): Hazel Sheffield, "Google Spends Years Figuring Out That the Secret to a Good Working Environment Is Just to Be Nice," *Independent*, March 7, 2016, http://www.independent.co.uk /news/business/news/google-workplace-wellbeing-perks-benefits -human-behavioural-psychology-safety-a6917296.html.

56 *intelligence was contribution:* A. W. Woolley, C. F. Chabris, A. Pentland, N. Hashmi, and T. W. Malone, "Evidence for a Collective Intelligence Factor in the Performance of Human Groups," *Science* 330, no. 6004 (2010): 686–88, doi:10.1126/science.1193147.

57 *"average social sensitivity" mattered most:* Charles Duhigg, "What Google Learned from Its Quest to Build the Perfect Team," *New York Times*, February 25, 2016, http://www.nytimes.com/2016/02/28/magazine /what-google-learned-from-its-quest-to-build-the-perfect-team.html.

"trade tasks": David J. Deming, "The Growing Importance of Social Skills in the Labor Market," working paper, Graduate School of Education, Harvard University and NBER, August 2015, http://scholar.harvard.edu /files/ddeming/files/deming_socialskills_august2015.pdf.

3. THE DEMOCRATIZATION OF TECHNOLOGY TOOLS

60 *weight of a satellite:* Tim Fernholz, "SpaceX Just Made Rocket Launches Affordable. Here's How It Could Make Them Downright Cheap," *Quartz*, December 4, 2013, http://qz.com/153969/spacex-just-made

-rocket-launches-affordable-heres-how-it-could-make-them-downright
-cheap/.

61 *for commercial shippers:* G. W. Bowersock, "Marcus Vipsanius Agrippa,"
Encyclopedia Britannica Online, https://www.britannica.com/biography
/Marcus-Vipsanius-Agrippa.

due to foul intent: Robert Vamosi, "Big Data Is Stopping Maritime
Pirates . . . from Space," *Forbes,* November 11, 2014, http://www.forbes
.com/sites/robertvamosi/2014/11/11/big-data-is-stopping-maritime
-pirates-from-space/#58993f1265fa.

missiles without warning: David E. Sanger and Martin Fackler, "N.S.A.
Breached North Korean Networks Before Sony Attack, Officials Say,"
New York Times, January 18, 2015, http://www.nytimes.com/2015/01/19
/world/asia/nsa-tapped-into-north-korean-networks-before-sony
-attack-officials-say.html.

trafficking narcotics: Associated Press, "US Blacklists Singapore Shipping
Firm over North Korean Weapons Smuggling," *Guardian,* July 23, 2015,
https://www.theguardian.com/world/2015/jul/24/us-blacklists-singapore
-shipping-firm-over-north-korean-weapons-smuggling.

nine days in July 2014: Claudia Rosett, "North Korean Ship Tests the
Waters Near America's Shores," *Forbes,* July 13, 2014, http://www
.forbes.com/sites/claudiarosett/2014/07/13/north-korean-ship-tests
-the-waters-near-americas-shores/#6ee2923e492a.

tracking on the open ocean: Automatic Identification System, § 33 CFR
401.20. See also International Maritime Organization (http://www.imo
.org/en/OurWork/safety/navigation/pages/ais.aspx) regarding the International Convention for the Safety of Life at Sea (SOLAS) maritime
treaty in effect since 1980.

over nine thousand tons of cargo: Scott A. Snyder, "Behind the *Chong Chon
Gang* Affair: North Korea's Shadowy Arms Trade," Council on Foreign
Relations, March 19, 2014, http://blogs.cfr.org/asia/2014/03/19/behind
-the-chong-chon-gang-affair-north-koreas-shadowy-arms-trade/;
"Vessel Details for: CHONG CHON GANG (General Cargo)—IMO
7937317, MMSI 445114000, Call Sign HMZF Registered in DPR Korea |
AIS Marine Traffic," MarineTraffic.com, August 29, 2016, http://www
.marinetraffic.com/ro/ais/details/ships/445114000.

62 *cigarettes and consumer goods:* Sheena Chestnut, "Illicit Activity and
Proliferation: North Korean Smuggling Networks," *International Security*
32, no. 1 (2007): 80–111, doi:10.1162/isec.2007.32.1.80.

(and the Washington Post *says it works):* Anna Fifield, "We Scrutinized
North Korean 'Viagra'—and Discovered It Might Actually Work,"

Washington Post, August 10, 2016, https://www.washingtonpost.com
/world/asia_pacific/we-scrutinized-north-korean-viagra—and
-discovered-it-might-actually-work/2016/08/10/ca181d0c-58d6-11e6
-8b48-0cb344221131_story.html.

"regime slush fund": Tom Burgis, "North Korea: The Secrets of Office
39," *Financial Times,* June 24, 2015, https://www.ft.com/content
/4164dfe6-09d5-11e5-b6bd-00144feabdc0.

nuclear weapons ambitions: "Commission Implementing Regulation (EU)
2015/1062," EUR-Lex Access to European Union Law, July 2, 2015, http://
eur-lex.europa.eu/legal-content/EN/TXT/?uri=CELEX:32015R1062; U.S.
Department of the Treasury, "Treasury Sanctions DPRK Shipping Companies Involved in Illicit Arms Transfers," news release, July 30, 2014,
https://www.treasury.gov/press-center/press-releases/Pages/jl2594.aspx.

63 *unannounced stop in Tartus, Syria:* Oren Dorell, "North Korea Ship Held
in Panama Has a Colorful Past," *USA Today,* July 18, 2013, http://www
.usatoday.com/story/news/world/2013/07/17/n-korea-ship-checkered
-history/2524479/.

thousands of people have died: Edward Delman, "The Link Between
Putin's Military Campaigns in Syria and Ukraine," *Atlantic,* October 2,
2015, http://www.theatlantic.com/international/archive/2015/10/navy
-base-syria-crimea-putin/408694/; Adam Taylor, "The Syrian War's
Death Toll Is Absolutely Staggering. But No One Can Agree on
the Number," *Washington Post,* March 15, 2016, https://www
.washingtonpost.com/news/worldviews/wp/2016/03/15/the-syrian
-wars-death-toll-is-absolutely-staggering-but-no-one-can-agree
-on-the-number/.

maintaining the base: Jeffrey Mankoff, and Andrew Bowen, "Putin
Doesn't Care if Assad Wins. It's About Russian Power Projection," *Foreign Policy,* September 22, 2015, http://foreignpolicy.com/2015/09/22
/putin-russia-syria-assad-iran-islamic-state/.

reasons that were again unclear: Dorell, "North Korea Ship Held in
Panama."

64 *sale of weapons to North Korea:* Rick Gladstone and David E. Sanger,
"Panama Seizes Korean Ship, and Sugar-Coated Arms Parts," *New York
Times,* July 16, 2013, http://www.nytimes.com/2013/07/17/world
/americas/panama-seizes-north-korea-flagged-ship-for-weapons.html.

or so he claimed: Juan O. Tamayo. "N. Korean Freighter Runs Aground off
Mexico After Stop in Havana," *Miami Herald,* July 15, 2014, http://www
.miamiherald.com/news/nation-world/world/americas/article1975612
.html.

waters along their coasts: "Spire Sense," Spire Sense, August 29, 2016, https://spire.com/products/sense/.

65 *fishing within its waters:* Steve Mollman, "Indonesia Has a New Weapon Against Illegal Fishing: Nano-satellites," *Quartz,* April 28, 2016, http://qz.com/672122/indonesia-has-a-new-weapon-against-illegal-fishing-nano-satellites/.

67 *at greatly reduced cost:* Connie Loizos, "Spire, Maker of Radio-Size Satellites, Tunes Into $40 Million in New Funding," TechCrunch, June 30, 2015, https://techcrunch.com/2015/06/30/spire-maker-of-bottle-size-satellites-tunes-into-40-million-in-new-funding/.

"by changing the software": Peter B. de Selding, "The World According to Spire's CEO," SpaceNews.com, July 15, 2015, http://spacenews.com/the-world-according-to-platzer/.

68 *network of over one hundred satellites:* Peter B. de Selding, "Spire Global Aims to Orbit 25 Smallsats in 2015," SpaceNews.com, March 17, 2015, http://spacenews.com/spire-global-aims-to-orbit-25-smallsats-in-2015/.

lower than in the year 2000: Marc Andreessen, "Why Software Is Eating the World," *Wall Street Journal,* August 20, 2011, http://www.wsj.com/articles/SB10001424053111903480904576512250915629460. See "In 2000, when my partner Ben Horowitz was CEO of the first cloud computing company, Loudcloud, the cost of a customer running a basic Internet application was approximately $150,000 a month. Running that same application today in Amazon's cloud costs about $1,500 a month."

successful IPO in June of 2016: Corrie Driebusch, "Twilio Raises More Than Expected in IPO," *Wall Street Journal,* June 22, 2016, http://www.wsj.com/articles/twilio-ipo-tests-markets-appetite-for-tech-companies-1466606076.

69 *innovative products and services:* Sajith Pai, "If API Technology Is Good Enough for Uber, It's Good Enough for Your Media Company," *Tech Trends* (blog), International News Media Association (INMA), September 16, 2015, http://www.inma.org/blogs/tech-trends/post.cfm/if-api-technology-is-good-enough-for-uber-it-s-good-enough-for-your-media-company.

"full stack integrators": Peter Yared, "The Rise and Fall of the Full Stack Developer," TechCrunch, November 8, 2014, https://techcrunch.com/2014/11/08/the-rise-and-fall-of-the-full-stack-developer/.

sequences to play chess: George A. Miller, "The Magical Number Seven, Plus or Minus Two: Some Limits on Our Capacity for Processing

Information," *Psychological Review* 63, no. 2 (1956): 81–97, doi:10.1037 /h0043158; Pedro Domingos, *The Master Algorithm: How the Quest for the Ultimate Learning Machine Will Remake Our World* (New York: Basic Books, 2015). See page 225 on "chunking."

"becoming an asset class": Scott Hartley, "Rise of the Global Entrepreneurial Class," *Forbes,* March 25, 2012, http://www.forbes.com/sites /scotthartley/2012/03/25/conspicuous_creation/#4e5e4cd66683.

70 *Microsoft, and Oracle:* Mike Gualtieri, Rowan Curran, Holger Kisker, and Sophia Christakis, *The Forrester Wave: Big Data Predictive Analytics Solutions,* Q2 2015, report, Forrester, April 1, 2015, https://www .forrester.com/report/The Forrester Wave Big Data Predictive Analytics Solutions Q2 2015/-/E-RES115697.

71 *to create the Behance platform:* Romain Dillet, "Adobe Acquired Portfolio Service Behance for More Than $150 Million in Cash and Stock," TechCrunch, December 21, 2012, https://techcrunch.com/2012/12/21 /adobe-acquired-portfolio-service-behance-for-more-than-150-million -in-cash-and-stock/.

"'more creativity and ideas'": Scott Belsky, interview by Ryan Essmaker and Tina Essmaker, *Great Discontent,* July 30, 2013, http:// thegreatdiscontent.com/interview/scott-belsky.

72 *eight million public design projects:* Carey Dunne, "Behance Cofounder Matias Corea on How He Built a Thriving Hub for Creatives," Co.Design, March 25, 2015, http://www.fastcodesign.com/3044210/behance -cofounder-matias-corea-on-how-he-built-a-thriving-hub-for-creatives.

features by business sector: Anna Escher, "UpLabs Thinks Designers and Developers Should Hang Out More," TechCrunch, March 7, 2016, https://techcrunch.com/2016/03/07/uplabs-thinks-designers-and -developers-should-hang-out-more/.

73 *"factory of the future" for product creators:* Sarah Kessler, "Shapeways's New 3-D-Printing Factory Brings Manufacturing Jobs into the Tech Scene," *Fast Company,* October 24, 2012, https://www.fastcompany .com/3002303/shapewayss-new-3-d-printing-factory-brings -manufacturing-jobs-tech-scene.

74 *$550 billion by 2025:* Daniel Cohen, Matthew Sargeant, and Ken Somers, "3-D Printing Takes Shape," *McKinsey Quarterly,* January 2014, http:// www.mckinsey.com/business-functions/operations/our-insights/3-d -printing-takes-shape.

leverage underutilized assets: Patrick Sisson, "Rent Your Own Assembly Line from a New Manufacturing Startup," Curbed, September 29, 2015,

http://www.curbed.com/2015/9/29/9916234/make-time-distributed
-manufacturing-machine-design.

available in the Arduino library: Zoe Romano, "A DIY Seizure Alarm
Based on Arduino Micro," *Arduino Blog*, August 11, 2015, https://blog
.arduino.cc/2015/08/11/a-diy-seizure-alarm-based-on-arduino-micro/.

74 *journalism at Southeastern Louisiana University*: Chad Hebert, "Arduino
Seizure Alarm," *Chad Hebert: Writer, Editor, Designer, Dad* (blog),
June 7, 2015, http://hebertchad34.wixsite.com/chad-hebert/single-post
/2015/06/07/Arduino-Seizure-Alarm.

distributed manufacturing: Sisson, "Rent Your Own Assembly Line."

five thousand to seventy-five thousand overnight: Eric Ries, "How DropBox
Started as a Minimal Viable Product," TechCrunch, October 19, 2011,
https://techcrunch.com/2011/10/19/dropbox-minimal-viable-product/.

launch its first satellite: Anthony Ha, "NanoSatisfi Raises $1.2M to
Disrupt the Aerospace Industry with Small, Affordable Satellites,"
TechCrunch, February 7, 2013, https://techcrunch.com/2013/02/07
/nanosatisfi-funding/.

76 *then measure, then learn*: Eric Ries, *The Lean Startup: How Today's
Entrepreneurs Use Continuous Innovation to Create Radically Successful
Businesses* (New York: Crown Business, 2011).

77 *about a nickel today*: Mary Meeker, *2016 Internet Trends Report*, report,
Kleiner Perkins, June 1, 2016, http://www.kpcb.com/blog/2016
-internet-trends-report.

210 million hours of video each year: "Hours of Video Uploaded to You-
Tube Every Minute as of July 2015," Statista, 2016, http://www.statista
.com/statistics/259477/hours-of-video-uploaded-to-youtube-every
-minute/.

78 *Ruby, and Python*: Pratap Ranade, interview by author, August 25, 2016.

"convention over configuration": Sam Cervantes, email interview by author, November 15, 2016.

79 *also on the Apple website*: Frederic Lardinois, "Apple Launches Swift Playgrounds for iPad to Teach Kids to Code," TechCrunch, June 13, 2016,
https://techcrunch.com/2016/06/13/apple-launches-swift-playgrounds
-for-ipad-to-teach-kids-to-code/.

president of Yale for twenty years: George Anders, "Yale's Ex-President
Heads West to Become CEO of Coursera," *Forbes*, March 24, 2014,
http://www.forbes.com/sites/georgeanders/2014/03/24/yales-ex
-president-heads-west-to-become-ceo-of-coursera/#6ef8bd897973.

one of the world's fifty best: Harry McCracken, "50 Best Websites 2012,"

Time, September 15, 2012, http://techland.time.com/2012/09/18/50
-best-websites-2012/slide/codeacademy/.

80 *Airbnb, and AOL use Treehouse:* "Start Learning at Treehouse for Free,"
Treehouse, 2016, https://teamtreehouse.com/.

"My broad liberal education": "Nathan Bashaw," LinkedIn, November 10,
2016, https://www.linkedin.com/in/nbashaw.

Brimer sagely commented: Matthew Brimer, interview by author, April 20,
2016.

81 *"you read the plates," he explained:* Rahul Sidhu, telephone interview by
author, May 24, 2016.

84 *"we had typewriters":* Michael Schirling, telephone interview by author,
October 26, 2016.

4. ALGORITHMS THAT SERVE — RATHER THAN RULE — US

86 *"fashionista Moneyball":* Ryan Mac, "Stitch Fix: The $250 Million Startup
Playing Fashionista Moneyball," *Forbes,* June 1, 2016, http://www.forbes
.com/sites/ryanmac/2016/06/01/fashionista-moneyball-stitch-fix
-katrina-lake/#58b1b2d72e2e.

to her trustworthy, stylish sister: Sophia Stuart, "How a Camping Trip
Gone Awry Turned into a Personal Shopping Start-Up," *PC Magazine,*
February 11, 2016, http://www.pcmag.com/article2/0,2817,2499142,00
.asp.

87 *Asia Pacific and Latin America Operations:* Heather Wood Rudulph, "Get
That Life: How I Founded an Online Personal Shopping Company,"
Cosmopolitan, May 31, 2016, http://www.cosmopolitan.com/career
/a59033/katrina-lake-stitch-fix-get-that-life/.

89 *to make the program work:* Mac, "Stitch Fix: The $250 Million Startup."

90 *and came on board:* Ibid.

to make it successful: D. J. Das, "At Stitch Fix, Data Scientists and A.I.
Become Personal Stylists | CIO," Big Data Cloud, May 13, 2016, http://
www.bigdatacloud.com/at-stitch-fix-data-scientists-and-a-i-become
-personal-stylists-cio/.

"expert-human judgment": Jay B. Martin, Eric Colson, and Brad Klingenberg, "Feature Selection and Validation for Human Classifiers," 2015,
http://www.humancomputation.com/2015/papers/60_Paper.pdf.

91 *earned through recommendations:* Morgan Quinn, "12 Sneaky Ways
Amazon Gets You to Pay More," *Time,* June 17, 2016, http://time.com
/money/4373046/how-amazon-gets-you-to-pay-more/.

can understand preferences: Mary Meeker, *2016 Internet Trends Report,*

report, Kleiner Perkins, June 1, 2016, http://www.kpcb.com/blog/2016
-internet-trends-report.

bohemian or classic: Ibid.

92 *decision-making by the human stylists:* Eric Colson, "Combining Machine
Learning with Expert Human Judgment," lecture, Data Driven NYC,
AXA Headquarters, New York, March 16, 2016.

93 *mitigate their bias:* Martin, Colson, and Klingenberg, "Feature Selection
and Validation for Human Classifiers."

a fast yearly clip: Meeker, *2016 Internet Trends Report.*

came to discover as Stitch Fix: Mac, "Stitch Fix: The $250 Million
Startup."

"best I've ever worked with," he's admitted: Bill Gurley, "Benchmark
Partner Bill Gurley: Too Much Money Is My Biggest Problem," interview
by Kara Swisher, Recode, September 12, 2016, http://www.recode
.net/2016/9/12/12882780/bill-gurley-benchmark-bubble-venture
-capital-startups-uber.

lifestyle brand Urban Outfitters: Jason Del Ray, "Why Sephora's Digital
Boss Joined Stitch Fix, the Personal Stylist Startup That's Growing Like
Mad," Recode, March 22, 2015, http://www.recode.net/2015/3/22
/11560546/why-sephoras-digital-boss-joined-stitch-fix-the-personal
-stylist.

94 *94 richest self-made women:* Rob Wile, "Meet the 34-Year-Old Founder
of Stitch Fix, Who Just Became One of America's Richest Self-Made
Women," *Time,* December 27, 2017, http://time.com/money/5080173
/katrina-lake-net-worth-stitch-fix/.

95 *calls himself an "AI realist":* Jon Cifuentes, "Kayak Founder Launches
Lola, an iOS Travel App Backed by $20 Million," VentureBeat, May 12,
2012, http://venturebeat.com/2012/05/12/kayak-founder-launches-lola
-an-ios-travel-app-backed-by-20-million/.

96 *46 percent of travel bookings:* Paul English and Tracy Kidder, "How Kayak
Co-founder Paul English Got Hit by a 'Truck Full of Money,'" interview
by Kara Swisher, Recode, November 14, 2016, http://www.recode.net
/2016/11/14/13618488/kayak-paul-english-tracy-kidder-truck-money
-biography-podcast.

"should we be building AI backed by humans": Ibid.

aims to "magically schedule meetings": Michael Wilkerson, "This Startup
Wants to Use AI to Schedule Your Meetings," Tech.co, November 20,
2014, http://tech.co/startup-wants-use-ai-schedule-meetings-2014–11.

97 *hard to "magically schedule meetings":* Ellen Huet, "The Humans Hiding
Behind the Chatbots," Bloomberg.com, April 18, 2016, http://www

.bloomberg.com/news/articles/2016-04-18/the-humans-hiding-behind
-the-chatbots.

deliver those cupcakes: Jessi Hempel, "Facebook Launches M, Its Bold
Answer to Siri and Cortana," *Wired,* August 26, 2015, http://www.wired
.com/2015/08/facebook-launches-m-new-kind-virtual-assistant/.

"no longer doing for me": Nick Bilton, "Is Silicon Valley in Another Bub-
ble . . . and What Could Burst It?," *Vanity Fair*—Hive, September 1, 2015,
http://www.vanityfair.com/news/2015/08/is-silicon-valley-in-another
-bubble.

"assisted living for millennials": Kara Swisher, quoted in Mark Sullivan,
"Inside Munchery's Big 'Plaid Box' Meal-Delivery Expansion," *Fast
Company,* May 18, 2016, https://www.fastcompany.com/3057351/inside
-muncherys-big-plaid-box-meal-delivery-expansion.

98 *data and data mining:* "SIGKDD Awards," 2014 SIGKDD Innovation
Award: Pedro Domingos, 2014, http://www.kdd.org/awards/view
/2014-sigkdd-innovation-award-pedro-domingos.

"prone to temper tantrums": Pedro Domingos, *The Master Algorithm: How
the Quest for the Ultimate Learning Machine Will Remake Our World* (New
York: Basic Books, 2015). See page 258 on "if computers are like idiot
savants."

99 *clapping-hands emoji:* Alistair Charlton, "Microsoft 'Makes Adjustments'
After Tay AI Twitter Account Tweets Racism and Support for Hitler,"
International Business Times, March 24, 2016, http://www.ibtimes
.co.uk/microsoft-makes-adjustments-after-tay-ai-twitter-account
-tweets-racism-support-hitler-1551445.

"some adjustments": Sarah Perez, "Microsoft Silences Its New A.I. Bot
Tay, After Twitter Users Teach It Racism [Updated]," TechCrunch,
March 24, 2016, https://techcrunch.com/2016/03/24/microsoft-silences
-its-new-a-i-bot-tay-after-twitter-users-teach-it-racism/.

"Who benefits?": John West, "Microsoft's Disastrous Tay Experiment
Shows the Hidden Dangers of AI," *Quartz,* April 2, 2016, http://
qz.com/653084/microsofts-disastrous-tay-experiment-shows-the
-hidden-dangers-of-ai/.

"would have seen this coming": Leigh Alexander, "The Tech Industry
Wants to Use Women's Voices—They Just Won't Listen to Them,"
Guardian, March 28, 2016, https://www.theguardian.com/technology
/2016/mar/28/tay-bot-microsoft-ai-women-siri-her-ex-machina.

100 *and went horribly wrong:* Michael Lewis, *Flash Boys: A Wall Street Revolt*
(New York: W. W. Norton, 2014).

in just thirty-six minutes: Tom Schoenberg, Suzi Ring, and Janan Hanna, "Flash Crash Trader E-Mails Show Spoofing Strategy, U.S. Says," Bloomberg.com, September 3, 2015, http://www.bloomberg.com/news /articles/2015-09-03/flash-crash-trader-sarao-indicted-by-grand-jury -in-chicago-ie4n4s0s.

those stocks in advance: Ibid.

101 *New York Stock Exchange (NYSE) and NASDAQ:* Steven Bertoni, "Flash-boy Brad Katsuyama on the Future of IEX After Winning SEC Ap-proval," *Forbes,* July 1, 2016, http://www.forbes.com/sites/stevenbertoni /2016/07/01/flashboy-brad-katsuyama-on-the-future-of-iex-after -winning-sec-approval/#da2f1214d0c8.

a "Blue Feed" and a "Red Feed": Jon Keegan, "Blue Feed, Red Feed," *Wall Street Journal,* May 16, 2016, http://graphics.wsj.com/blue-feed-red -feed/.

wider range of perspectives: Brian Barrett, "Your Facebook Echo Chamber Just Got a Whole Lot Louder," *Wired,* June 29, 2016, http://www.wired .com/2016/06/facebook-embraces-news-feed-echo-chamber/.

102 *"humans failed, not Big Data":* Aaron Timms, "Is Donald Trump's Surprise Win a Failure of Big Data? Not Really," *Fortune,* November 14, 2016, http://fortune.com/2016/11/14/donald-trump-big-data-polls/.

the most tenured employee: Jessica Guynn, "Naomi Gleit Helps Keep Face-book Growing," *Los Angeles Times,* December 22, 2012, http://articles .latimes.com/2012/dec/22/business/la-fi-himi-gleit-20121223.

103 *"expand on that system," he explained:* Soleio Cuervo, telephone interview by author, March 29, 2016.

104 *exceeding 25 percent:* Elizabeth Dwoskin, "Lending Startups Look at Borrowers' Phone Usage to Assess Creditworthiness," *Wall Street Journal,* November 30, 2015, http://www.wsj.com/articles/lending -startups-look-at-borrowers-phone-usage-to-assess-creditworthiness -1448933308.

are often left behind: Shivani Siroya, "Helping Developing Entrepreneurs Lift Their Communities Out of Poverty," *Huffington Post* (blog), October 19, 2010, http://www.huffingtonpost.com/shivani-siroya/inventure -empowers-develo_b_767994.html.

clarity around the market: John Aglionby, "US Fintech Pioneer's Start-Up in Kenya," *Financial Times,* July 5, 2016, https://www.ft.com/content /05e65d04-3c7a-11e6-9f2c-36b487ebd80a.

105 *tend to be better borrowers:* Dwoskin, "Lending Startups Look at Borrow-ers' Phone Usage."

was around 5 percent: Aglionby, "US Fintech Pioneer's Start-Up."

satisfied with their first experience: David Lidsky, "Most Innovative Companies 2015: Inventure," *Fast Company,* February 9, 2015, http://www.fastcompany.com/3039583/most-innovative-companies-2015/inventure.

between 6 and 12 percent: Dwoskin, "Lending Startups Look at Borrowers' Phone Usage."

106   *qualifications to be approved:* "Leveraging Technology Solutions in Credit and Verification," Lenddo, 2016, https://www.lenddo.com/.

subconscious appeal of images: Deborah Gage, "Neon Labs Raises $4.1M to Figure Out the Subconscious Appeal of Images," *Venture Capital Dispatch* (blog), *Wall Street Journal,* July 15, 2014, http://blogs.wsj.com/venturecapital/2014/07/15/neon-labs-raises-4-1m-to-figure-out-the-subconscious-appeal-of-images/.

conscious of making the choice: Alexandre N. Tuch, Eva E. Presslaber, Markus Stöcklin, Klaus Opwis, and Javier A. Bargas-Avila, "The Role of Visual Complexity and Prototypicality Regarding First Impression of Websites: Working Towards Understanding Aesthetic Judgments," *International Journal of Human-Computer Studies* 70, no. 11 (2012): 794–811, doi:10.1016/j.ijhcs.2012.06.003.

that work into a patent: Sophie Lebrecht, Moshe Bar, Lisa Feldman Barrett, and Michael J. Tarr, "Micro-Valences: Perceiving Affective Valence in Everyday Objects," *Frontiers in Psychology* 3 (2012), doi:10.3389/fpsyg.2012.00107.

107   *neuroscience-based machine learning:* Lauren Schwartzberg, "Most Creative People 2015: Sophie Lebrecht," *Fast Company,* May 11, 2015, https://www.fastcompany.com/3043930/most-creative-people-2015/sophie-lebrecht.

the thirty-first Olympiad: "NBCUniversal to Provide Record 6,755 Hours from Rio Olympics," NBC Olympics, June 28, 2016, http://www.nbcolympics.com/news/nbcuniversal-provide-record-6755-hours-rio-olympics.

as many as two thousand images each: David Pierce, "Inside the Daunting Job of a Super Bowl Photographer," The Verge, February 3, 2013, http://www.theverge.com/2013/2/3/3947574/inside-the-daunting-job-of-a-super-bowl-photographer; Richard Deitsch, "Inside NBC's Production Truck for Super Bowl XLIX's Wild Finish," *Sports Illustrated,* February 2, 2015, http://www.si.com/nfl/2015/02/02/super-bowl-xlix-broadcast-nbc-patriots-seahawks.

5. MAKING OUR TECHNOLOGY MORE ETHICAL

109 *"user-centered design"*: Donald A. Norman, *The Psychology of Everyday Things* (New York: Basic Books, 1988). See subsequent title, *The Design of Everyday Things* as well.

110 *"to humanize technology"*: Donald A. Norman, *Turn Signals Are the Facial Expressions of Automobiles* (Reading, MA: Addison-Wesley, 1992).
semaphores between drivers: Will Knight, "10 Breakthrough Technologies 2015: Car-to-Car Communication," *MIT Technology Review,* 2015, https://www.technologyreview.com/s/534981/car-to-car-communication/; Ron Miller, "Volvo Brings Cloud to the Car to Transmit Safety Data Automatically," TechCrunch, March 4, 2015, https://techcrunch.com/2015/03/04/volvo-brings-cloud-to-the-car-to-transmit-safety-data-automatically/.
developing at Nissan: Brett Berk, "How Nissan's Using Anthropology to Make Autonomous Cars Safe," The Drive, November 24, 2015, http://www.thedrive.com/tech/999/how-nissans-using-anthropology-to-make-autonomous-cars-safe.

111 *"that make our heart sing"*: Jonah Lehrer, "Steve Jobs: 'Technology Alone Is Not Enough,'" *The New Yorker,* October 7, 2011, http://www.newyorker.com/news/news-desk/steve-jobs-technology-alone-is-not-enough.
products leading the way: Mark Zachry, "An Interview with Donald A. Norman," *Technical Communication Quarterly* 14, no. 4 (2005): 469–87, doi:10.1207/s15427625tcq1404_5.
that overwhelm us: Edward Tenner, *Why Things Bite Back: Technology and the Revenge of Unintended Consequences* (New York: Knopf, 1996).
company called Tiny Speck: Maya Kosoff, "The Amazing Life of Stewart Butterfield, the CEO of One of the Fastest-Growing Business Apps Ever," Business Insider, September 1, 2015, http://www.businessinsider.com/amazing-life-of-slack-ceo-stewart-butterfield-2015-9/.

112 *over 2.7 million daily users:* Josh Constine, "Slack's Growth Is Insane, with Daily User Count up 3.5X in a Year," TechCrunch, April 1, 2016, https://techcrunch.com/2016/04/01/rocketship-emoji/.
19 percent in information gathering: James Manyika, Michael Chui, and Hugo Sarrazin, "Social Media's Productivity Payoff," *Harvard Business Review,* August 21, 2012, https://hbr.org/2012/08/social-medias-productivity-pay.
"they're going to give you back time": "Silicon Valley's Homogeneous 'Rich Douchebags' Won't Win Forever, Says Investor Chamath Palihapitiya," interview, *Recode Decode* (podcast), March 21, 2016, http://www

.recode.net/2016/3/21/11587128/silicon-valleys-homogeneous-rich
-douchebags-wont-win-forever-says.

tools built with human-centered technology: Gentry Underwood, "Beyond
Ethnography: How the Design of Social Software Obscures Observation and Intervention," lecture, July 8, 2010, https://www.parc.com
/event/1134/beyond-ethnography.html.

113   *requires all of us to participate:* Don Norman and Bruce Tognazzini, "How
Apple Is Giving Design a Bad Name," FastCo Design, November 10,
2015, https://www.fastcodesign.com/3053406/how-apple-is-giving
-design-a-bad-name.

efficiency in product design: Brian X. Chen, "Simplifying the Bull: How
Picasso Helps to Teach Apple's Style," *New York Times,* August 10,
2014, http://www.nytimes.com/2014/08/11/technology/-inside-apples
-internal-training-program-.html.

and UC Berkeley: Andrew Cohen, "Leading Political Theorist Joshua Cohen Joins Berkeley Law Faculty," Berkeley Law, March 26, 2015, https://
www.law.berkeley.edu/article/leading-political-theorist-joshua-cohen
-joins-berkeley-law-faculty/.

114   *more pastoral settings:* John Schwenkler, "The Democratic Beauty of
Central Park," *Commonweal* (blog), January 3, 2013, https://www
.commonwealmagazine.org/blog/democratic-beauty-central-park.

foster the human good: Tristan Harris, "How Better Tech Could Protect
Us from Distraction," lecture, June 2014, https://www.ted.com/talks
/tristan_harris_how_better_tech_could_protect_us_from_distraction.

115   *Persuasive Technology Laboratory (PTL):* Ibid.

how people develop habits: "10 New Gurus You Should Know: BJ Fogg,"
Fortune, November 8, 2008, http://archive.fortune.com/galleries/2008
/fortune/0811/gallery.10_new_gurus.fortune/.

Psychology of Facebook: B. J. Fogg, "Mass Interpersonal Persuasion: An
Early View of a New Phenomenon," *Persuasive Technology Lecture Notes
in Computer Science* (2008): 23–34, doi:10.1007/978-3-540-68504-3_3.

"paths to global peace": Jordan Larson, "The Invisible, Manipulative
Power of Persuasive Technology," *Pacific Standard,* May 14, 2014,
https://psmag.com/the-invisible-manipulative-power-of-persuasive
-technology-df61a9883cc7.

116   *company, which he called Apture:* April Joyner, "30 Under 30 2009:
Apture—Tristan Harris, Can Sar, and Jesse Young," Inc.com, 2009,
http://www.inc.com/30under30/2009/profile_apture.html.

a reported $18 million: Brad McCarty, "Google Pays $18 Million to Shut-
ter Apture, CloudFlare Clones It in 12 Hours," The Next Web, Decem-

ber 19, 2011, http://thenextweb.com/insider/2011/12/19/google-pays
-18-million-to-shutter-apture-cloudflare-clones-it-in-12-hours/; Amir
Efrati, "Google Acquisition Binge Continues with Apture, Katango,"
Wall Street Journal, November 10, 2011, http://www.wsj.com/articles
/DJFVW00020111110e7bal79xd.

called Time Well Spent: Jo Confino, "Google Seeks Out Wisdom of Zen
Master Thich Nhat Hanh," *Guardian,* September 5, 2013, https://www
.theguardian.com/sustainable-business/global-technology-ceos
-wisdom-zen-master-thich-nhat-hanh.

concentrated creative thought: Harris, "How Better Tech Could Protect
Us."

117 *about diverting the eye:* Tristan Harris, "How Technology Hijacks People's
Minds — from a Magician and Google's Design Ethicist," *Medium* (blog),
May 18, 2016, https://medium.com/swlh/how-technology-hijacks
-peoples-minds-from-a-magician-and-google-s-design-ethicist
-56d62ef5edf3.

hijacking people's attention: Tristan Harris, "Distracted? Let's Demand a
New Kind of Design," YouTube video, lecture, April 1, 2015, https://
www.youtube.com/watch?v=3OhMJh8IKbE. See 2015 conference,
Wisdom 2.0.

"attention of its recipients": "Herbert Simon," *Economist,* March 20, 2009,
http://www.economist.com/node/13350892. See also "The Economist
Guide to Management Ideas and Gurus."

118 *services that respect our time:* Harris, "How Technology Hijacks People's
Minds."

"bicycles for our minds": Tristan Harris, "Is Technology Amplifying Human Potential, or Amusing Ourselves to Death?" *Tristan Harris* (blog),
March 6, 2015, http://www.tristanharris.com/2015/03/is-design-for
-amplifying-human-potential-or-amusing-ourselves-to-death/.

"continuous partial attention": Thomas L. Friedman, "The Age of Interruption," *New York Times,* July 5, 2006, http://www.nytimes.com/2006
/07/05/opinion/05friedman.html.

continually, partially attuned: Linda Stone, "Continuous Partial Attention," *Linda Stone* (blog), https://lindastone.net/qa/continuous-partial
-attention/.

moments every single day: Lisa Eadicicco, "Americans Check Their
Phones 8 Billion Times a Day," *Time,* December 15, 2015, http://time
.com/4147614/smartphone-usage-us-2015/.

119 *"interruption science":* Bob Sullivan and Hugh Thompson, "Brain, Inter-

rupted," *New York Times,* May 3, 2013, http://www.nytimes.com/2013
/05/05/opinion/sunday/a-focus-on-distraction.html.

regain focus on a task: Rachel Emma Silverman, "Workplace
Distractions: Here's Why You Won't Finish This Article," *Wall
Street Journal,* December 11, 2012, http://www.wsj.com/articles
/SB10001424127887324339204578173252223022388.

closer to every forty seconds: Gloria Mark, telephone interview by author,
April 6, 2016.

120 *are more productive:* Gloria Mark, Shamsi T. Iqbal, Mary Czerwinski,
Paul Johns, Akane Sano, and Yuliya Lutchyn, "Email Duration,
Batching and Self-interruption," *Proceedings of the 2016 CHI Conference on Human Factors in Computing Systems—CHI '16,* May 7, 2016,
doi:10.1145/2858036.2858262.

focus more on work: Kermit Pattison, "Worker, Interrupted: The
Cost of Task Switching," *Fast Company,* July 28, 2008, https://www
.fastcompany.com/944128/worker-interrupted-cost-task-switching.

however, is stress: Gloria Mark, Daniela Gudith, and Ulrich Klocke, "The
Cost of Interrupted Work," *Proceedings of the Twenty-Sixth Annual CHI
Conference on Human Factors in Computing Systems—CHI '08,* 2008,
doi:10.1145/1357054.1357072.

121 *known to be highly addictive:* Nir Eyal, "Want to Hook Your Users? Drive
Them Crazy," TechCrunch, March 25, 2012, https://techcrunch
.com/2012/03/25/want-to-hook-your-users-drive-them-crazy/.

rate of other gambling: Natasha Dow Schüll, *Addiction by Design: Machine
Gambling in Las Vegas* (Princeton, NJ: Princeton University Press, 2012).

today's one-finger bandits: "one-armed bandit," Dictionary.com, http://
www.dictionary.com/browse/one-armed-bandit; Christine Ammer, *The
American Heritage Dictionary of Idioms* (New York: Houghton Mifflin
Harcourt).

"is part of the design": Tristan Harris, "Smartphone Addiction: The Slot
Machine in Your Pocket," Spiegel Online, July 27, 2016, http://www
.spiegel.de/international/zeitgeist/smartphone-addiction-is-part-of
-the-design-a-1104237.html.

"what's going to come next": Harris, "Distracted? Let's Demand a New
Kind of Design."

122 *"navigating toward their goals":* Harris, "How Technology Hijacks People's Minds."

"the way you want it to": Harris, "Distracted? Let's Demand a New Kind
of Design."

123   *ubiquitous in technology products*: Joe Edelman, "Choicemaking and the
      Interface," *NXHX.org* (blog), 2014, http://nxhx.org/Choicemaking/.

124   *"chooses from the options given"*: Joe Edelman, "Is Anything Worth Maxi-
      mizing?," *Medium* (blog), April 12, 2016, https://medium.com/@edelwax
      /is-anything-worth-maximizing-d11e648eb56f.

125   *"consciousness filter"*: Bianca Bosker. "The Binge Breaker," *Atlantic*,
      November 2016, http://www.theatlantic.com/magazine/archive/2016/11
      /the-binge-breaker/501122/.
      had on passenger behavior: Kareem Haggag and Giovanni Paci, "Default
      Tips," *American Economic Journal: Applied Economics* 6, no. 3 (2014): 1–19,
      doi:10.1257/app.6.3.1.

126   *just because of the menu*: Cass Sunstein, "Check Here to Tip Taxi Drivers
      or Save for 401(k)," Bloomberg.com, April 9, 2013, https://www
      .bloomberg.com/view/articles/2013-04-09/check-here-to-tip-taxi
      -drivers-or-save-for-401-k-.
      contact with this lock screen: Joe Edelman, "Empowering Design (Ending
      the Attention Economy, Talk #1)," lecture, 2015, https://vimeo
      .com/123488311. See also Tristan Harris's interpretation in "How Tech-
      nology Hijacks People's Minds—from a Magician and Google's Design
      Ethicist."

127   *"disinterested in social concerns"*: Norman, *Turn Signals Are the Facial
      Expressions*.
      to point at an arrow: Daniel S. Venolia and Shinpei Ishikawa, Three
      Degree of Freedom Graphic Object Controller. US Patent US5313230 A,
      filed July 24, 1992, and issued May 17, 1994.

128   *psychology professor Daniel Kahneman*: Richard H. Thaler and Cass R.
      Sunstein, *Nudge: Improving Decisions About Health, Wealth, and Happiness*
      (New Haven, CT: Yale University Press, 2008).

129   *"being our intellectual surrogates"*: Damon Horowitz, "From Technologist
      to Philosopher," *Chronicle of Higher Education*, July 17, 2011, http://www
      .chronicle.com/article/From-Technologist-to/128231/.
      $50 million in 2010: Michael Arrington, "Google Acquires Aardvark for
      $50 Million (Confirmed)," TechCrunch, February 11, 2010, https://
      techcrunch.com/2010/02/11/google-acquires-aardvark-for-50-million/.

130   *the world was binary*: Sean Duffy, interview by author, April 11, 2016.

131   *Duffy wasn't so sure*: Christina DesMarais, "How Self-Tracking Can Bene-
      fit Business," Inc.com, March 14, 2011, http://www.inc.com/managing
      /articles/201103/how-self-tracking-can-benefit-business.html.

132   *diabetes fell by 58 percent*: Diabetes Prevention Program Research Group,

"Reduction in the Incidence of Type 2 Diabetes with Lifestyle Intervention or Metformin," *New England Journal of Medicine* 346, no. 6 (2002): 393–403, doi:10.1056/nejmoa012512.

preserved the human touch: Ibid.

133 *"challenge of the twenty-first century":* *The Power of Prevention: Chronic Disease . . . the Public Health Challenge of the 21st Century,* report, National Center for Chronic Disease Prevention and Health Promotion, Centers for Disease Control (CDC), 2009, http://www.cdc.gov/chronicdisease /pdf/2009-power-of-prevention.pdf.

134 *"resembles a symphony":* Sean Duffy, interview by author, April 11, 2016.

135 *"behavior change so difficult":* Steven Johnson, "Recognising the True Potential of Technology to Change Behaviour," *Guardian,* December 13, 2013, https://www.theguardian.com/sustainable-business/behavioural -insights/true-potential-technology-change-behaviour.

136 *over three hundred thousand users:* Talkspace, 2016, https://www .talkspace.com/.

become a therapist herself: Teresa Novellino, "Talkspace Raises $9.5M to Let Users Text Their Therapists," *New York Business Journal,* May 13, 2015, http://www.bizjournals.com/newyork/news/2015/05/13/therapy -via-text-startup-raises-9-5-m-series-a.html.

deterrent in many circles: Ibid.

under $130 a month: Joseph Rauch, "How Much Does Therapy Cost? (And Why Is It So Expensive?)," *Talkspace* (blog), October 29, 2015, https://www.talkspace.com/blog/2015/10/how-much-does-therapy -cost-and-why-is-it-crazy-expensive/.

137 *Alpha Tau Omega:* Sara Ashley O'Brien, "Frat Brothers Get Free Text Therapy," CNN, September 22, 2016, http://money.cnn.com/2016/09 /22/technology/text-therapy-talkspace-ato-fraternity/.

students, or alumni: Oren Frank, email interview by author, September 26, 2016.

138 *session with a therapist:* Jordyn Taylor, "We Texted a Therapist from an Inflatable Igloo in Madison Square Park Today," *Observer,* November 5, 2014, http://observer.com/2014/11/we-texted-a-therapist-from-an -inflatable-igloo-in-madison-square-park-today/.

sidewalk at the park's edge: Talkspace, "Talkspace #ReflectReality Funhouse Mirror," YouTube (video blog), October 5, 2015, https://www .youtube.com/watch?t=5&v=NsLfu4Sko0U.

"The roof is on fire!": Natt Garun, "Talkspace Wants You to Combat Social Media Addiction by Texting a Therapist," The Next Web, September

16, 2015, http://thenextweb.com/apps/2015/09/16/does-this-filter-make
-me-look-skinny/#gref.

139 *"experience it, thank you"*: Norman, *Turn Signals Are the Facial Expressions*.

6. ENHANCING THE WAYS WE LEARN

140 *learning and problem solving*: Jim Wilson, "Old-School in Silicon Valley," *New York Times*, October 22, 2011, http://www.nytimes.com/slideshow/2011/10/22/business/20111023-WALDORF-4.html. See 75 percent of parents of students at Los Altos, California, Waldorf school had a strong high-tech connection.
    Waldorf method of instruction: Matt Richtel, "A Silicon Valley School That Doesn't Compute," *New York Times*, October 22, 2011, http://www.nytimes.com/2011/10/23/technology/at-waldorf-school-in-silicon-valley-technology-can-wait.html.
    philosophy of Rudolf Steiner: "Waldorf Education: An Introduction," Association of Waldorf Schools of North America—Waldorf Education, https://waldorfeducation.org/waldorf_education.

141 *"not set up for that"*: Claire Cain Miller, "Why What You Learned in Preschool Is Crucial at Work," *New York Times*, October 16, 2015, accessed August 2016, http://www.nytimes.com/2015/10/18/upshot/how-the-modern-workplace-has-become-more-like-preschool.html?_r=0.
    nursing, and business management: David J. Deming, "The Growing Importance of Social Skills in the Labor Market," working paper, Graduate School of Education, Harvard University and NBER, August 2015, http://scholar.harvard.edu/files/ddeming/files/deming_socialskills_august2015.pdf.

142 *evaluated by standardized tests*: Valerie Strauss, "Teacher: What Third-Graders Are Being Asked to Do on 2016 Common Core Test," *Washington Post*, April 12, 2016, https://www.washingtonpost.com/news/answer-sheet/wp/2016/04/12/teacher-what-third-graders-are-being-asked-to-do-on-2016-common-core-test/.
    nature of the solar system: David Deming, telephone interview by author, August 16, 2016. "Dark matter" was the apt cosmological metaphor Deming used for educational soft skills.
    leadership, and confidence?: Tom Wolfe, *The Right Stuff* (New York: Farrar, Straus and Giroux, 1979).
    address K–12 education: *Following EdTech Money*, report, 2016, https://www.edsurge.com/research/special-reports/state-of-edtech-2016/funding.

143 *indicators of success:* Eric Ries, "Why Vanity Metrics Are Dangerous," *Startup Lessons Learned* (blog), December 23, 2009, http://www
.startuplessonslearned.com/2009/12/why-vanity-metrics-are
-dangerous.html.

students who graduate: Motoko Rich, "Online School Enriches Affiliated Companies If Not Its Students," *New York Times,* May 18, 2016, http://
www.nytimes.com/2016/05/19/us/online-charter-schools-electronic
-classroom-of-tomorrow.html.

that of physical schools: "U.S. High School Graduation Rate Hits New Record High," *Homeroom: U.S. Department of Education* (blog), 2015,
http://blog.ed.gov/2015/12/u-s-high-school-graduation-rate-hits-new
-record-high/; *2016 Building a Grad Nation Report,* report, America's Promise Alliance, May 9, 2016, http://www.gradnation.org/report
/2016-building-grad-nation-report.

144 *with her math homework:* Helena de Bertodano, "Khan Academy: The Man Who Wants to Teach the World," *Telegraph,* September 28, 2012,
http://www.telegraph.co.uk/education/educationnews/9568850
/Khan-Academy-The-man-who-wants-to-teach-the-world.html.

in order to facilitate it: Esther Wojcicki and Lance T. Izumi, *Moonshots in Education: Launching Blended Learning in the Classroom* (San Francisco: Pacific Research Institute, 2014).

145 *for blended learning:* Heather Staker, *The Rise of K–12 Blended Learning: Profiles of Emerging Models,* report, Innosight Institute, May 2011,
http://www.christenseninstitute.org/wp-content/uploads/2013/04
/The-rise-of-K-12-blended-learning.emerging-models.pdf.

cofounder Sergey Brin: Nellie Bowles, "Tech Celebs Join Esther Wojcicki as New Media Center Opens at Palo Alto High," Recode, October 20,
2014, http://www.recode.net/2014/10/20/11632026/tech-celebs-join
-esther-wojcicki-as-new-media-center-opens-at-palo.

146 *methods being developed:* "Esther Wojcicki," Creative Commons, 2016, https://creativecommons.org/author/estherwojcicki/.

potential of the approach: Rhode Island School of Design (RISD), "Writer Hilton Als to Deliver Keynote Address at Rhode Island School of Design's 2016 Commencement," news release, May 11, 2016, http://www
.risd.edu/press-releases/2016/Writer-Hilton-Als-to-Deliver-Keynote
-Address-at-Rhode-Island-School-of-Design's-2016-Commencement/.

148 *"Paly invests in the arts":* Bowles, "Tech Celebs Join Esther Wojcicki."

given the answers: Esther Wojcicki, interview by author, October 23, 2015.

fully techie approaches: Barbara Means, Yukie Toyama, Robert Murphy, Marianne Bakia, and Karla Jones, *Evaluation of Evidence-Based Practices in Online Learning: A Meta-Analysis and Review of Online Learning Studies,* report, U.S. Department of Education, September 2010, https://www2 .ed.gov/rschstat/eval/tech/evidence-based-practices/finalreport .pdf.

149   *across multiple programs:* "Proof Points: Blended Learning Success in School Districts," Christensen Institute, September 2015, http://www .christenseninstitute.org/publications/proof-points/; Emily Deruy, "New Data Backs Blended Learning," *Atlantic,* September 23, 2015, http://www .theatlantic.com/politics/archive/2015/09/new-data-backs-blended -learning/432894/.
       "reflection and creative thinking": Karen E. Willcox, Sanjay Sarma, and Philip H. Lippel, *Online Education: A Catalyst for Higher Education Reforms,* report, Online Education Policy Initiative, Massachusetts Institute of Technology (MIT), April 2016, https://oepi.mit.edu/files /2016/09/MIT-Online-Education-Policy-Initiative-April-2016.pdf.

150   *tools and approaches:* "Moonshots in Education," *EdTechTeam* (blog), https://www.edtechteam.com/moonshots/. See also schedule of Google Apps for Education Summits: https://www.gafesummit.com/.
       game in Edmonton, Canada: James Sanders, telephone interview by author, May 16, 2016.

151   *strategy for the Chromebook:* James Sanders, "Chromebooks in the Class-room," YouTube video, September 9, 2012, https://www.youtube.com /watch?v=rlLME325S-g.

152   *schools by 2018:* White House, Office of the Press Secretary, "FACT SHEET: ConnectED: Two Years of Delivering Opportunity to K-12 Schools & Libraries," news release, June 25, 2015, https://www .whitehouse.gov/the-press-office/2015/06/25/fact-sheet-connected -two-years-delivering-opportunity-k-12-schools; "Presidential Innova-tion Fellows," White House, 2016, https://www.whitehouse.gov /innovationfellows.

153   *giving them credit:* Greg Toppo, "Low-Tech 'Breakout EDU' Looks to Invigorate Education One Wooden Box at a Time," *USA Today,* July 1, 2016, http://www.usatoday.com/story/tech/2016/06/30/low-tech -breakout-edu-looks-invigorate-education-one-wooden-box-time /86580464/.
       open physical locks: "Games," Breakout EDU, September 2016, http:// www.breakoutedu.com/games/.

154   *inventor of kindergarten:* Mitchel Resnick, "Technologies for Lifelong Kindergarten," *Educational Technology Research and Development* 46, no. 4 (1998): 43–55, doi:10.1007/bf02299672.

Slumdog Millionaire: Lucy Tobin, "Slumdog Professor," *Guardian*, March 2, 2009, https://www.theguardian.com/education/2009/mar/03/professor-sugata-mitra.

155 *teachers are less necessary*: Nathan J. Matias, "Is Education Obsolete? Sugata Mitra at the MIT Media Lab," *MIT Center for Civic Media* (blog), May 16, 2012, https://civic.mit.edu/blog/natematias/is-education-obsolete-sugata-mitra-at-the-mit-media-lab; Sugata Mitra, "Build a School in the Cloud," speech, February 2013, https://www.ted.com/talks/sugata_mitra_build_a_school_in_the_cloud.

in December 2013: Mitra, "Build a School in the Cloud."

156 *all done over Skype*: Ibid.

"is going obsolete": Sugata Mitra, "Meet an Education Innovator Who Says Knowledge Is Becoming Obsolete," interview by Paul Solman, *PBS Newshour*, November 13, 2015, http://www.pbs.org/newshour/making-sense/meet-an-education-innovator-who-says-knowledge-is-becoming-obsolete/.

157 *"beyond their immediate concerns"*: Michał Paradowski, "Classrooms in the Cloud or Castles in the Air?," *IATEFL Voices* 239 (July/August 2014): 8–10, http://www.academia.edu/7475327/Classrooms_in_the_cloud_or_castles_in_the_air.

black-and-white correct answer: Katrina Schwartz, "Messy Works: How to Apply Self-Organized Learning in the Classroom," MindShift, October 7, 2015, https://ww2.kqed.org/mindshift/2015/10/07/messy-works-how-to-apply-self-organized-learning-in-the-classroom/. See also the SOLE toolkit developed by Sugata Mitra: http://ww2.kqed.org/mindshift/2013/12/11/ready-to-ignite-students-curiosity-heres-your-toolkit/

158 *will need in working life*: Schwartz, "Messy Works."

"school of the future": David Osborne, "The Schools of the Future," *U.S. News and World Report*, January 19, 2016, http://www.usnews.com/opinion/knowledge-bank/articles/2016-01-19/californias-summit-public-schools-are-the-schools-of-the-future.

a working-class city: Nichole Dobo, "Despite Its High-Tech Profile, Summit Charter Network Makes Teachers, Not Computers, the Heart of Personalized Learning," The Hechinger Report, March 1, 2016, http://hechingerreport.org/despite-its-high-tech-profile-summit-charter-network-makes-teachers-not-computers-the-heart-of-personalized-learning/.

159 *accepted into four-year colleges*: Osborne, "The Schools of the Future."

"learn and grow": Ibid.

yoga, film, and music: Nichole Dobo, "How This Bay Area Charter School

Network Is Reinventing Education," *Los Angeles Times*, March 1, 2016, http://www.latimes.com/local/education/la-me-silicon-school -20160229-story.html.

more affluent students: Osborne, "The Schools of the Future."

160 *how their students are doing:* Ibid.

161 *free to schools nationwide:* Chris Cox, "Introducing Facebook and Sum-mit's K-12 Education Project," *Facebook Newsroom* (blog), September 3, 2015, http://newsroom.fb.com/news/2015/09/introducing-facebook -and-summits-k-12-education-project/; Vindu Goel and Motoko Rich, "Facebook Takes a Step into Education Software," *New York Times*, September 3, 2015, http://www.nytimes.com/2015/09/04/technology /facebook-education-initiative-aims-to-help-children-learn-at-their -own-pace.html.

build their own playlists: Summit Basecamp, 2016, http:// summitbasecamp.org/explore-basecamp/.

other schools in the area: Strauss, "Teacher: What Third-Graders Are Being Asked to Do"; Osborne, "The Schools of the Future."

admitted to four-year colleges: Osborne, "The Schools of the Future."

double the national average: "Our Approach—Our Results," Summit Public Schools, 2016, http://summitps.org/approach/results.

early signs of promise: Ibid.

162 *have a real impact:* Rachel Lockett, telephone interview by author, April 20, 2016.

164 *parents, and students use it:* Jessica Hullinger, "Remind Launches New Slack-Like App for Schools," *Fast Company*, February 17, 2016, https:// www.fastcompany.com/3056642/most-creative-people/remind -launches-new-slack-like-app-for-schools; "School Messaging App Remind Lands on a Business Model," FastCo News, August 23, 2016, https://news.fastcompany.com/school-messaging-app-remind-lands -on-a-business-model-4017528.

contributed to these findings: Peter Bergman, "Peter Bergman—Home-page," Teachers College Columbia University, 2016, http://www .columbia.edu/~psb2101/.

teachers, and with their children: Susan Dynarski, "Helping the Poor in Education: The Power of a Simple Nudge," *New York Times*, January 17, 2015, http://www.nytimes.com/2015/01/18/upshot/helping-the-poor-in -higher-education-the-power-of-a-simple-nudge.html.

165 *drop the cost far further:* Peter Bergman, "Parent-Child Information Frictions and Human Capital Investment: Evidence from a Field Exper-

iment," working paper, Teachers College, Columbia University, June 23, 2015, http://ssrn.com/abstract=2622034.

develop literacy skills: Benjamin N. York and Susanna Loeb, "One Step at a Time: The Effects of an Early Literacy Text Messaging Program for Parents of Preschoolers," NBER working paper no. 20659, November 2014, http://www.nber.org/papers/w20659.

more words than poorer children: Betty Hart and Todd R. Risley, *Meaningful Differences in the Everyday Experience of Young American Children* (Baltimore: P. H. Brookes, 1995).

166 *"What sound does it make?":* Susanna Loeb and Ben York, "Helping Parents Help Their Children," Brookings, February 18, 2016, https://www.brookings.edu/research/helping-parents-help-their-children/.

require substantial time: Motoko Rich, "To Help Language Skills of Children, a Study Finds, Text Their Parents with Tips," *New York Times,* November 14, 2014, http://www.nytimes.com/2014/11/15/us/to-help -language-skills-of-children-a-study-finds-text-their-parents-with -tips.html.

167 *"engaged the whole community":* Paul-Andre White, "Using Remind at Leal Elementary School," telephone interview by author, May 27, 2016.

170 *college students and African American students:* Richard Pérez-Peña, "Active Role in Class Helps Black and First-Generation College Students, Study Says," *New York Times,* September 2, 2014, http://www.nytimes .com/2014/09/03/education/active-learning-study.html.

"higher course structure": S. L. Eddy and K. A. Hogan, "Getting Under the Hood: How and for Whom Does Increasing Course Structure Work?," *CBE—Life Sciences Education* 13, no. 3 (2014): 453–68, doi:10.1187/cbe .14-03-0050.

171 *human learning and memory:* Henry L. Roediger III, "How Tests Make Us Smarter," *New York Times,* July 18, 2014, http://www.nytimes .com/2014/07/20/opinion/sunday/how-tests-make-us-smarter.html.

paragraphs to memorize: J. D. Karpicke and J. R. Blunt, "Retrieval Practice Produces More Learning Than Elaborative Studying with Concept Mapping," *Science* 331, no. 6018 (February 11, 2011): 772–75, doi:10.1126 /science.1199327.

7. BUILDING A BETTER WORLD

173 *"good for humanity":* Gabo Arora, interview by author, May 24, 2016.

United Nations General Assembly: "Gabo Arora," VR Days, November 2016, http://vrdays.co/people/gabo-arora/.

174 *antipoverty campaigns:* Melina Gills, "Gabo Arora on Making VR with
     Vrse.works and the United Nations," Tribeca, March 31, 2016, https://
     tribecafilm.com/stories/tribeca-virtual-arcade-my-mothers-wing
     -gabo-arora-chris-milk-interview.

175 *"augment or improve it":* David Carr, "Unease for What Microsoft's
     HoloLens Will Mean for Our Screen-Obsessed Lives," *New York Times,*
     January 25, 2015, http://www.nytimes.com/2015/01/26/business/media
     /unease-for-what-microsofts-hololens-will-mean-for-our-screen
     -obsessed-lives.html.
     twice as effective: John Gaudiosi, "UN Uses Virtual Reality to Raise
     Awareness and Money," *Fortune,* April 18, 2016, http://fortune.com
     /2016/04/18/un-uses-virtual-reality-to-raise-awareness-and-money/.
     most of them scoffed: Gabo Arora, interview by author, May 24, 2016.

176 *technology at VPL Research:* Jennifer Kahn, "The Visionary," *The New
     Yorker,* July 11, 2011, http://www.newyorker.com/magazine/2011/07
     /11/the-visionary.

177 *such as a living room wall:* Tom Simonite, "Microsoft's HoloLens Will
     Put Realistic 3-D People in Your Living Room," *MIT Technology
     Review,* May 20, 2015, https://www.technologyreview.com/s/537651
     /microsofts-hololens-will-put-realistic-3-d-people-in-your-living-room/.
     crowd-funding site Kickstarter: Max Chafkin, "Why Facebook's $2 Billion
     Bet on Oculus Rift Might One Day Connect Everyone on Earth," *Vanity
     Fair*—Hive, October 2015, http://www.vanityfair.com/news/2015/09
     /oculus-rift-mark-zuckerberg-cover-story-palmer-luckey.
     VR startup Magic Leap: Dan Primack, "Google-Backed Magic Leap Rais-
     ing $827 Million," *Fortune,* December 9, 2015, http://fortune.com/2015/
     12/09/google-backed-magic-leap-raising-827-million/.
     "We will all become virtual humans": Monica Kim, "The Good and the
     Bad of Escaping to Virtual Reality," *Atlantic,* February 18, 2015, http://
     www.theatlantic.com/health/archive/2015/02/the-good-and-the-bad
     -of-escaping-to-virtual-reality/385134/.
     "teaching artificial minds": Donald A. Norman, *Turn Signals Are the
     Facial Expressions of Automobiles* (Reading, MA: Addison-Wesley, 1992),
     13–14.

178 *"hurting face-to-face conversation":* Lauren Cassani Davis, "The Flight
     from Conversation," *Atlantic,* October 7, 2015, http://www.theatlantic
     .com/technology/archive/2015/10/reclaiming-conversation-sherry
     -turkle/409273/.
     "we become more human": Chris Milk, "How Virtual Reality Can Create
     the Ultimate Empathy Machine," speech, March 2015, https://www.ted

.com/talks/chris_milk_how_virtual_reality_can_create_the_ultimate
_empathy_machine.

rewards of face-to-face interaction: Sherry Turkle, "Design and Technology in Interpersonal Relationships," lecture, Fitbit Headquarters, San Francisco, May 31, 2016.

180 *such as the electrical power grid:* Ralph Langner, "Cracking Stuxnet, a 21st-Century Cyber Weapon," speech, March 2011, https://www.ted.com /talks/ralph_langner_cracking_stuxnet_a_21st_century_cyberweapon.

pipelines, and power plants: Ellen Nakashima and Joby Warrick, "Stuxnet Was Work of U.S. and Israeli Experts, Officials Say," *Washington Post,* June 2, 2012, https://www.washingtonpost.com/world/national-security /stuxnet-was-work-of-us-and-israeli-experts-officials-say/2012/06/01 /gJQAlnEy6U_story.html.

use and reuse: Gwen Ackerman, "Sony Hackers Used a Half-Dozen Recycled Cyber-Weapons," Bloomberg.com, December 19, 2014, http://www .bloomberg.com/news/2014-12-19/sony-hackers-used-a-half-dozen -recycled-cyber-weapons.html.

181 *"another person's experience":* Drew Faust, "To Be 'A Speaker of Words and a Doer of Deeds:' Literature and Leadership," speech, United States Military Academy, West Point, March 24, 2016, http://www.harvard.edu /president/speech/2016/to-be-speaker-words-and-doer-deeds-literature -and-leadership.

182 *"prior days of glory":* Karl W. Eikenberry, "The Humanities and Global Engagement," address, March 18, 2013, https://www.amacad.org /content/publications/pubContent.aspx?d=1306.

tolerant and inclusive country: Katherine Boyle, "For Real 'Monument Woman,' Saving Afghan Treasures Is Unglamorous but Richly Rewarding," *Washington Post,* February 14, 2014, https://www.washingtonpost .com/entertainment/museums/for-realmonument-woman-saving -afghan-treasures-is-unglamorous-but-richly-rewarding/2014/02/13 /af543588-9267-11e3-84e1-27626c5ef5fb_story.html.

rebuild tattered states: Faust, "To Be 'A Speaker of Words.'"

"surrender their moral judgment": Jeffrey Fleishman, "At West Point, Warriors Shaped Through Plutarch and Shakespeare," *Los Angeles Times,* May 11, 2015, http://www.latimes.com/entertainment/great-reads/la-et -c1-literature-of-war-20150511-story.html.

183 *the front lines of war:* Emily Miller, telephone interview by author, May 19, 2016.

185 *across the fuzzy-techie divide:* "Stanford H4D—Spring 2016," Stanford University, March 2016, http://hacking4defense.stanford.edu/.

186 *facilitate creative collaboration:* Ibid.

187 *defense and intelligence communities:* Steve Blank, "The Innovation Insurgency Scales—Hacking for Defense (H4D)," *Steve Blank* (blog), September 19, 2016, https://steveblank.com/2016/09/19/the-innovation -insurgency-scales-hacking-for-defense-h4d/.
     solutions for the State Department: "Hacking 4 Diplomacy," Stanford University, accessed June 2016, http://web.stanford.edu/class/msande298 /index.html.
     helping cities manage waste: Maya Kosoff, "Why Did Leo DiCaprio Join a Garbage Start-Up—Literally?," *Vanity Fair*—Hive, June 2, 2016, http:// www.vanityfair.com/news/2016/06/rubicon-trash-disposal-startup.

188 *when it comes to accepting the status quo:* Robert Safian, "'We Need a New Field Manual for Business': Casey Gerald," *Fast Company,* October 14, 2014, https://www.fastcompany.com/3036583/generation-flux/we-need -a-new-field-manual-for-business-casey-gerald.
     developing world with digital work: Sarah Kessler, "Sama Group Is Redefining What It Means to Be a Not-for-Profit Business," *Fast Company,* February 16, 2016, https://www.fastcompany.com/3056067/most -innovative-companies/sama-group-for-redefining-what-it-means-to -be-a-not-for-profit-bus.

189 *could be completely eradicated:* Sam Jones, "World Food Programme Pins Hopes on App to Nourish 20,000 Syrian Children," *Guardian,* November 12, 2015, https://www.theguardian.com/global-development /2015/nov/12/world-food-programme-share-the-meal-app-syrian -children.
     schoolchildren in Lesotho: Ibid.

190 *technology into other platforms:* Scott Hartley, "How You Can Share Thanksgiving with Syrian Refugees," Inc.com, November 12, 2015, http:// www.inc.com/scott-hartley/how-you-can-share-thanksgiving-with -syrian-refugees.html.
     how to convert oil drums: "Rural Information Access (Digital Drum)," Stories of UNICEF Innovation, 2012, http://www.unicefstories.org/tech /digital_drum/.
     Cooper Hewitt, Smithsonian Design Museum in New York: "UNICEF's Digital Drum Chosen as a Time Magazine Best Invention of 2011," UNICEF USA, https://www.unicefusa.org/press/releases/unicef's-digital-drum -chosen-time-magazine-best-invention-2011/8085.
     in a 2011 Forbes *interview:* Rahim Kanani, "An Interview with Erica Kochi on UNICEF's Tech Innovation," *Forbes,* September 18, 2011, http://www

.forbes.com/sites/rahimkanani/2011/09/18/an-interview-with-erica
-kochi-on-unicefs-tech-innovation/#6c5d0bf05049.

191 *health care and education:* Stan Higgins, "UNICEF Eyes Blockchain as
Possible Solution to Child Poverty Issues," CoinDesk, February 3, 2016,
http://www.coindesk.com/unicef-innovation-chief-blockchain-child
-poverty/.

192 *"institutions that govern their lives":* Zachary Bookman and Juan-Pablo
Guerrero Amparán, "Two Steps Forward, One Step Back: Assessing the
Implementation of Mexico's Freedom of Information Act," *Mexican
Law Review* 1, no. 2 (2009): 3–51, http://info8.juridicas.unam.mx/pdf
/mlawrns/cont/2/arc/arc1.pdf.

193 *"shop that holds the Leatherman":* Zachary Bookman, telephone interview
by author, March 25, 2016.

194 *2012 piece he wrote for the* New York Times: Zachary Bookman, "Settling
Afghan Disputes, Where Custom Holds Sway," *At War: Notes from the
Front Lines* (blog), *New York Times,* June 4, 2012, http://atwar.blogs
.nytimes.com/author/zachary-bookman/.

195 *Over one thousand state and local governments:* T. S. Last, "Updated: Santa
Fe Unveils Web Platform for Budget Transparency," *Albuquerque
Journal,* August 10, 2016, https://www.abqjournal.com/823796/santa-fe
-unveils-new-budget-transparency-web-platform.html.

197 *"I was the darling of the city":* Charlie Francis, telephone interview by
author, April 29, 2016.

8. THE FUTURE OF JOBS

202 *for well over a hundred years:* Jon Yeomans, "Australia's Mining Boom
Turns to Dust as Commodity Prices Collapse," *Telegraph,* February 6,
2016, http://www.telegraph.co.uk/finance/newsbysector/industry
/mining/12142813/Australias-mining-boom-turns-to-dust-as-commodity
-prices-collapse.html.
improved efficiency by 15 to 20 percent: Sharon Masige, "Self Driving
Mining Truck Capable of 90km Speed," *Australian Mining,* April 15, 2016,
https://www.australianmining.com.au/news/self-driving-mining-truck
-capable-of-90km-speed/.
reduced rubber consumption: Jamie Smyth, "Rio Tinto Shifts to Driverless
Trucks in Australia," *Financial Times,* October 19, 2015, https://www
.ft.com/content/43f7436a-7632-11e5-a95a-27d368e1ddf7.
six hundred standard automobile tires: Robert Johnson, "This Is What a
$42,500 Tire Looks Like," Business Insider, May 31, 2012, http://www

.businessinsider.com/this-is-what-a-42500-tire-looks-like-the
-5980r63-xdr-2012-5.

203 *so humans don't have to:* "Mine of the Future," Rio Tinto, http://www
.riotinto.com/documents/Mine_of_The_Future_Brochure.pdf.
Rise of the Robots: Martin Ford, *Rise of the Robots: Technology and the
Threat of a Jobless Future* (New York: Basic Books, 2015).
the next one to two decades: Carl Benedikt Frey and Michael A. Osborne,
"The Future of Employment: How Susceptible Are Jobs to Computerisation?," publication, Oxford Martin School, Oxford University, September 17, 2013, http://www.oxfordmartin.ox.ac.uk/downloads/academic
/The_Future_of_Employment.pdf.

204 *"new uses for labor":* John Maynard Keynes, quoted in Erik Brynjolfsson
and Andrew McAfee, *The Second Machine Age: Work, Progress, and Prosperity in a Time of Brilliant Technologies* (New York: W. W. Norton, 2014),
174.

205 *shrinking the fastest:* David Deming, "About Me," http://scholar.harvard
.edu/ddeming/biocv.

206 *strong social skills:* David J. Deming, "The Growing Importance of Social
Skills in the Labor Market," working paper, Graduate School of Education, Harvard University and NBER, August 2015, http://scholar.harvard
.edu/files/ddeming/files/deming_socialskills_august2015.pdf.
candidates with those requisite skills: Kate Davidson, "Employers Find
'Soft Skills' Like Critical Thinking in Short Supply," *Wall Street Journal,*
August 30, 2016, http://www.wsj.com/articles/employers-find-soft
-skills-like-critical-thinking-in-short-supply-1472549400.
according to CNN: Sara Ashley O'Brien, "Zuckerberg Backs Andela, a
Startup More Elite Than Harvard," CNNMoney, June 16, 2016, http://
money.cnn.com/2016/06/16/technology/andela-24-million-chan
-zuckerberg-foundation/.

208 *"practically a sport":* Valerie Strauss, "Enough with Trashing the Liberal
Arts. Stop Being Stupid," *Washington Post,* March 5, 2016, https://www
.washingtonpost.com/news/answer-sheet/wp/2016/03/05/enough-with
-trashing-the-liberal-arts-stop-being-stupid/.
"market for Greek philosophers is tight": Christopher J. Scalia, "Conserva-
tives, Please Stop Trashing the Liberal Arts," *Wall Street Journal,* March
27, 2015, http://www.wsj.com/articles/christopher-scalia-conservatives
-please-stop-trashing-the-liberal-arts-1427494073.
"deal with new situations": Lawrence Katz, "Get a Liberal Arts B.A., Not a
Business B.A., for the Coming Artisan Economy," *PBS Newshour,* July 15,

2014, http://www.pbs.org/newshour/making-sense/get-a-liberal-arts
-b-a-not-a-business-b-a-for-the-coming-artisan-economy/.

209 *"type of work they entail"*: Michael Chui, James Manyika, and Mehdi
Miremadi, "Where Machines Could Replace Humans—and Where They
Can't (Yet)," McKinsey & Company, July 2016, http://www.mckinsey
.com/business-functions/business-technology/our-insights/where
-machines-could-replace-humans-and-where-they-cant-yet.
30 percent of activities: James Manyika, Daniela Rus, Edwin Van Bommel,
and John Paul Farmer, "Robots and the Future of Jobs: The Economic
Impact of Artificial Intelligence," lecture, Council on Foreign Relations,
New York, November 14, 2016.

210 *framework for making that evaluation:* D. H. Autor, F. Levy, and R. J. Murnane, "The Skill Content of Recent Technological Change: An Empirical
Exploration," *Quarterly Journal of Economics* 118, no. 4 (2003): 1279–333,
doi:10.1162/003355303322552801.
at least for quite some time: Daron Acemoglu and David Autor. "Skills,
Tasks and Technologies: Implications for Employment and Earnings,"
Handbook of Labor Economics 4b (2011): 1043–171, doi:10.1016/s0169
-7218(11)02410-5.

211 *cost of labor is significantly higher there:* Ben Bland, "China's Robot Revolution," *Financial Times*, June 6, 2016, https://www.ft.com/content
/1dbd8c60-0cc6-11e6-ad80-67655613c2d6.

213 *a moment-to-moment basis:* Andreas Xenachis, telephone interview by
author, May 25, 2016.
will still be done by humans: David J. Snowden and Mary E. Boone, "A
Leader's Framework for Decision Making," *Harvard Business Review,*
November 2007, https://hbr.org/2007/11/a-leaders-framework-for
-decision-making.

214 *sensor technology:* Chui, Manyika, and Miremadi, "Where Machines
Could Replace Humans."

216 *could be done through technology:* Ibid.

217 *"highways and freeways"*: Andreas Koller, quoted in Michael Pooler, "Man
and Machine Pair Up for Packing," *Financial Times*, September 6, 2016,
https://www.ft.com/content/376f9fa0-33d5-11e6-bda0-04585c31b153.

218 *"parallel automation"*: Manyika et al., "Robots and the Future of Jobs."
for the next twenty years: Julie Johnsson, "Boeing Sees Need for 30,850
New Pilots a Year as Travel Soars," Bloomberg.com, July 25, 2016,
https://www.bloomberg.com/news/articles/2016-07-25/boeing-sees
-need-for-30–850-new-pilots-a-year-as-travel-soars.

219 *a superb air force pilot:* William Langewiesche, "Anatomy of a Miracle," *Vanity Fair,* June 2009, http://www.vanityfair.com/culture/2009/06 /us_airways200906.

"stall the wings and lose lift": Chesley B. Sullenberger III and Jeffrey Zaslow, *Sully: My Search for What Really Matters* (New York: William Morrow, 2016).

years and years in the future: K. Mugunthan, "Human-Level Artificial General Intelligence Still Long Way to Go: David Silver, Google's DeepMind Scientist," *Economic Times,* March 23, 2016, http:// economictimes.indiatimes.com/opinion/interviews/human-level -artificial-general-intelligence-still-long-way-to-go-david-silver -googles-deepmind-scientist/articleshow/51522993.cms.

220 *a program called AlphaGo:* Catherine Shu, "Google Acquires Artificial Intelligence Startup DeepMind for More Than $500M," TechCrunch, January 26, 2014, https://techcrunch.com/2014/01/26 /google-deepmind/.

human world champion: Sam Byford, "DeepMind Founder Demis Hassabis on How AI Will Shape the Future," The Verge, March 10, 2016, http://www.theverge.com/2016/3/10/11192774/demis-hassabis-interview -alphago-google-deepmind-ai.

brute-force computational power: Cade Metz, "The Sadness and Beauty of Watching Google's AI Play Go," *Wired,* March 11, 2016, http://www .wired.com/2016/03/sadness-beauty-watching-googles-ai-play-go/.

ten-year jump in AI: William Hoffman, "Elon Musk Says Google Deepmind's Go Victory Is a 10-Year Jump for A.I.," *Inverse,* March 9, 2016, https://www.inverse.com/article/12620-elon-musk-says-google -deepmind-s-go-victory-is-a-10-year-jump-for-a-i.

the dawn of artificial general intelligence: Clemency Burton-Hill, "The Superhero of Artificial Intelligence: Can This Genius Keep It in Check?," *Guardian,* February 16, 2016, https://www.theguardian.com /technology/2016/feb/16/demis-hassabis-artificial-intelligence -deepmind-alphago.

221 *the best possible move:* "The Dream of AI Is Alive in Go," interview, *Andreessen Horowitz* (podcast), March 11, 2016, http://a16z.com/2016 /03/11/artificial-intelligence-alphago/; David Silver and Demis Hassabis, "AlphaGo: Mastering the Ancient Game of Go with Machine Learning," *Google Research Blog,* January 27, 2016, https://research.googleblog .com/2016/01/alphago-mastering-ancient-game-of-go.html.

222 *"more than we can tell":* Michael Polanyi, *The Tacit Dimension* (Garden City, NY: Doubleday, 1966).

choices that the machine made: Cade Metz, "In Two Moves, AlphaGo and Lee Sedol Redefined the Future," *Wired,* March 16, 2016, http://www .wired.com/2016/03/two-moves-alphago-lee-sedol-redefined-future/.

223   *great deal of what it knows:* Cade Metz, "How Google's AI Viewed the Move No Human Could Understand," *Wired,* March 14, 2016, http:// www.wired.com/2016/03/googles-ai-viewed-move-no-human -understand/.

true AGI is "decades away": Mugunthan, "Human-Level Artificial General Intelligence."

involved in doing so: Paul Sawers, "With 10M Downloads on iOS, Prisma Now Lets Android Users Turn Their Photos into Works of Art," VentureBeat, July 25, 2016, http://venturebeat.com/2016/07/25/with-10 -million-downloads-on-ios-prisma-now-lets-android-users-turn-their -photos-into-works-of-art/.

224   *understanding love or desire:* Lindsey J. Smith, "Google's AI Engine Is Reading 2,865 Romance Novels to Be More Conversational," The Verge, May 5, 2016, http://www.theverge.com/2016/5/5/11599068/google-ai -engine-bot-romance-novels.

What Computers Can't Do: Hubert L. Dreyfus, *What Computers Can't Do: A Critique of Artificial Reason* (New York: Harper & Row, 1972).

"poorer versions of them": Sean Dorrance Kelly and Herbert Dreyfus on limits of AI: Stanley Fish, "Watson Still Can't Think," *New York Times,* February 28, 2011, http://opinionator.blogs.nytimes.com/2011/02/28 /watson-still-cant-think/.

"in vitro phase": Daniel Susskind, "AlphaGo Marks Stark Difference Between AI and Human Intelligence," *Financial Times,* March 21, 2016, https://www.ft.com/content/8474df6a-ed0b-11e5-bb79-2303682345c8; "When Humanity Meets A.I.," interview, *Andreessen Horowitz* (podcast), June 28, 2016, http://a16z.com/2016/06/29/feifei-li-a16z-professor -in-residence/.

"working in shoe stores": Jay Yarow, "Marc Andreessen at the DealBook Conference," Business Insider, December 12, 2012, http://www .businessinsider.com/marc-andreessen-at-the-dealbook-conference -2012-12.

225   *"abstraction and creativity":* Will Knight, "AI's Language Problem," *MIT Technology Review,* August 9, 2016, https://www.technologyreview.com /s/602094/ais-language-problem/.

"and thus for human possibility": Drew Faust, "To Be 'A Speaker of Words and a Doer of Deeds': Literature and Leadership," speech, United States Military Academy, West Point, March 24, 2016, http://www.harvard

.edu/president/speech/2016/to-be-speaker-words-and-doer-deeds
-literature-and-leadership.

CONCLUSION: PARTNERSHIP GOES BOTH WAYS

227 *we see, that counts:* Scott Hartley, "Why the Way We Use Computers Is
About to Change Again," Inc.com, December 10, 2015, http://www
.inc.com/scott-hartley/what-tomorrow-s-james-bond-villain-will-look
-like.html; Geoffrey A. Fowler, "Siri: Once a Flake, Now Key to Apple's
Future," *Wall Street Journal,* June 14, 2016, http://www.wsj.com/articles
/siri-once-a-flake-now-key-to-apples-future-1465905601.

228 *entrepreneurs in developing ideas:* Seung Lee, "Why Amazon Echo, Not
the iPhone, May Be the Key to Internet's Future," *Newsweek,* June 1,
2016, http://www.newsweek.com/why-amazon-echo-not-iphone-may
-be-key-internets-future-465487.
perform basic conversations: Haje Jan Kamps, "ToyTalk Renames to Pull-
String, Repositions as Authoring Tool for Bots," TechCrunch, April 26,
2016, https://techcrunch.com/2016/04/26/pullstring-bot-authoring/.
put to use in incredible ways: Jon Fingas, "Google AI Builds a Better
Cucumber Farm," Engadget, August 31, 2016, https://www.engadget
.com/2016/08/31/google-ai-helps-cucumber-farm/.

229 *today's greatest tool: a smartphone:* Kelley Holland, "45 Million Americans
Are Living Without a Credit Score," CNBC, May 5, 2015, http://www.
cnbc.com/2015/05/05/credit-invisible-26-million-have-no
-credit-score.html.
to move beyond the U.S.: Scott Martin, "PayJoy Picks Up $18M for Smart-
phone Financing Plans," *Wall Street Journal,* July 11, 2016, http://www
.wsj.com/articles/payjoy-picks-up-18m-for-smartphone-financing
-plans-1468236609.

230 *"produce creative chances":* C. P. Snow, *The Two Cultures* (Cambridge:
Cambridge University Press, 1993).

231 *have not yet been created:* Cathy N. Davidson, *Now You See It: How the
Brain Science of Attention Will Transform the Way We Live, Work, and
Learn* (New York: Viking, 2011).

232 *"education should be," he recounts:* Tom Wasow, interview by author, April
20, 2016.
"talented people in the world": Eugene Kim, "This Popular Major at Stanford Produced Some of the Biggest Names in Tech," Business Insider,
January 21, 2016, http://www.businessinsider.com/stanford-symbolic
-systems-major-alumni-2016-1/#reid-hoffman-is-the-cofounder-and

-chairman-of-linkedin-he-graduated-in-1989-with-a-degree-in-symbolic
-systems-and-cognitive-science-1.

233 *physical buildings and roads:* Melissa Delaney, "Schools Shift from STEM to STEAM," *EdTech,* April 2, 2014, http://www.edtechmagazine.com/k12 /article/2014/04/schools-shift-stem-steam.

making this a national priority: "STEAM Hits Capitol Hill," Rhode Island School of Design (RISD) News, February 18, 2013, http://www.risd.edu /about/news/steam_hits_capitol_hill/.

234 *his 1952 book,* Player Piano: Kurt Vonnegut, *Player Piano* (New York: Delacorte Press, 1952).

Index

THE
MILLENNIUM
PROBLEMS

The Seven Greatest Unsolved
Mathematical Puzzles of Our Time

KEITH DEVLIN

Basic Books
A Member of the Perseus Books Group

Designed by BookComp, Inc.

A cataloging-in-publication record for this book is available from the Library of Congress.

ISBN-13: 978-0-465-01729-4 (hc.)   ISBN-13: 978-0-465-01730-0 (pbk.)
ISBN-10: 0-465-01729-0 (hc.)   ISBN-10: 0-465-01730-4 (pbk.)

15 14 13 12 11 10